A Glimpse of Indian Knowledge Tradition

Cognizance of Continuity

VITTHAL GORE

A Glimpse of Indian Knowledge Tradition - Cognizance of Continuity

ISBN: 979-8-89519-910-7 (Paperback)
ISBN: 979-8-89556-402-8 (Hardbound)

Publisher: Notion Press - India, Singapore, Malaysia.
First Published: 5 September 2024.
Revised Edition: 10 November 2024.

Contents

Acknowledgments

By the blessings of Lord Venkateshwara and the goodwill of many people around, I could undertake many responsibilities in personal and professional life. One of them is the completion of this edited volume that owes me an extreme degree of indebtedness and appreciation to a host of 'souls-in-deed' for whom my love and respect will ever increase.

- I am deeply grateful to all those who have contributed to the realization of this book on Indian Knowledge Tradition. First and foremost, I extend my heartfelt thanks to my virtual mentor and guide, Prof. Kapil Kapoor, whose wisdom, and knowledge have been invaluable throughout this journey.

- I am indebted to honourable Prof. Kapil Kapoor sir for writing FOREWORD to this book. Irrespective of his very busy schedule, he could do it on time and enabled the publisher to publish the book.

- I am indebted to the scholars and experts in the field whose groundbreaking research provided the foundation for this work. Special thanks to each of the contributors of this edited volume, whose insights illuminated many aspects of Indian knowledge systems.

- Editing a book on Indian Knowledge Tradition is a journey that has been filled with learning, reflection, and heartfelt exploration of the intricacies of indigenous value system and wisdom. I am deeply grateful to all those who have supported me and contributed to this endeavour.

- First and foremost, I would like to express my sincere gratitude to my own parents, Late. Mrs. Manorama and

Late. Mr. Gangadharrao Gore whose love, patience, and wisdom continue to inspire me every day. Their guidance laid the foundation for my understanding of this world. No thanks can make me free from indebtedness to my parents who are the constant source of motivation.

- I am thankful to my spouse, Mrs. Rajashri, for her unwavering support and understanding during the time spent for editing this book. Her encouragement kept me focused and motivated. I am always bound in love and gratitude to my beloved children Ms. Vedashri and Master Vedant whose silent support made it possible for me to pursue and complete the book.

- I extend my appreciation to the experts in the field whose works have shaped my perspective and informed the content of this book. Special thanks to Prof. Kapil Kapoor, who has been constantly preaching and generously sharing his insights and expertise for the upliftment of the common people in this world with the domain knowledge of the Bharat bhoomi.

- I am also indebted to Adv. Gunvantrao Patil Haibatpurkar, President, Bharat Liberal Education Society, Udgir and Mr. Umesh Patil Deonikar, Secretary, Bharat Liberal Education Society, Udgir and all the honourable office bearers and members of Bharat Liberal Education Society, Udgir for their constant encouragement and directorial support.

- I am indebted to my publisher and the editorial team at Notion Press, Chennai whose professionalism and enthusiasm have been instrumental in bringing this project to fruition. Their professional guidance and expertise have been invaluable throughout the course of developing book.

- To my friends and colleagues who provided encouragement, feedback, and understanding throughout this process,

I am truly grateful to everybody. Their support has meant more to me than words can express. I also express my gratitude to all my friends, colleagues and well-wishers for their love and support time and again.

- This book is dedicated to every Indian who strives to nurture and guide the succeeding generations with indigenous knowledge and wisdom.

I am fortunate that this book is being published on my BIRTHDAY.

Once again, I express my thankfulness to Lord Venkateshwara for cherishing my vision to explore my capability to strive hard for achieving all pinnacles in life.

Vitthal Gore
5th September 2024.

Foreword

India's rich and diverse cultural heritage is a tapestry of wisdom, philosophical social, and artistic with its roots stretching back thousands of years offering insights into reality, cosmos and the lived experience. This tradition represents one of the most enduring and profound legacies of humanity one that is living and relevant in the contemporary world.

This book, *A Glimpse of Indian Knowledge Tradition - Cognizance of Continuity* is a timely comprehensive exploration of and a testament to the resilience and adaptability of Indian thought which has seamlessly integrated with contemporary knowledge and has solutions for some of the most pressing challenges of our age.

The book invites readers to explore India's intellectual and spiritual heritage. The articles compiled in this book provide insights into the various streams of knowledge that have shaped Indian civilization. The importance of preserving and understanding these traditions cannot be overstated. In a world that often emphasizes technological advancement and material progress, the ādhyātmik a core of the Indian knowledge foregrounds balance, harmony and loka-saṅgraha. In this era of rapid change, the Indian Knowledge Systems argue harmony between the material and the spiritual, the individual and the collective, the local and the universal.

As the readers delve into the book, they will not only enter a scholarly resource but also a source of inspiration for one seeking to deepen one's understanding of the world and one's place in it.

A Glimpse of Indian Knowledge Tradition - Cognizance of Continuity is more than just an academic exploration; it is a call to recognize and embrace this rich intellectual heritage. By engaging with these ideas, readers are invited to not only appreciate the depth and breadth of Indian knowledge but also to draw inspiration from it as they navigate the complexities of the contemporary world. It will, apart from enriching knowledge, broaden the perspective and instil a respect for the Indian civilization and a deep self-respect.

I am confident that this book will serve as a valuable resource for scholars, students, and anyone interested in understanding the enduring legacy of our knowledge heritage and traditions.

Prof. Kapil Kapoor
Padma Bhushan (2023)
Former Chancellor, MGIHU Wardha, and Pro-Vice Chancellor,
Jawaharlal Nehru University, New Delhi.
Former Professor, Centre for Linguistics and English,
Professor, Centre for Sanskrit Studies, JNU New Delhi.
28 August 2024.

Preface

India, a land of myriad cultures, languages, and traditions, stands as a beacon of ancient wisdom that has illuminated the paths of seekers and scholars for millennia. A Glimpse of Indian Knowledge Tradition: Cognizance of Continuity endeavours to unveil the profound intellectual heritage that has shaped India's identity and continues to resonate in global discourse today.

The genesis of this book lies in a deep-rooted fascination with India's rich tapestry of knowledge. It is a tribute to the enduring intellectual legacy that spans from the ancient Vedic texts to the modern interpretations of Indian philosophy, science, and spirituality. As we embark on this journey through time, it becomes evident that India's contribution to human knowledge transcends mere historical chronicles; it embodies a living tradition that evolves and adapts yet remains anchored in its philosophical underpinnings.

Equally significant is India's pioneering contribution to science and mathematics. The ancient Indian mathematicians made seminal discoveries in algebra, geometry, and arithmetic, laying the foundations for advancements that would influence scholars across continents. The concept of zero, the decimal system, and the works of mathematicians like *Aryabhatta* and *Brahmagupta* attest to India's mathematical genius, which continues to underpin modern scientific inquiry.

At the heart of this exploration are the foundational texts that form the bedrock of Indian thought - the *Vedas, Upanishads, Bhagavad Gita, Indian Philosophies* and the treatises of ancient sages and scholars. These texts not only articulate profound metaphysical insights but also serve as guides to ethical living, scientific inquiry, and spiritual realisation. They represent a holistic worldview that integrates the material and the spiritual, the empirical and the metaphysical, offering a comprehensive framework for understanding existence and the cosmos.

Central to the narrative are the philosophical systems that have flourished in India over centuries, from the rationalistic approaches of Hinduism, Buddhism, Jainism, Sikhism, and Veer Shaivism to the profound metaphysics and different schools of thought, which have contributed unique perspectives on reality, consciousness, and the nature of the self. Through rigorous debate and dialectical reasoning, these philosophies have enriched intellectual discourse and provided enduring answers to perennial questions about the nature of existence.

Moreover, India's holistic approach to health and well-being, as expounded in Ayurveda and Yoga, remains remarkably relevant in today's world. Ayurveda, with its emphasis on balance and harmony, offers a comprehensive system of medicine that integrates diet, herbal remedies, and lifestyle practices to promote physical and mental well-being. Similarly, *Yoga*, through its practices of *asanas* (postures), pranayama (breath control), and meditation, provides pathways to spiritual growth and inner transformation.

This book also sheds light on India's cultural and artistic achievements from its vibrant literary traditions. These cultural expressions not only reflect the aesthetic sensibilities of their creators but also embody profound philosophical and spiritual themes, illustrating the inseparable connection between art, culture, and knowledge in Indian civilisation.

As we navigate through these realms of Indian knowledge tradition, it becomes evident that its influence extends far beyond geographical boundaries. The teachings of Indian philosophy have inspired thinkers from ancient Greece to Renaissance Europe, shaping intellectual currents and fostering cross-cultural dialogue. Today, as the world grapples with complex challenges, from environmental sustainability to global health crises, the holistic worldview of Indian knowledge tradition offers insights and solutions rooted in centuries of wisdom and experience.

In compiling this book, our aim is not merely to recount historical achievements but to celebrate the enduring relevance of Indian knowledge tradition in a rapidly changing world. Through meticulous research, scholarly analysis, and thoughtful reflection, we endeavour to illuminate the timeless wisdom embedded in India's cultural fabric and to inspire a renewed appreciation for its contributions to human civilisation.

All the esteemed scholars who contributed their seminal research articles have enriched this volume to the next level. As we embark on this journey together, may this book illuminate the richness of India's knowledge tradition and inspire a deeper appreciation for the timeless wisdom embedded within its cultural fabric.

We invite readers to board on this journey of discovery, to delve into the depths of India's intellectual heritage, and to join us in celebrating the profound insights and enduring legacy of A Glimpse of Indian Knowledge Tradition: Cognizance of Continuity.

Dr. Vitthal Gore
5th September 2024.

Chapter 1

Indian Knowledge System: Two Major Aspects and Sources

Pankaja Ghai Kaushik,
Associate Professor, Department of Sanskrit,
Lady Shri Ram College for Women, Delhi.

In India, the New Education Policy 2020 (NEP 2020) has been implemented in all spheres of education. NEP 2020 has three-fold targets:

1. Align with 21st-century education goals
2. Promoting India's traditions and value system
3. Reconstruct regulation and governance

In order to accomplish the second target of NEP 2020 by promoting India's traditions and value system among the young citizens of the country, the Indian Knowledge System is introduced in the curricula at all levels of education as NEP 2020 derives its values from Indian heritage and cultural sources. Indian thinkers have furnished 2 aspects which bring a holistic approach towards human life: attaining the highest worldly achievements without getting attached to them and indulging in them. This is possible when an appropriate balance is maintained between the achievements of worldly subjects and inner consciousness. This balance is prominently visible in the Indian Knowledge System through various sets of sources.

Objective

The paper aims to review the relevance of inclusion of Indian Knowledge System in the field of education, 2 major aspects of Indian

Knowledge System and its various sources in special context of texts compiled in Sanskrit language.

Knowledge and Education

As human beings march in their journey towards progress through newer developments, they need to be guided by a core set of ideals and principles of living. Knowledge is a powerful tool for accomplishing the physical and spiritual worlds. We all construct knowledge in many ways. Knowledge can be acquired through experience, inner perception, experiments, observations and measurements, inference, rational intuitions, and testimony, etc. Knowledge has a central role and place in education. Knowledge is relevant in education, specifically to the issue of choosing which knowledge should be passed on to the students. Achievement to fall the aims of education intrinsically depends on knowledge. We have been exposed to a certain set of knowledge systems for our education, which is largely imported from out of this country (Knowledge constructed in the western part of the globe). In the context of education, Indians have been sort of deprived of traditional Indian knowledge. Many generations in India are not even aware of the fact that a corpus of knowledge evolved by the people of ancient India exists. There has been, in ancient India, the tradition of contemplation of all the elements of this universe. Indian thinkers, scholars, and laypeople have explored the universe through their different methods and established numerous genres of knowledge, wisdom, and scientific knowledge. This corpus was prepared with the kind intention of the welfare of humanity along with the conservation of nature.

Education and Indian Knowledge System (IKS)

Indian Knowledge System has a significant role in education as a corpus of Indian traditional knowledge that is constructed through all methods - empirical, introspection, scientific, testimony, etc.

(Vibrant Tradition of Epistemology). Indian Knowledge System fulfils the requirements of instrumental and intrinsic values of knowledge. Corpus of Indian knowledge is not a thing of the past; it is relevant in contemporary times in many ways. Indian Knowledge System has a lot to offer in attaining aims of rational thinking, health, and well-being. It has a natural potential to inculcate ethical and moral values, pride, and rootedness in India through education. Indian knowledge is based on a holistic approach - worldly achievements and (*Abhyudaya* and *Niḥśreyasa*) divine enlightenment. At present, Indian students may be introduced to the world as the guiding force for sustainable development through their environment-friendly knowledge system. Studying the Indian Knowledge System as a part of modern education can foster interdisciplinary research, resulting in a harmonious blend of various knowledge systems.

Introducing the Indian Knowledge System into higher education can attract international students seeking to explore the depth and wisdom of India. Young minds have the capability to convert the older system and get it fit into contemporary moulds and, finally, benefit from it; hence, exposure to Indian traditional knowledge should be offered to them. The introduction of the Indian Knowledge System will bring snippets of the Indian Knowledge Systems by providing a fresh look at the corpus and culling out relevant portions that may generate renewed interest in the subject and motivate several students in a deeper study of the knowledge repository of India.

Indian Knowledge System: Two Major Aspects

There are some opinions that Indians were least interested in worldly subjects. They were more inclined towards philosophical and spiritual enlightenment. When we see the Indian knowledge corpus, we find that 2 paths were ordained simultaneously known as Pravṛttirviṣaya and Nivṛttiviṣaya. These 2 paths were to guide the people active in social life and people active in spiritual accomplishment. After achieving material gains, a person gets exhausted and finds ways to come out of it. In the Indian system, there are various sources for both kinds of accomplishments. Based on this, Indian Knowledge System can be understood from 2 aspects:-

1. Knowledge related to all physical subjects (Pravṛttirviṣayaka) प्रवृत्तिविषयाः Jyñāna and Vijyñāna
2. Jyñāna - Empirical, textual knowledge – social – political – legal – economic - religious, Dharma (Norms and Ethics), etc.
3. Vijyñāna – Sciences, mathematics, astronomy, philosophy, yoga, architecture, medicine, agriculture, engineering, linguistics, literature, sports, games, art forms, etc.
4. Knowledge related to inner consciousness (Nivṛttiviṣayaka) निवृत्तिविषयाः Jeevan Darṣana, Philosophy, Spirituality, Liberation, Salvation, Self-realisation, Sanctity of real and unreal.

Sources of Indian Knowledge System

Indian Knowledge System is a huge term; the following are comprised under the umbrella term Indian Knowledge System:

- Texts compiled in Sanskrit
- Compiled in vernacular languages
- Indian knowledge translated into foreign languages
- Tribal traditional knowledge
- Other unrecorded knowledge in the form of social customs and rituals.

The texts compiled in Sanskrit, Pāli and Prākṛta languages are the main sources of Indian Traditional Knowledge. The ancient research and knowledge related to all areas are preserved in these texts in their original form. Along with the original texts, commentaries written on the texts are also a great source of evolvement of the ideas. Corpus compiled in these languages may be classified into 2 categories:

1. Literary (Text) Sources
2. Archaeological Sources

There are 14 places of knowledge which are mentioned in treatises mentioned in Purāṇa Nyāya Mimānsā Dharma Śāstrāṅga Miśritāh Vedāh Sthānāni Vidyānaṁ Dharmasya Cha Chaturdaśa Yājñavalkya Smṛti - 1.3. These **Chaturdaśavidyāsthānāni (14)** consisting of

- **Four Vedas** - *Ṛigveda, Yajurveda, Sāmaveda, Atharvaṇaveda*
- **Six Vedāṅgas** - *Śikṣā, Kalpa, Vyākaraṇa, Chhandas, Niruktam* and *Jyotiṣa*
- **Itihāsa** - *Rāmāyaṇa, Mahābhārata* and *Purāṇa* (18 Puranas Viṣṇupurāṇa, Bhāgavata, etc.)
- **Dharmaśāstra** - *Manusmṛti, Yājñavalkyasmṛti, Parāśarasmṛti,* etc.)
- **Mimānsā –** Hermeneutics
- **Nyāya-** logic and Epistemology

Four Vedas

Four Vedas, *Ṛigveda, Yajurveda, Sāmaveda, and Atharvaṇaveda*, can be further classified into 4 parts to get complete knowledge of Vedic Literature:

1. Saṁhitās - worshipping natural entities and other social values
2. Brāhmaṇas - for rituals and other yajñās
3. Āraṇyakās - spiritual practices
4. Upaniṣads - self-realisation.

Six Vedāṅgas

1. **Jyotiṣa**: Lagadha is the main name associated with Vedāṅga-jyotiṣa, but there are many other several contributions to this field by Parāśara, Vṛddha-garga, Āryabhaṭa (*Āryabhaṭīyam*), Varāhamihira (*Bṛhajjātakam, Pañcasiddhāntikam*), Brahmagupta

(*Brahmasphuṭa-siddhānta*), Nīlakaṇṭha Somayājī (*Tantra-saṅgraha*), Sāmanta Candraśekhara to name a few along with their main contributions in brackets.

2. **Vyākaraṇa:** Pāṇini's name comes first when talking about Sanskrit Vyākaraṇa (Grammar). He has written *Aṣṭādhyāyī*, from which we come to know that there had been many grammarians before Pāṇini, but Pāṇini came up with a minimal set of rules that described the Sanskrit language in just about 4000 sutras (aphorisms). Patañjali's *Mahābhaṣya* Bhartṛhari's *Vākyapadiyaṁ* are other sources for deep grammatical knowledge.

3. **Nirukta:** The oldest surviving text of *Nirukta* is by Yāska. Nirukta covers etymology and is the systematic creation of a glossary discussing how to understand uncommon words. Although not classified under Nirukta, notable later contributions in the general areas of glossary/dictionary/thesaurus are Amarasiṁha's *Amarakośa* (serving as dictionary-thesaurus, where synonyms are given in a verse constrained by prosody) and *Śabda-kalpa-drama*.

4. **Chandas**: The oldest extant work on Chandas is Piṅgala's *Chandas-Sūtra*, while a much later work is Kedāra Bhaṭṭa's *Vṛtta-Ratnākara*. The most exhaustive compilations of Sanskrit prosody describe over 600 metres, the highest for any language with a tradition of metrical compositions.

5. **Śikṣā:** Śikṣā deals with phonetics, and since the Vedas were transmitted orally through a Guru-Śiṣya-Paramparā, Śikṣā becomes very important. There could be slight differences in utterances of different syllables in the different śākhās (branches) of the Vedas; hence, those are covered in what is known as prātiśākhyas. However, Pāṇini's *Śikṣa* gives succinct and brief knowledge for most practical purposes.

6. **Kalpa:** Kalpa-sūtras includes śrauta-sūtras (which systematises the Vedic rituals), gṛhya-sūtras (which describes the various rituals to be performed by a gṛhastha by himself along with his wife), Dharma-sūtras (which include the various political, social, and legal duties to be performed) and śulva-sūtras (which discuss the construction of various fire altars, literally śulva means a thread).

Itihāsa and Purāṇa

A popular saying in the tradition is *"Itihāsapurāṇābhyāṁ vedaṁ samupabṛṁhayet"* (Vedic virtues and values are to be communicated through Itihāsa and Purāṇa).

The *Rāmāyaṇa* and *Mahābhārata* (Itihasa)

The *Rāmāyaṇa* and *Mahābhārata* are basic texts of Indian culture. All kinds of knowledge have been gathered in one place in the form of 2 epics. The *Rāmāyaṇa* is known as the epitome of Indian values and ideals. The *Mahābhārata* is an encyclopaedia of Indian traditional knowledge. These 2 epics have served as inspiration for numerous kāvyas (poetic literature) and nāṭakas (dramas) in Saṁskṛt and other Indian languages. The *Rāmāyaṇa* and *Mahābhārata* serve as a great repository of communicating knowledge through the medium of storytelling. We see that over a period of time, these inspired *Pañcatantra*, *Hitopadeśa* and other ancient Indian storybooks, which are great sources of several kinds of knowledge.

Purāṇa Literature

Eighteen Purāṇas – Vishnu Purana, Naradiya Purana, Padma Purana, Garuda Purana, Varaha Purana, Bhagavata Purana, Matsya Purana, Kurma Purana, Linga Purana, Shiva Purana, Skanda Purana, Agni Purana, Brahmanda Purana, Brahmavaivarta Purana, Markandeya

Purana, Bhavishya Purana, Vamana Purana, and Brahma Purana - are great source of history of Indian social, political, and religious culture.

Dharmaśāstra

Dharmaśāstras are sources of ancient Indian sociology, polity, and legal jurisprudence. They deal with the following 3 main areas of society:

1. Ācāra – Ācāra deals with a code of conduct prescribed for every individual in the form of the Āśrama system and for all the civilians in the form of the Varṇa system.

2. Vyavahāra – Vyavahāra deals with Law and order, legal procedure, and penal code. Various types of civil and criminal disputes and their procedures are mentioned in this part of Dharmaśāstra texts. Nuances of ancient Indian Polity are also mentioned in this part.

3. Prāyaścitta – Prāyaścitta are the remedial actions which are to be done if the ācāra or constitutional actions are skipped.

Four Upavedas

1. Āyurveda (Healthcare, Medicine)
   - Suśruta Saṁhitā
   - Charaka Saṁhitā
1. Dhanurveda (Archery),
2. Gandharva-veda (Dance, Music, etc.)
   - Nātyaśāstra
1. Sthāpatya-veda (Architecture).

Philosophy

Those darśanas which accept the Veda as a valid source of knowledge are 6 in number and are called Āstika-darśanas (orthodox). They are:

1. Nyāya
2. Vaiśeṣika
3. Sāṅkhya
4. Yoga
5. Pūrva-mīmāṁsā
6. Uttara-mīmāṁsā

There are other darśanas which do not accept the Veda as a valid means of knowledge. They are called Nāstika-darśanas (Heterodox):-

1. Sautrāntika
2. Vaibhāṣika
3. Yogācāra
4. Mādhyamika
5. Svetāmbara
6. Digambara

Political, Administrative, Economic, and Interstate affairs

*   Kautilyarthaśāstra
*   Śukraniti
*   Kāmandakīya Nitiśātra

Scientific Texts

Astronomy and Mathematics

1. Āryabhatiyam
2. Suryasiddhanta
3. Śulbasutras
4. Lilāvati
5. Bṛhtsaṁhitā
6. Lagadha Ganita
7. Vedic Ganita

Conclusion

Indian Knowledge System is a huge corpus. The more someone digs, the more she/he gets. In order to bring the tremendous hard work and wisdom of our ancestors and make Indians proud, traditional knowledge should be introduced to students through education. This is the treasure through which not only Indians but the entire world can be benefited.

References

Arya, Vedveer (2014), *Indian Contribution to Mathematics and Astronomy.* Aryabhat Publication, Hyderabad.

Balshastri (2013), *Panchatantram,* Chaukhmba Surabharati Prakashan, Varanasi.

Dutta, Amatya Kumar (2002), *Mathematics in Ancient India: An overview.* Resonance, Journal of Science Education Vol. 7 Issue 4, Indian Academy of Sciences Bangalore, India.

Kane, P.V. (1975), *History of Dharmashastra.* Bhandarkar Oriental Research Institute, Pune.

Kieth, A. Berriedale (1982), *A History of Sanskrit Literature.* Motilal Banarsidas, Delhi.

Macdonell, Arthur (2012), *A History of Sanskrit Literature.* Motilal Banarsidas, Delhi.

Mathur, Ashutosh Dayal (2007) *Medieval Hindu Law.* Oxford University Press, New Delhi.

Purāṇanyāyamimānsādharmaśāstrāṅgamiśritāḥ Vedāḥ sthānāni vidyānāṁ dharmasya cha chaturdaśa Yājñavalkya smṛti - 1.3

Sastri, Gaurinath (2015), *A Concise History of Classical Sanskrit Literature.* Oxford University Press, Delhi

Semwal, Krishna (2009) *Sanskrit Vanmaya Mein Vijyana.* Delhi Sanskrit Academy, Delhi.

Sharma, Umashankar 'Rishi' (2012) *Sarvadarshan Sangrah.* Chaukhamba Vidyabhavan, Varanasi.

Swami, Ramsukhdas (2047 Samvat) *Gita Prabodhini.* Geeta Press, Gorakhpur.

Upadhyaya, Baldeva (1978) *Sanskrit Sahitya Ka Bruhd Itihas.* Sharda Niketan, Varanasi.

Chapter 2

A Repertoire of Indian Culture and Traditions

L. V. Padmarani Rao,
Professor and Head, P. G. Department of English, and Research Centre,
Yeshwant Mahavidyalaya, Nanded, Maharashtra.

It is a culture that withstands shocks, not a simple mass of knowledge.
—Swami Vivekananda

Culture is the expression of man's nature in the modes of living and thinking, which may be seen in literature, in religious practices, and in recreation and enjoyment. All the achievements of human beings as members of social groups can be called 'culture.' Art, music, literature, architecture, sculpture, philosophy, religion, and science can be seen as aspects of culture. However, culture also includes the customs, traditions, festivals, ways of living and one's outlook on various issues of life. Culture and traditions thus refer to a human-made environment which includes all the material and non-material products of collective life that are transmitted from one generation to the next. The material component of culture consists of objects that are related to the material aspect of human life, such as clothing, food, and household goods, while the non-material culture refers to ideas, ideals, thoughts, and beliefs. Culture varies from place to place and country to country. Its development is based on the historical process operating in a local, regional, or national context. Hence, the people of any country are characterised by their distinctive cultural traditions.

In very simple terms, culture is the embodiment of the way in which one thinks and does things, as well as the things that people have inherited as members of society. This is practically the same as 'Sanskriti' of the Sanskrit language. The term 'Sanskriti' has been derived from the root' Kri (to do) of the Sanskrit language. Sanskriti embodies the essence of a society's cultural identity, heritage, and values, serving as a source of pride, inspiration, and continuity for future generations. It represents the collective wisdom, creativity, and resilience of people, transcending geographical boundaries and connecting individuals to their cultural roots.

The word 'culture' has its origin in Latin. It is derived from the Latin word cultura,' which is derived from the verb' colere,' meaning 'to till' or 'to cultivate.' Initially, in ancient Rome, 'cultura' was used in an agricultural sense, referring to the cultivation of crops or the tending of plants. Over time, the term 'cultura' took on broader meanings beyond agriculture. It began to encompass the ideas of nurturing, fostering, and refining, extending to intellectual and spiritual pursuits as well. In Medieval Latin, 'cultura' came to refer to the cultivation of the mind, education, and refinement of the arts and sciences. In English, the word 'culture' entered the language during the 15th century, borrowed directly from Latin. Initially, it retained its agricultural connotations but gradually evolved to encompass the broader range of meanings associated with human intellectual, artistic, and social development. Today, 'culture' encompasses a wide array of human activities, beliefs, customs, and achievements, reflecting the diverse aspects of society and civilisation.

The word 'tradition' originates from the Latin word 'traditio,' which is derived from the verb 'tradere,' meaning 'to hand over' or 'to deliver.' In ancient Rome, 'traditio' referred to the act of transmitting or handing down something from one person or generation to another. Over a period of time, the meaning of 'tradition' evolved to encompass customs, practices, beliefs, and rituals that are passed down within a society or community over generations. These traditions often carry symbolic or cultural significance, playing a role in shaping social identity, cohesion, and continuity. In English, the word 'tradition' entered the language in the late Middle Ages, borrowed from Old French and Latin roots. It originally retained its sense of transmission or handing down, but it gradually acquired broader meanings related to cultural heritage, customs, and historical practices. Today, 'tradition' refers to both the act of passing down customs and the customs themselves, reflecting the enduring influence of the past on present day societies and cultures.

'Sanskriti' is a Sanskrit word that translates to 'culture' in English. In Indian languages, including Hindi, *Sanskriti* refers to the sum total of a society's customs, traditions, values, arts, and way of life. It encompasses all aspects of societal and cultural expression, like the customs, rituals, ceremonies, and practices that are passed down through generations within a society, which may include religious ceremonies, rites of passage, festive celebrations, and social rituals that reflect the values and beliefs of the community. *Sanskriti* also has a wider connotation of morals, Values, Language and Communication, Education, Knowledge Systems, Arts, Literature, Architecture, Heritage, Social Structure and Community life.

Society and culture in India are intertwined threads that shape the fabric of everyday life. From the bustling streets of cities to the tranquil villages of the countryside, Indian society is a mosaic of diverse customs, traditions, and social structures. At its heart lies a rich tapestry of cultural practices, rituals, and beliefs that bind communities together and provide a sense of identity and belonging. Through an exploration of caste, religion, language, family, and gender dynamics, we gain insights into the complexities and nuances of Indian society and culture, revealing the resilience and diversity of the human experience.

–Nadeem Hasnain

Indian Culture

Indian culture is incredibly diverse and rich, encompassing a wide range of traditions, languages, religions, cuisines, and arts. India is known for its religious diversity, with Hinduism, Islam, Christianity, Sikhism, Buddhism, and Jainism being the major religions. Each religion has its own customs, rituals, and festivals, contributing to the vibrant tapestry of Indian culture. It is rightly said by Meghnad Desai, "Indian culture and tradition are a vibrant tapestry woven from the threads of ancient wisdom, diverse customs, and timeless rituals. They reflect the resilience of a civilisation that has endured millennia, embraced complexity and diversity while remaining anchored in core values of compassion, spirituality, and community."

India celebrates a myriad of festivals throughout the year, each with its own significance and rituals. Diwali, Holi, Eid, Durga Puja, Navratri, and Christmas are just a few examples of the diverse festivals celebrated across the country. These festivals often involve vibrant decorations, traditional attire, music, dance, and delicious food. Indian cuisine is known for its diverse flavours, spices, and regional variations.

In the rich tapestry of Indian mythology lie the timeless tales of gods and goddesses, heroes and demons, creation, and destruction. These myths serve as mirrors reflecting the complexities of human nature and the cosmic order, offering profound insights into the mysteries of existence. Through symbols and rituals, these myths are woven into the fabric of everyday life, shaping cultural identities and spiritual practices across the sub-continent.

–Devdutt Pattanaik

Each region of India has its own speciality dishes and cooking techniques. Staples like rice, wheat, lentils, and vegetables are common, but the use of spices like cumin, turmeric, coriander, and cardamom add depth and complexity to Indian dishes. Traditional Indian clothing varies across regions and communities. Saree, salwar kameez, kurta-pyjama, dhoti, and sherwani are some of the traditional garments worn by both men and women. These garments often feature intricate embroidery, vibrant colours, and luxurious fabrics, reflecting India's rich textile heritage. India boasts a rich tradition of art and dance forms, each with its own unique style and history. Classical dance forms such as Bharatanatyam, Kathak, Odissi, Kuchipudi, and Manipuri are deeply rooted in Indian mythology and spirituality. Indian art encompasses various forms, including paintings, sculpture, pottery, and textile arts, with regional styles such as Madhubani, Warli, Tanjore, and Pattachitra gaining recognition. India is home to numerous languages, with Hindi and English being the official languages at the national level. Each state has its own official language, and there are hundreds of regional languages and dialects spoken across the country. Indian literature is vast and diverse, ranging from ancient epics like the Ramayana and Mahabharata to modern works by authors such as Rabindranath Tagore, Vikram Seth, and Arundhati Roy.

Indian literature is a treasure trove of creativity and imagination, spanning centuries of literary excellence and cultural diversity. From the ancient epics of the Ramayana and Mahabharata to the modern works of Rabindranath Tagore and R.K. Narayan, Indian literature reflects the richness of its linguistic heritage and the depth of its philosophical insights. Through poetry, prose, drama, and fiction, Indian writers have explored the human condition, capturing the essence of life in all its beauty, complexity, and contradictions. This anthology showcases the breadth and depth of Indian literary tradition, offering readers a glimpse into the soul of a nation through its words and stories.

–A.N.D. Haksar

India is the birthplace of yoga and Ayurveda, ancient systems of wellness and healing. Yoga emphasises physical postures, breathing techniques, and meditation to promote holistic well-being, while Ayurveda focuses on natural remedies, herbal medicine, and dietary practices to maintain health and balance. Family plays a central role in Indian culture, with strong bonds between generations. Respect for elders, hospitality, and communal living are important values. Indian society is structured around various caste, class, and community affiliations, which influence social interactions and relationships. Overall, Indian culture is a tapestry woven from diverse threads, reflecting the country's long history, cultural exchanges, and spiritual traditions. It continues to evolve and adapt while retaining its essence and richness. That is the reason Sarina Singh says, "Culture is the heart and soul of India, a tapestry woven from the myriad threads of tradition, diversity, and creativity. From the vibrant colours of its festivals to the serene melodies of its music, Indian culture embodies a rich heritage that spans millennia. It is a celebration of life, a symphony of languages, customs, and beliefs that unite the nation in its shared humanity and collective spirit of resilience and innovation."

Indian Traditions

Indian tradition encompasses a wide array of customs, beliefs, rituals, and practices that have been passed down through generations. Upinder Singh's emphasis is appropriate when he says, "From the Stone Age to the early medieval period, India's history is a saga of innovation, conflict, and cultural exchange, where diverse people and ideas intersected to create a rich and complex mosaic of human experience."

Traditionally, Indian families often lived together in a joint family system, comprising multiple generations living under one roof. This system fosters strong family bonds, with elders being respected and playing a central role in decision-making and guidance. Respect for elders is a fundamental value in Indian tradition. Children are taught to defer to elders, seek their blessings, and care for them in their old age. Elders are considered repositories of wisdom and experience, and their advice is highly valued. Indian tradition is deeply rooted in values of family, community, spirituality, and cultural heritage, providing a rich tapestry of customs and rituals that continue to shape contemporary Indian society.

A repertoire of Indian Culture and Traditions

India is rich in its cultural diversity and rich traditional heritage and hence A.L. Basham opines, "Indian culture is perhaps the most ancient of all living cultures, and it has always been influential far beyond its borders."

From the standpoint of Languages and Literature, India is a land of linguistic diversity, with hundreds of languages spoken across the country. Hindi and English are the official languages, but each state has its own regional language(s). Indian literature spans millennia, from ancient texts such as the Vedas Upanishads and epics like the Ramayana and Mahabharata to modern works by authors like Rabindranath Tagore, R.K. Narayan, and Salman Rushdie.

Religion and Spirituality point of view, Hinduism is the predominant religion in India, followed by Islam, Christianity, Sikhism, Buddhism, and Jainism. India is home to numerous sacred sites, temples, mosques, churches, gurudwaras, and monasteries, attracting pilgrims and tourists from around the world. Spiritual practices such as yoga, meditation, and Ayurveda have their roots in ancient Indian traditions.

Indian Art and Architecture mark its distinctive and unique position in the entire world. Indian art and architecture showcase a blend of indigenous styles and influences from various cultures and dynasties. Architectural marvels such as the Ajanta and Ellora Caves, Khajuraho Temples, and Hampi ruins reflect India's rich heritage. Traditional Indian art forms include painting (Madhubani, Tanjore, Miniature), sculpture, pottery, weaving (Banarasi silk, Kanchipuram sarees), and jewellery making. Indian classical music, with its intricate rhythms and melodies, includes genres like Hindustani (North Indian) and Carnatic (South Indian) music. Classical dance forms like Bharatanatyam, Kathak, Odissi, Kuchipudi, Mohiniyattam, and Manipuri are steeped in mythology, spirituality, and intricate footwork. Folk music and dance forms vary from region to region, reflecting local traditions and cultural practices.

Cuisines and Culinary traditions of India today are world-known and liked across the globe. Indian cuisine is renowned for its diverse flavours, aromatic spices, and regional specialities. Staple foods include rice, wheat, lentils, and vegetables, with each region boasting its own signature dishes. Street food, such as chaat, samosas, dosas, and kebabs, offer a tantalising culinary experience.

Indian festivals and celebrations are based on agricultural harvests and celebrations. India celebrates a multitude of festivals throughout the year, ranging from religious and cultural events to harvest festivals and national holidays. Diwali, Holi, Eid, Christmas, Navratri, Durga Puja, Raksha Bandhan, and Pongal are among the major festivals celebrated with fervour and enthusiasm across the country. Indian attire varies widely based on region, climate, and occasion. Traditional clothing includes sarees, salwar kameez, lehengas, dhotis, kurta-pyjamas, and sherwanis. Handcrafted textiles, embroidery (such as zari, chikankari, and bandhani), and intricate jewellery are integral to Indian fashion and adornment.

The social customs and etiquette followed in India are typical and unique when compared to any other part of the world. Indian society places importance on hospitality, respect for elders, and familial ties. Customs such as touching elders' feet as a sign of respect, greeting with a *namaste*, and offering food and drinks to guests are common. Rituals and ceremonies marking life events such as birth, marriage, and death are deeply ingrained in Indian culture.

Indian societies place a strong emphasis on collective identity, social harmony, familial bonds, respect for elders, filial piety, and a strong affinity to customs, traditions, morals, and values, which are integral for shaping social interactions, family dynamics, and societal norms. The Indian sub-continent is incredibly diverse, with a wide range of languages, traditions, faiths, and cultural practices. Each region and community within the country has its own unique customs, traditions, and identity, shaped by historical, geographical, and socio-political factors, but still is together as a single country. Nowhere else in the world does one find such diversity and togetherness, which truly presents 'Unity in diversity' and forms *Vasudhaiva Kutumbakam*.

Culture and Traditions in the post-modern world

Culture in the post-modern world, particularly after the advent of Liberalisation, Privatisation, and Globalisation (LPG), has undergone significant transformations. Post-modern culture is characterised by increased interconnectedness and cultural exchange on a global scale. Advances in communication technology, transportation, and media have facilitated the spread of ideas, values, and cultural products across borders, leading to a more interconnected and multicultural world, leading to cultural globalisation that celebrates diversity and hybridity, blurring traditional boundaries between cultures, identities, and artistic styles. Cultural fusion, appropriation, and remixing are common phenomena, leading to the emergence of new cultural forms, expressions, and identities that defy easy categorisation.

The rise of consumerism and mass media has led to the commodification of culture, with cultural products and experiences increasingly marketed and consumed as commodities. Consumer culture shapes not only economic practices but also identities, lifestyles, and social relationships in the post-modern world. The proliferation of digital technologies has transformed the way culture is created, disseminated, and experienced. Digital culture encompasses online communities, social media platforms, digital art, gaming, virtual reality, and other forms of digital expression that shape contemporary social interactions and cultural practices.

Post-modern culture is marked by a critical stance towards traditional cultural norms, hierarchies, and power structures. Cultural critics challenge dominant narratives, question authority, and advocate for social justice, diversity, and inclusivity in cultural representations and institutions. Pop culture has become ubiquitous in the post-modern world, influencing everything from fashion and entertainment to politics and advertising. Media saturation and celebrity culture shape public discourse and collective imagination, blurring the lines between reality and fiction. Post-modern culture is characterised by fragmentation and pluralism, with multiple, often conflicting, cultural narratives, identities, and truths coexisting in the public sphere. This fragmentation challenges notions of cultural unity and authenticity, leading to debates about cultural relativism and moral relativism.

Post-modern culture has witnessed the rise of identity politics, with marginalised groups asserting their rights, visibility, and cultural representation in the public sphere. Issues of race, gender, sexuality, ethnicity, and religion play a central role in contemporary cultural debates and struggles for social justice. In response to the rapid pace of change and globalisation, post-modern culture often exhibits a sense of nostalgia and longing for the past. Cultural artefacts, traditions, and memories are preserved, remixed, and reimagined as people seek to make sense of their place in an ever-changing world.

Overall, culture in the post-modern world is characterised by complexity, fluidity, and constant flux, reflecting the diverse and interconnected nature of contemporary society. While post-modern culture presents challenges and contradictions, it also offers opportunities for creative expression, cultural exchange, and collective transformation in the globalised era.

Cultural Globalisation Vs Indigenous Culture

Indian history has a long stand of more than 15 thousand years and has seen many invasions and cults, and Romila Thapar justifies this diversity absolutely:

Indian history is a complex tapestry woven from the threads of ancient civilisations, diverse cultures, and dynamic social structures. From the dawn of civilisation to the early medieval period, India witnessed the rise and fall of numerous kingdoms, the flourishing of arts and sciences, and the interplay of diverse religious and philosophical traditions. Through the lens of archaeology, literature, and historical records, we uncover the fascinating story of India's past, exploring its rich heritage and enduring legacies.

If culture is not given importance, it can have significant consequences on individuals, communities, and society as a whole, the biggest effect being loss of identity. Culture forms the foundation of individual and collective identity; without a strong cultural framework, people may feel disconnected from their roots, traditions, and heritage, leading to a loss of identity and a sense of belonging.

The second effect could be the erosion of traditions. Culture serves as a repository of traditions, customs, and values passed down through generations. Neglecting cultural practices and traditions can result in their gradual erosion or extinction, depriving future generations of their cultural heritage. Thus, it results in a lack of social cohesion. Culture plays a vital role in fostering social cohesion and community solidarity. Shared cultural values and norms provide a sense of unity and belonging among members of a society. Without a strong cultural foundation, social cohesion may weaken, leading to increased social fragmentation and conflict. Moreover, cultural diversity enriches society by providing a variety of perspectives, experiences, and ways of life. Neglecting cultural importance can lead to the marginalisation or suppression of minority cultures, resulting in a loss of diversity and vitality in society.

The most important disadvantage of cultural globalisation is the loss of traditional wisdom and knowledge. Traditional cultures often contain valuable knowledge, wisdom, and skills that have been accumulated over centuries. Ignoring cultural importance can lead to the neglect or loss of this valuable cultural heritage, depriving society of insights into sustainable living, ecological stewardship, and holistic well-being.

The economic impact of this is that, normally, culture contributes to economic development through tourism, creative industries, and cultural exports. Neglecting cultural importance can undermine these economic opportunities, leading to the decline of cultural industries and diminishing economic benefits associated with cultural heritage. Culture provides individuals with a sense of meaning, purpose, and connection to something greater than themselves. Neglecting cultural values and practices can result in a sense of spiritual emptiness, existential alienation, and emotional disconnection.

Overall, culture is a fundamental aspect of human existence that shapes our identities, relationships, and societies. Failing to recognise the importance of culture can have far-reaching consequences, impacting everything from individual well-being to social cohesion and economic prosperity. Therefore, it is essential to value, preserve, and celebrate cultural diversity and heritage in all its forms.

Indian culture in the post-modern world: A challenge

Globalisation has led to increased cultural homogenisation, where western cultural norms and values are often prioritised over the indigenous ones. This can lead to a dilution of traditional Indian cultural practices and values, as they may be perceived as outdated or inferior in the face of dominant global trends. So, it is essential to emphasise the importance of preserving and promoting indigenous cultural practices and traditions. Encourage initiatives that celebrate cultural diversity and highlight the unique aspects of Indian culture in a global context.

We are living in a homogenised culture where everything is the same.

–An American author and social critic, Chuck Palahniuk

The rise of consumer culture and materialism can erode traditional values such as simplicity, austerity, and spiritual fulfilment. The pursuit of wealth and material possessions may overshadow the importance of spiritual and moral purity in Indian culture. The solution could be to advocate for a balanced approach to development that prioritises sustainable and equitable growth over unchecked consumerism. Promote values of contentment, compassion, and mindfulness as essential components of a meaningful life.

With money, we buy things that we don't need

–Victor Hugo.

Western media, entertainment, and lifestyle choices often influence Indian youth, leading to a disconnect from traditional cultural practices and values. Westernisation can challenge notions of purity in Indian culture, particularly in areas such as dress, language, and social behaviour. It has become increasingly indispensable to foster critical thinking and cultural literacy among youth to help them navigate and critically evaluate the influences of western culture. Encourage dialogue between generations to bridge the gap between traditional and modern values.

You shouldn't judge people based on appearances and your preconceptions.

–British author Jacqueline Wilson

The globalised economy has facilitated the spread of multinational corporations and consumer brands, which may prioritise profit over cultural sensitivity. This can lead to cultural commodification and appropriation, where traditional Indian symbols and practices are commercialised for mass consumption. It is necessary to support local artisans, craftsmen, and cultural practitioners to preserve and promote traditional Indian crafts, arts, and cultural practices. Encourage ethical consumption practices that respect the integrity and authenticity of indigenous cultures.

Be VOCAL for the LOCAL

–Narendra Modi, Prime Minister of India

Advances in technology and digital media have transformed the way culture is produced, consumed, and shared. While technology offers opportunities for cultural preservation and dissemination, it also presents challenges such as cultural misinformation, digital divide, and loss of traditional knowledge. Sensibly, leverage technology to digitise and archive traditional cultural practices, languages, and heritage. Promote digital literacy and access to technology in rural and marginalised communities to ensure equitable participation in the digital age.

Technology is best when it brings people together.

–An American entrepreneur and web developer,

Matt Mullenweg

One needs to '**be glocal**,' which is a concept that encapsulates the idea of blending global awareness with local action. It is a broader philosophy embraced, advocating for sustainable development, community empowerment, and global citizenship by maintaining individual identity.

Conclusion

Overall, maintaining purity in Indian culture and tradition in the post-modern LPG world requires a multi-faceted approach that balances cultural preservation with adaptation to changing realities. By fostering pride in indigenous culture, promoting cultural literacy, and embracing cultural diversity, Indian society can navigate the challenges of globalisation while preserving the richness and integrity of its cultural heritage. Embracing one's cultural identity fosters a sense of pride, confidence, and self-esteem. Celebrating cultural heritage and achievements promotes a positive sense of self and empowers individuals to assert their identities with dignity and respect. Only such notions do ancient Indian wisdom and cultural heritage manage to navigate the complexities of the modern world. Otherwise, nothing like 'Indian Culture' would be left to pass on as 'Indian tradition' to the forth-coming generations for preserving 'Bharatiya Sanskruti' under the umbrella term of 'Cultural Globalisation.' It is time for all to think and act.

References

Basham, A.L. *The Wonder That Was India*. Picador, 2004.

Desai, Meghnad. *The Rediscovery of India: A New Sub-continent*. Penguin Books, 2009.

Hasnain, Nadeem. *Indian Society and Culture*. Anmol Publications, 2010.

Haksar, A.N.D. (Editor). *Indian Literature: An Anthology*. Penguin Books, 1997.

Pattanaik, Devdutt. *Indian Mythology: Tales, Symbols, and Rituals from the Heart of the Sub-continent*. Inner Traditions, 2003.

Singh, Sarina (Editor). *India: The Cultural Companion*. Interlink Books, 2011.

Singh, Upinder. *A History of Ancient and Early Medieval India: From the Stone Age to the 12th Century.* Pearson Education, 2008.

Thapar, Romila. *The Penguin History of Early India: From the Origins to AD 1300.* Penguin Books, 2003.

Web Sources

It is a culture that withstands shocks, not a simple mass of knowledge.
—Swami Vivekananda

We are living in a homogenised culture where everything is the same.
—An American author and social critic, Chuck Palahniuk

You shouldn't judge people based on appearances and your preconceptions.
—British author Jacqueline Wilson

Be VOCAL for the LOCAL
—Narendra Modi, Prime Minister of India

Technology is best when it brings people together.
—An American entrepreneur and web developer, Matt Mullenweg.

Chapter 3

Tattvajñāna: A Constructive Outline of Indian Metaphysics

Ambika Datta Sharma,
Senior Professor & Head, Department of Philosophy,
Dr. Harisingh Gour Vishwavidyalaya Sagar, Madhya Pradesh.

Rajan,
Assistant Professor of Philosophy,
School of Education, Azim Premji University, Bhopal, Madhya Pradesh.

---

yāvadantargataḥsargaḥsaṃsthito'ṅkuritopamaḥ |
kusūlasyevabījasyasiktasyevāṅkurohṛdi || ||

(Yoga-Vasistha; 7.87.2)

This means that as I introspected and mediated deeply, I realised that the world resides in my heart, blooming like seeds in a granary when watered by rain.

Preamble and Quest

The essence of metaphysical practices and themes reveals much about specific cultural values and principles, exerting influence on both individual and collective consciousness. Following this premise, a theoretical question arises: whether Indian culture, where metaphysics, translated as Tattvamīmāṃsā or Tattvajñāna, holds prominence, should fundamentally be characterised by spiritualism, materialism, or argumentation in essence rather than merely in process or practice. Influenced by this inquiry, this composition examines a constructive outline of Indian metaphysics, emphasising its interconnectedness with epistemology, ethics, religion, and language, thus constructing a cohesive knowledge system. Through the examination of selected themes and inquiries, our aim is to highlight the consistency and spiritual essence inherently embedded within it. Correspondingly, by drawing on insights from classical sources like Advaita Vedanta, Buddhism, and Jainism, as well as contemporary Indian academicians such as T.R.V. Murti, C.D. Śarmā, BiswambharPahi, and R.K. Tripathi, we navigate through a diverse display of Indian metaphysical discourses and frameworks while maintaining coherence.

1. Beyond Historicism: Open-Ended Horizons of Indian Metaphysics

From a thinking perspective, it is indeed fascinating to contemplate the vastness and complexity of both the outer and inner worlds, each filled with infinite possibilities and dimensions to be explored. The inner world is as vast as the infinite expanse of cosmic entities such as galaxies, seas, and skies. Now, whether they are separate or interconnected, the wonder of existence persists, inviting exploration and contemplation. This experiential aspect of reality has constantly been a matter of wonder among thinkers, sages, and seers, transcending cultural barriers. They all encounter almost the same kind of questions: What is the nature of reality? What is that one or more thing that, if known, can help us understand the entire world, whether inner or outer? [1] How did this world come into existence, and why? Why is there something rather than nothing? Is there

---

1. As came in Brihadaranyaka Upanishad: *Maitreyī ātmano vā are darśanena śravaṇena matyā vijñānenedaṁ sarvaṁ viditam*: "If you can grasp the significance of what this ātman is, you have known everything; and then, you have possessed everything; you have become all things. There is nothing left to desire afterwards. And if this is not to be achieved, what is going to be your fate? See - Krishnananda, S. (Trans.). (1983). *Brihadaranyaka Upanishad*. The Divine Life Society, Sivananda Ashram, Rishikesh, India. p.204.

really something, or is it just a veil of Maya and the rest? Likewise, as glimpsed philosophically in the famous creation hymn of Rig-Veda:

Who really knows? Who can here proclaim it? When was it produced? Whence is this creation? The gods came afterwards with the creation of this universe. Who then knows whence it has arisen? Whence this creation has arisen—perhaps it formed itself, perhaps it did not—the one who looks down on it, in the highest heaven, only he knows, or perhaps he does not know (Rig-Veda; 10: 129; Sen, 2012: 22).

The series of questions concerning reality and existence, which we explore in metaphysics (Tattvamīmāṃsā), will continue, and if these inquiries align with your pursuit, Indian culture presents a vast ocean of wisdom wherein we can research to discover countless answers without succumbing to confusion. Moreover, to respond to the initial scepticism, it is crucial to recognise that philosophy, including its branches such as metaphysics, resides within its domain as long as dialectical inquiry persists and Vada among systems continues. Conversely, once definitive answers are reached, they transcend the realm of philosophy (Russell, 2001: 90).

Therefore, if conclusive solutions to metaphysical questions remain subtle, it signifies the dynamic nature of any philosophical thought. This aspect not only reflects the richness of philosophical discourse but also underscores the continual evolution and exploration innate in Indian philosophical traditions. Moving to the next sceptical stance, critics may question whether hymns, myths, metaphors, and prayers are suitable for inclusion within the realm of metaphysics, which is a systematic study of theories of reality. Moreover, they may challenge the attempt to fit such entities, including the Rig-Veda, into the typical historiographical framework, which prioritises chronology over the consistency of ideas and themes. For such sceptics, consistency is still all about chronology.

Fortunately, these sceptical viewpoints can be effectively addressed. For instance, regarding the influence of cultural narratives on metaphysical speculation, it can be argued that humans possess the capacity to transcend chronologies and rigid frameworks. Through mediums such as hymns, myths, arts, metaphors and poems, individuals can gain insight into the reality of the world beyond mere mechanistic understanding, or at the very least; these mediums provide a window to "Truth" and "Reality." It is now widely acknowledged that history is equally accompanied by narratives found in mythology, theology, and other cultural expressions (Munslow, 2018). Remarkably, these narratives, whether individual or collective, can serve as valuable tools for research. Western historiographers have acknowledged this aspect, which supports the notion that history cannot be solely constructed from a chronology of events (Roberts, 2001). Furthermore, it is also worth noting that no mature culture remains solely confined within the boundaries of certain literature; it continually explores new possibilities towards truth and reality. This exploratory principle centrally applies to Indian metaphysics as well. As Stephen Phillips, while writing about Indian metaphysics, claims:

Vedic poems and hymns express various themes, some of which are philosophical and important to the speculation of later periods. But the Upanishads, the "secret doctrines" of the ancient culture, are what decisively launched Indian philosophy—especially Indian idealism. Early Upanishads (from 800 to 300 BCE) represent a break with previous literature in the freeing of an abstract intellect from myth and ritual. Prose appears, and the poetry is usually discursive, didactic, and less imagistic than that of the Veda. Though argument and elaborations of positions are not as pronounced and professionalised as in later periods, even the earliest Upanishads employ self-conscious argumentation. They contain several reports of debates on metaphysical topics held in the courts of kings (*Phillips, 1997: 8*).

Correspondingly, by remaining open to interdisciplinary approaches and methods, we can appreciate that Indian philosophical thought can be understood within both pre-systematic phases, encompassing the Vedas and Upanishads, and systematic phases, incorporating all the Darshanas (schools of thought), up to contemporary philosophical studies (Hiriyanna, 1995). In fact, the majority of Indian philosophical discourse and practice can be understood within this systematic-pre-systematic and contemporary framework, whether we consider the popular emergence of theistic and atheistic philosophical schools of thought or the continuity of similar types of questions throughout the culture within the argumentative tradition, regardless of theoretical standpoint (Nicholson, 2010). Moreover, its progress in the medieval, colonial, and post-colonial periods indeed represents a philosophical triumph worth appreciating (Ganeri, 2011; Deshpande, 2015; Raghuramaraju, 2007). Consistency, as we shall see, is deeply embedded in Indian thought, including within metaphysics, provided we acknowledge this without imperialistic or ideological biases. To be precise, Indian metaphysics, as we shall see, despite enduring theoretic dialectics, maintains its core themes and inquiries without yielding to the temptation of creating modish trends and ideology. Resisting external pressures, it adapts while staying true to foundational principles, integrating experiential knowledge and rational inquiry (Mohanty, 1992).

Within this rational convention and line of thought, major Indian philosophy schools and corresponding religions are intricately intertwined, offering a unique legacy on Indian metaphysics (Perrett, 2001). Unlike western traditions, which often distanced themselves from religious discourses and practices after the medieval period or claimed to do so, Indian philosophy maintains a deep connection with the religious fabric of the sub-continent (Padhi, 2005). This practical integration is influenced by several factors. Firstly, prominent schools such as Buddhism, Jainism, Vedanta, Samkhya, yoga, and Nyaya engage in shared debates on fundamental existential and experiential questions, closely aligning with the inquiries found in religions or culminating into the same. These discussions address issues such as the problem of suffering and evil, as well as the mystery of life after death, among others. Likewise, both Indian philosophy and religions share central concepts such as karma, reincarnation, liberation, and ultimate reality, encompassing Hinduism, Buddhism, and Jainism, further blurring the lines between philosophy and religion. (Radhakrishnan, 1989). Moreover, contemplative practices like meditation, yoga, worship, and asceticism serve dual purposes of philosophical inquiry and spiritual growth, deeply entwined with religious observances (Bilimoria & Sherma, 2020).

Overall, the interconnectedness of Indian philosophy schools and religions stems from shared history, concepts, practices, texts, and cultural dynamics, challenging their distinct categorisation. There is a rationale behind this assertion, rooted in the understanding that the philosophical study of religion is inherently metaphysical in nature and vice versa. These realms cannot be adequately explored solely through physical means.

1. Questions of Self and Causation in Indian Metaphysics: Few Inquiries into the Inner and Outer World

Metaphysics, the philosophical inquiry into the fundamental nature of reality and existence, encompasses a wide array of themes, among which the concepts of Self, Creation, and Causation are of great interest among thinkers and sages (Loux, Crisp, 2017). These themes are not only central to western philosophical traditions but also hold significant importance in Indian metaphysics (Perrett, 2013; Phillips, 1997). In Indian philosophy, these themes serve as initial windows into the metaphysical domain, offering unique projects and insights into the nature of reality and existence in one way or another. Through the long Vada (dialogical) tradition centred on these fundamental themes,

Indian metaphysics has developed rich and diverse perspectives on the nature of existence, consciousness, causation, and the fundamental principles governing the universe. Various schools of Indian philosophy, such as Vedanta, Nyaya, Vaisheshika, Samkhya, Buddhism, Jainism, Charvaka, and Kashmir Shaivism, among others, offer profound insights into these metaphysical inquiries (Mādhava, 1996). Despite the diversity in their theoretical standpoints and outcomes, these schools exhibit remarkable consistency in addressing these questions, albeit through different lenses and methodologies. Likewise, Roy W. Perrett beautifully outlines a focus of Indian metaphysics:

Metaphysics is concerned with the counterpart to pramana theory, i.e., prameya theory. Whereas the sramanas are the means of knowledge, the prameyas are the knowable, cognisable entities that constitute the world. With respect to the number and kinds of such entities, there was a very wide variety of opinions among classical Indian philosophers - including variants of monism, dualism, and pluralism about both entities and kinds. *Many metaphysical topics were debated, but 2 of the most important were causation and the nature of the self*. The competing theories offered about these 2 issues also raised other questions about the metaphysics of wholes and parts, substances and properties, and universals and particulars (Perrett, 2013: X, italics emphasised).

In line with this thought, to begin inquiries into the nature of self in Indian philosophy, the notion of self, often referred to as "atman" or "purusha," is deeply intertwined with the quest for understanding one's true nature and ultimate reality. The classical questions from the Upanishads such as "Ko Aham" (Who am I?), "Kuta Ajata" (where from (it) appeared? Or where did I come from?), and "Kim iyamvisriti" (What is this universe?) are not merely abstract inquiries but serve as profound windows into metaphysical inquiry and the nature of reality itself. These questions prompted sages and seers to delve deeply into the nature of self, existence, and the cosmos, leading to profound insights and understanding beyond conventional knowledge. Thus, rather than fading away, these questions continue to inspire seekers on the path of self-discovery and spiritual realisation, giving birth to speculative metaphysics. As inquired in Aitareya Upanishad:

If speaking is done through speech; if breathing-out is done through the out-breath; if seeing is done through sight; if hearing is done through hearing; if touching is done through the skin; if thinking is done through the mind; if breathing is done through the in-breath; and if procreation is done through the reproductive organs – then who am I? (Olivelle, 1998: 319; ĀU 1.3.11)

This foundational question has been a perpetual inquiry in Indian metaphysics and has given birth to the synonymity of "I" with Self or Atman: whether one affirms the existence of the self or not is a different matter. Likewise, all the responses, whether they give rise to naturalism, dualism, pantheism, monism, or nihilism, pertaining to this inquiry are quite interesting and contribute to making Indian metaphysics more dialogical, providing perspectives to look at Indian culture through new streams of thought. For instance, one answer is illustrated in the Brihadaranyaka Upanishad:

Ātmāvā is draṣṭavyaḥśrotavyomantavyonidididhyāsitavyaḥ: "O, Maitreyī, it is the ātman that is to be beheld; it is the ātman that is to be known; it is the ātman that is to be searched for; it is the ātman which is to be heard about; it is the ātman which is to be thought in the mind; it is the ātman which is to be meditated upon. There is nothing else worthwhile thinking, nothing else worthwhile possessing because nothing worthwhile exists other than This (Krishnananda, 1983)."

Of equal importance, as affirmed, within the discourse surrounding the concept of the self in Indian philosophical traditions, various schools of thought present divergent viewpoints, thereby highlighting the dialectical and dynamic nature of Indian metaphysical thought (Ganeri, 2007; Ram Prasad, Kuznetsova, & Ganeri, 2016). To briefly outline about them, one perspective, epitomised by the Charvaka system, contends that the self is not an independent entity but rather synonymous with the body, which possesses consciousness as a by-product of material elements. This view underscores perception as the primary source of knowledge and dismisses the existence of a self beyond sensory experience. According to Charvaka, self-ceases exist upon the demise of the body, with no notion of transmigration. Modern naturalism movement centrally beholds this physics in its worldview (Ganeri, 2012). In contrast with this stance, Samkhya-yoga philosophy offers yet another angle, delineating purusha (soul) and Prakriti (matter) as 2 different fundamental realities. Purusha, akin to the Upanishadic concept of Atman, is posited as omnipresent and devoid of qualities. Samkhya-yoga acknowledges the plurality of selves and delineates between pure self and empirical self (jiva), with the former representing transcendent consciousness.

Furthermore, the Nyaya-Vaisesika philosophical tradition introduces the concept of the self as an enduring entity possessing cognitive abilities and desires. They characterise the self, or ātmā, as distinct due to its qualities such as desire, aversion, volition, pleasure, pain, and cognition. According to Nyaya-Vaisesika, the existence of the self is affirmed through inference (anumāna), and it serves as the inherent cause of cognitive experiences. Additionally, the self is perceived as an object of mental perception. Notably, in these schools of thought, consciousness is considered an accidental attribute of the self, arising from interactions with the mind and sense organs. Outlining another important school, the Mīmāṃsaka philosopher conceptualises the self (ātman) as an eternal, unbroken entity characterised by pure consciousness, akin to light, and inherently self-existent and self-revealing. However, contrary to the Sāṅkhya School's assertion that the self is inseparable from the intellect (buddhi), it is viewed as a dynamic principle undergoing constant change while retaining its core identity throughout various stages of transition. Similarly, the self maintains its essence as an unaltered consciousness amidst the diverse experiences of pleasure or pain encountered throughout its journey of metempsychosis. It neither completely vanishes with transient states, as posited by Buddhists, nor remains entirely unchanged, as argued by the Naiyāyikas.

In Advaita Vedanta, a unified perspective emerges, positing the reality of one self-identified with Brahman or the Absolute. While it recognises the empirical reality of the individual self, Advaita Vedanta denies its ontological reality, emphasising the unity of Atman and Brahman. In contrast, Vishishtadvaita Vedanta acknowledges the ontological reality of the individual self, considering it an inseparable part of Brahman. In Jainism, an alternative perspective emerges, affirming the existence of a permanent self, or jiva, endowed with infinite attributes such as knowledge, perception, and bliss. Unlike Charvaka and Buddhism, Jainism asserts the reality of the self beyond the material body. This view acknowledges the coexistence of liberated and bound selves and distinguishes between pure self and empirical self, with the former remaining unaffected by worldly experiences. Contrarily, Buddhist philosophy challenges the notion of a permanent self, advocating for the impermanence of all phenomena. Buddhism posits that the self is a transient composite of 5 aggregates, and upon the dissolution of the body, nothing enduring persists. Instead, Buddha characterises the self as a stream of consciousness, constantly evolving from one moment to the next. Rebirth, in Buddhist doctrine, is a consequence of karma rather than the transference of a soul. Through these varied perspectives and debates, the discourse on the self in Indian philosophical traditions highlights the complexity and richness of philosophical inquiry into the nature of existence and consciousness. With the above brief outlines, we obtain a comprehensive summary of Indian metaphysics regarding the self, which can be consolidated as follows:

What is the essential nature of sentient beings such as people? The main traditions of classical Indian philosophy can be categorised into 4 groups based on their answers to this metaphysical question. The first group, consisting solely of the Charvakas, asserted that a person is merely a body and the attributes or qualities associated with that body. Consequently, they denied the possibility of life continuing after death. Conversely, all other traditions maintained that people possess a nonphysical component, which constitutes their core identity and persists beyond the death of the body. Do these immaterial entities remain permanently distinct from each other, or do they merge into a greater whole upon liberation? The latter viewpoint was espoused by those in the second group: Advaita Vedantins, Non-dualistic Shaivas, and certain Pancaratrika Vaishnavas. According to them, individual souls are identical with, or emanations, evolutes, effects, or contractions of an Oversoul or Absolute Self, known as Brahman, Shiva, and Narayana in their respective traditions. The 2 remaining groups agree that the nonphysical aspects of people remain forever distinct from each other; however, they disagree on whether to characterise them as souls or selves. According to Buddhists, they should not be characterised as such, while those in the final fourth group—such as Nyaya, Vaisheshika, Mimamsa, Samkhya, Shaiva Siddhanta, and Jainism—assert that they should (Watson, 2017: 293).

With the above discussion, one of the central issues of Indian metaphysics that emerges is the debate on self and non-self, which has engaged the insights of great metaphysicians and dialecticians from antiquity to modern times. T.R.V. Murti, C.D. Śarmā, Biswambhar Pahi and Jonardan Ganeri, contemporary Indian thinkers, have made significant contributions to this debate, offering distinct perspectives on Indian metaphysics (Murti, 1955; Śarmā, 1996; Ganeri, 2007). Selecting Murti among these thinkers, he affirms this debate just cited and distinguishes Indian metaphysics into 2 main traditions: "one centred on the ātma doctrine found in the Upanishads, and the other rooted in the anātma doctrine of Buddhism" (Murti, 1955: 26).

Subsequently, these traditions present contrasting views of reality. The Upanishads and related Brahmanical systems perceive reality as comprising an unchanging inner essence (ātman) within a world of flux and impermanence, termed the substance view. This perspective, exemplified in Advaita Vedanta, denies the ultimate reality of the apparent world. While Sāṁkhya leans towards substance, Nyāya-Vaiśeṣika accords significance to both substance and modes. Ātman is central to their philosophical framework to explain the nature of reality. Conversely, Buddhism rejects the notion of substance (ātman), asserting the transient nature of existence devoid of an unchanging core. And in the words of Murti, this discourse implies that:

Indian philosophy must be interpreted as the flow of these 2 vital streams—one having its source in the ātma doctrine of the Upaniṣads ṣ and the other in the anātmavāda of Buddha...Throughout the course of their development, they remain true to their original inspirations. The Brāhmanical systems took the real as Being, Buddhism as Becoming; the former espoused the universal, existential, and static view of reality, the latter the particular, sequential, and dynamic; for one space, for the other time, is the archetype. The Brāhmanical systems are relatively more categorical and positive in their attitude (vidhimukhena), while the Buddhists are more negative (niṣedhamukhena) (Murti, 1955: 28).

However, it is important to note that the discussion does not end with these 2 traditions alone. While the dialogue certainly commences with them, dialectics pave the way for the exploration of additional perspectives. The synthesis of these 2 views does not replace them but rather forms a third perspective. For instance, Murti finds a solution within Buddhism itself, particularly within the branch known as Mādhyamika Sunyavāda. Furthermore, scholars like T.M.P. Mahadevan argue that non-dual metaphysics has the capacity to encompass all views, including those of Buddhism and dualism (Chatterjee, 1998; Mahadevan, 1976). Additionally, protagonists of the Jaina system argue that it had relatively little influence on the trajectory of Indian philosophy and remained unaffected by other systems. Therefore, they contend that Jainism offers a viable solution for the compatibility issues arising from debates such as Self and Non-self or Being and Becoming through their anekantavada metaphysical stance (Matilal, 1981). Now, to culminate this debate on self or non-self, it is crucial to acknowledge that the nature of self in any particular philosophical school fundamentally informs their metaphysics of soteriology, which is essentially a collective goal of all schools except Charvaka. This is an extensive issue, and therefore, we maintain the discussion open-ended as we progress forward.

However, before we shift the discourse, we can also consider Prof. Biswambhar Pahi's theory, another recent Indian philosophy academician, who offers a comprehensive analysis of the evolution of Indian metaphysical thought, with a particular emphasis on the influence of Śākyamuni Gautama Buddha's teachings (Pahi, 2000). By scrutinising Vedic doctrines such as Nityānavāda, Ātmavāda, and Ucchedavāda, Buddha established the groundwork for the Santānavādi Tattvamīmāṃsā tradition. This tradition, as noted by Murti as well, is characterised by its emphasis on Pratītyasamutpāda theory, which highlights non-selfism, immaterialism, and the transient nature of existence, rejecting eternalism, selfism, and materialism. This is a stream of Indian metaphysics, much like Murti's stance. Then, we have the Upanishadic way of doing metaphysics. In line with this tradition, Pahi delineates 2 primary schemas of thought: "the Yājñavalkya tradition and the Kānādiya tradition" (Pahi, 2000: 1-3). The former underscores the distinction between the subjective and objective realms, drawing from sources like the Bṛhadāraṇyaka Upaniṣad. Vedānta, Sāṅkhya, and yoga philosophies align with this tradition, emphasising the disparity between subject and object. In contrast, the Kānādiya tradition emphasises the essential opposition between substantialism and non-substantialism, developing theories in response to Buddhist transientism and anātmism. The Vaiśeṣika tradition, alongside Nyāya and Mīmāṃsā, employs the Dharma-Dharmī framework to delineate subjective and objective elements. Pahi also points out that, unlike the Yājñavalkya tradition, Mīmāṃsā incorporates generalisation, space, and time into its philosophical framework. The Kānādiya tradition, in contrast, grappled with Buddhist doctrines, refining its theories over centuries. And that is why, in modern times, the debate between Buddhist and Nyāya schools of thought is so popular.

Transitioning from the exploration of the inner world to the contemplation of the external world, Indian metaphysics further investigates a rich discourse concerning the questions of causation. Similar to the extensive debate on the nature of the self, the problem of causation plays an especially significant role in Indian metaphysical discourse. This problem manifests in Indian thought in various forms, whether in the cosmogonic speculations of the Vedas and Upanishads or the Vedic emphasis on ritual action (karma) and its causal mechanisms, to name a few (Perrett, 1998). Likewise, with the acceptance of liberation (moksha) as the ultimate goal by the majority of Indian philosophical schools, these concerns intertwined, driving a deep interest in causation. The issue is so prominent in Indian metaphysics that Buddhism, one of the popular schools of thought, is often interpreted as emphasising the idea of causation, encapsulated in the concept of dependent origination (pratītyasamutpāda) (Kalupahana, 1975). While it is true that the Charvaka materialists rejected causation altogether, orthodox Hindu philosophers, as well as heterodox Buddhists and Jainas, accepted both causation and liberation, albeit with differing interpretations. Indian theories of causation are typically categorised based on whether the effect is considered a mode of the cause. In other words, Indian thinkers are primarily concerned with the interplay between the material cause and its effect. The crux of the debate lies in contrasting perspectives on the essence of the effect and its relation to the cause.

In other words, Indian metaphysicians ponder whether the material cause permeates any essence into its effect or if the essence emerges entirely external to the cause. For instance, does the seed impart any essence to the sprouting plant, or does the essence arise from nothingness, suggesting that the effect is created ex nihilo? This fundamental query delineates the 2 main theories of Indian causation: Satkarya-Vada, positing the existence of the effect's essence prior to formal manifestation, and Asatkarya-Vada, proposing the non-existence of the effect's essence before its formal emergence. Within these frameworks, various philosophical schools, such as Nyaya-Vaisesika, Sankhya-Yoga, Vedanta, and Buddhists, offer diverse interpretations, further enriching the discourse. Satkarya-Vada proposes that the effect exists in a latent or potential state before manifesting itself in reality. This perspective encompasses 2 main doctrines: "Parinama-Vada, which posits a genuine transformation from cause to effect as endorsed by Sankhya-Yoga, and Vivarta-Vada, which suggests a perception of illusory change, a concept championed by the Sankara school of Vedanta" (Perrett, 1998: 121).

Conversely, Asatkarya-Vada maintains that the effect is entirely new and devoid of pre-existing essence within its cause. This divergence leads to differing views on the continuity of the cause after the emergence of the effect, with Nyaya-Vaisesika proposing Arambha-Vada, where the cause persists alongside the effect, and Buddhists advocating for the annihilation of the cause post-effect. The classification of Indian theories of causation thus underscores the rich legacy of philosophical inquiry, offering nuanced insights into the nature of existence, causality, and reality within the Indian metaphysical tradition. Interestingly, within this discourse of causation, we also encounter an important metaphysical issue known as the problem of relation, which exists in various domains, such as between cause and effect, mind, and body, as well as God and man, among others. R.K. Tripathi, a well-known Indian philosophy scholar, even asserts that all other problems, such as liberation, causation, and creation, are surficial; the central issue in Indian metaphysics is that of relation (Tripathi, 1969). Tripathi argues that while Indian philosophers examine questions about topics like the self, God, causation, and substance, these inquiries are specific to each school and not universal. Neither the creation nor the substance problem applies to all schools. For instance, Buddhism and Jainism do not bother about the problem of creation at all.

Following this, Tripathi argues that the problem of relation emerges as a promising central theme of Indian metaphysics. It is being argued that this problem lies at the core of each system's unique logic and is crucial for understanding their entire philosophical framework, demonstrating the diverse aspects of Indian metaphysics beyond spirituality and mysticism. This issue stems from our everyday experience, where we encounter the concepts of identity and difference in both us and the objects around us. Likewise, as noted above, these 2 features, found in various pairs of categories such as substance and quality, subject and object, or body and soul, form the basis of our understanding. However, it is not merely the coincidence of identity and difference that intrigues philosophers, but rather their relationship to each other, which cannot be addressed simply by doing physics but rather requires metaphysics. In line with this argument, Tripathi further helps us to grasp that this question of the realness of this relationship leads to 4 possible approaches: "that both identity, difference, and their relation are equally real; that while identity and difference are real, their relation is false; that either identity or difference, along with their relation, must be false; or that all 3 are equally false" (Tripathi, 1969: 40-42). Realist systems of Indian philosophy assert the equal reality of identity, difference, and their relation. This perspective, evident in schools like Nyaya-Vaisesika and Mimamsa, maintains that a pluralist view of reality necessitates the acceptance of the reality of relation.

However, this view is challenged by thinkers like those of the Samkhya-yoga school, who argue that while identity and difference are real, their relation is false. They contend that a relationship cannot be of the same status as a relatum and can be dispelled through discriminating knowledge. Further complexity arises with the perspectives of Advaita Vedanta and Buddhism. Advaita Vedanta advocates for the reality of identity over difference, while Buddhism emphasises the reality of difference as it can explain change. These contrasting views highlight the intricate nature of the problem of relation and its implications for Indian philosophical thought. It not only forms the basis of their fundamental logic but also influences their main doctrines. Hence, Tripathi argues that the central problem of Indian metaphysics shapes the very essence of philosophical inquiry within the Indian tradition. However, the main issue with this thesis is that it focuses solely on the process and practice of one aspect of metaphysics, neglecting the ultimate goal that thinkers strive towards, whether it is moksha or another objective. This once again raises the fundamental metaphilosophical question: should we determine the central philosophy of any system based on the process or the end result? Therefore, the nature of Indian philosophy remains a subject of debate. Nonetheless, Tripathi offers a fresh perspective on Indian metaphysics that warrants further research.

1. **Mystery of 2 Truths: The Revisionary Realm of Indian Metaphysics**

The Buddha's teaching of the Dharma is based on 2 truths: a truth of worldly conventions and an ultimate truth. — (Nagarjuna, Mulamadhyamakakdrika 24: 8)

If there is something rather than nothing, then prima facie, there is one question that troubles any sincere scholar: Do we perceive that something, which we may call reality, as it truly is or differently? If we perceive reality indirectly, as a large number of thinkers accept, then it becomes the task of metaphysicians to quest for the real. Philosophy and religion have a long and intertwined history, especially concerning the concept of the "true world" theory, which is prominently manifested in the two-truth theories of Indian philosophy. This theory has existed in various forms throughout antiquity and remains relevant in modern times. It appears in various philosophical systems and religious teachings, such as Plato's distinction between 'Forms and Ideas,' Kant's differentiation of 'Phenomena and Noumena,' Martin Heidegger's 'Being' and 'beings,' and the Indian philosophical concepts of 'Pratibhāsika' (apparent) and 'Paramārthika' (real), or 'saṃvṛtisatya' (conventional truth) and 'paramārthasatya' (ultimate truth). In his work "Central Philosophy of Buddhism," Professor T. R. V. Murti points out that absolutist views, whether found in Madhyamika Buddhism, Advaita Vedanta, or F. H. Bradley's philosophy, draw a clear line between an ultimate reality (referred to as the Absolute) and a realm that is merely pragmatically real (the world of our everyday experiences), leading to the development of a '2 truths' doctrine and an illusion theory (Murti, 1955: 104).

And not merely as esoteric problems in Indian philosophy. The issues that emerge from probing the questions of mithya and samvrti, Brahman and paramilrthasatya are human and indefeasible; they have weight for philosophers everywhere. They have been central in the Indian tradition and, until recently, peripheral in the western, which can tell us much about the 2 traditions. The Indians have 2 truths as a philosophical problem because they do not sunder faith and reason but embrace all questions, including what in the west would be 'religious' questions - within reach of philosophical thought. Hence, religious experience and insight thrust forward the problem of 2 truths indefeasibly. In the west, because, for the greater part, we have held our religious faith to be of a different order than our philosophical convictions, we have had little need to see things in terms of 2 truths: we are content with one truth and one faith (Sprung, 2012:5).

In its essence, the true world theory posits that there exists a reality beyond the surface appearances of this seeming and often chaotic world. It offers a number of ideal utopias, such as the notion that life has a higher purpose, transcending the mundane and sometimes bewildering aspects of existence, or that there is an epistemic world beyond cognition and perception. As Vasubandhu's The Principles of Exegesis (Vyākhyāyukti) points out: "The Buddha taught the 2 truths: conventional truth, which is the object of correct mundane cognitions, and ultimate truth, which is the object of world-transcending cognition" (Thakchoe, 2023: 55). This perspective not only offers a revisionary conceptual framework distinct from the simple descriptive standpoint but also instils hope by suggesting the possibility of overcoming the perpetual cycle of earthly suffering (Garfield, 2010).[2] At least, this has been the case with Vedanta and Buddhism. The true world theory points towards an ultimate destination or telos, a grand purpose or goal that goes beyond the limitations of our material reality. At its core, this doctrine posits that concerning liberation from samsara, reality remains singular.

Put differently, achieving liberation does not entail "escaping" from samsara to an alternate realm of boundless freedom, although such expressions may be metaphorically used. As per the "2 truths" doctrine, enlightenment is inherent because liberation signifies liberation from

---

2. Tsong Khapa, following Candrakīrti closely, writes that "'Convention' refers to a lack of understanding or ignorance; that is, that which obscures or conceals the way things really are" {Ocean of Reasoning 480-481). Candrakīrti himself puts the point this way: Obscurational truth 3 is posited due to the force of afflictive ignorance, which constitutes the limbs of cyclic existence. The srāvakas, pratyekabuddhas and bodhisattvas, who have abandoned afflictive ignorance, see compounded phenomena to be like reflections, to have the nature of being created; but these are not truths for them because they are not fixated on things as true. Fools are deceived, but for those others - just like an illusion - in virtue of being dependency originated, they are merely obscurational. See - Garfield, J. L. (2010). Taking Conventional Truth Seriously: Authority Regarding Deceptive Reality. *Philosophy East and West*, *60*(3), 341–354.

ignorance and the erroneous perception of reality. The universe inhabited by an enlightened sage is identical to that of ordinary individuals, yet the perception of the enlightened sage transcends the false confines of time, space, and subjectivity. Enlightened sages apprehend reality in its true essence—a noumenal reality. It suggests that one day, the enlightened will emerge from the constraints of dogma, transcending our conceptual and linguistic frameworks, much like awakening from sleep.

However, for debate's sake, it is indeed a significant distinction that what is categorised as ignorance in Buddhism is viewed as truth and reality in Vedanta, and vice versa. However, the narrative remains the same as depicted in the above quote. In simpler terms, while change is acknowledged as real in Buddhism, it is deemed unreal in Vedanta because it does not align with their metaphysical framework. In Buddhism, impermanence (change) is a core tenet encapsulated in the concept of "anicca" (Śarmā, 1952). The recognition of the ever-changing nature of existence is fundamental to the Buddhist understanding of reality. Embracing impermanence is pivotal to overcoming suffering and attaining enlightenment. Conversely, in Vedanta, particularly in certain non-dualistic schools like Advaita Vedanta, the ultimate reality (Brahman) is considered changeless and eternal. Within this metaphysical framework, the perceived changes in the phenomenal world are seen as illusory and not ultimately real. The emphasis lies on transcending the apparent changes to realise the unchanging truth of Brahman. What it implies is that the two-truth theory has been a pervasive and significant concept in Indian philosophy in general and metaphysics in particular, whether a school accepts it, like Advaita Vedanta and Buddhism, or rejects it, like Charvaka. Interestingly, Indian thought language has also been taken into this metaphysical discourse of 2 truths (Chakrabarti, 2017:43-46).

However, if any 2 schools of thought have made this metaphysical discourse of 2 truths famous, they are none other than Advaita

Vedanta and Buddhism. Interestingly, there is a debate about whether these 2 schools are on the same page regarding this problem or if they hold different perspectives. To be precise, while both schools agree that what you perceive is not ultimately real, they give birth to diverse perspectives to look at this particular discourse of 2 truths. A typical Advaitin argues that perceiving change is unreal, whereas a typical Buddhist argues that perceiving unchanged is unreal. Here again, we would bring T.R.V Murti into the domain. In his discourse, Murti challenges the prevailing notion that the disparities between Madhyamika sunyata and Brahman are merely shallow, suggesting instead that they run deep into dialectics. He posits that despite apparent similarities in terminology and structure, the disparities between the 2 philosophies are profound. In other words, both Madhyamika and Advaita Vedanta assert the transcendence of the absolute from language and thought and its emptiness of empirical determinations. Likewise, as C.D. Sarma also confirms, they concur on the non-dual nature of reality and the illusory nature of phenomena (Śarmā, 1996).

However, Murti highlights their differing approaches to metaphysics in general and avidya (ignorance) and the absolute in particular. He explains that each system negates a distinct aspect of illusion: "Madhyamika negates conceptualism, Vijnanavada negates objectivity, and Vedanta negates the very idea of difference" (Murti, 1973:9-10). Moreover, Murti elucidates that each system formulates the distinction between reality and Appearance and acknowledges the 2 truths (paramartha and vyavaharika). To be precise, their epistemic and ontic stances are not compatible at all. Of equal importance, Murti does not leave the discourse in conflict; rather, he shows the way to synthesis. According to him, despite these differences, "all these systems share an ideal of spiritual discipline centred on knowledge (prajna) as the means to liberation (mukti or nirvana), with other factors serving as supplementary" (Murti, 1973:10). Actually, this standpoint of Murti is centrally supported by his theory or standpoint established in his work "*Central Philosophy of Buddhism: A Study of the Madhyamika System*," as noted above in the form of the ātma doctrine and theanātma doctrine. But it also does not necessarily mean that looking from the binaries point of view, like that of Murti, actually depicts the full picture. An Advaitin would never agree with such a standpoint, as for them, this very binary viewpoint would be based on ignorance. Likewise, without rejection, the Jain school of thought would also declare this standpoint contextual and partial.

Of equal importance, what we can honestly say about this important metaphysical debate in Indian philosophy is that it represents a richer outlook of Indian revisionary metaphysics that binds all the systems together. To make sense of this claim, in metaphysics, various approaches can be distinguished based on their objectives and methodologies. Descriptive metaphysics, as mentioned, focuses on analysing the structure of reality as it appears within our current conceptual framework. It seeks to understand how our existing concepts align with the actual nature of reality. Typically, realist thinkers like those of Nyaya-Vaisesika and Mimamsa fall into this category in Indian philosophy. On the contrary, revisionary metaphysics aims to go beyond the confines of our current conceptual scheme. It questions whether our existing conceptual framework accurately reflects the true nature of reality and proposes potential modifications or alternative conceptual schemes to better align with reality.

As Vasubandhu's the Principles of Exegesis (Vyākhyāyukti) points out: The Buddha taught the 2 truths: conventional truth, which is the object of correct mundane cognitions, and ultimate truth, which is the object of world-transcending cognition (Thakchoe, 2023).

This approach is considered revisionary because it challenges established concepts and seeks to refine our understanding of reality through conceptual innovation or adjustment. The above-mentioned schools concerning the two-truth debate are fitting examples of the revisionary metaphysics category, as they engage in questioning and potentially reshaping our conceptual frameworks to better correspond with the true nature of reality, thereby providing a unified normative perspective to examine them. In other words, conventionally true entities rely on linguistic and conceptual conventions for their existence, while ultimately, true entities, as posited by any of the schools mentioned in this context, exist independently of convention. These real existent entities are fundamentally irreducible, independent, and unconstructed, unlike conventional entities, which demonstrate qualities of reducibility, derivation, and construction. Ultimate truths resist physical destruction and logical analysis, exist independently of external influences, and are not products of mental constructions. Murti's stance is certainly plausible, as it adds dialectical depth to the Indian metaphysical discourse. However, this debate could become even more engaging if we seek proximity among all these schools that discuss truth rather than creating binaries among them. This approach leaves room for further research and exploration into the interconnectedness and shared insights among these philosophical traditions.

Conclusion, Challenges and Cosmopolitan Future of Indian Metaphysics

After outlining the major themes of Indian metaphysics, namely the nature of self, the centrality of the problem of causation and relation, and the idea of 2 truths and their revisionary aspects, we come to the end of this composition. It implies that these themes can provide a comprehensive window to a range of Indian philosophical standpoints on "Truth" and "Reality," which is actually the central aim of any metaphysical inquiry in one way or another. However, since philosophers are known for their critical reflection, certain inquiries are left unanswered, which would make this composition more comprehensive. We leave those questions open-ended for further research. Specifically, a socio-cultural and political question arises regarding the appropriateness of reordering one cultural discourse into another cultural vocabulary, such as revisionary and descriptive metaphysics, realism, and idealism, which Indian traditionalists might argue are byproducts of a foreign culture. This issue is sensitive and has sparked lengthy debates. Additionally, challenges from postmodernists and naturalists, such as logical positivists, who critique the notion of metaphysics in general and transcendental metaphysics in particular, further complicate the discourse of cosmopolitan metaphysical pursuits. Likewise, the comments of orientalists like Hegel, Albert Schweitzer, William Archer, and others on Indian metaphysics being primarily a spiritualist and otherworldly tradition is indeed a contested subject of inquiry. The proximity of Indian metaphysics with spirituality, attributed to its soteriological goals and inquiry into the nature of self and the revisionary world beyond perception, cannot be ignored.

Without delving into detailed responses, a few outlines can be mentioned regarding the above questions. Concerning language disputes, it can be said that language is a unique component of human essence, serving as a window to truth and reality. It should not be bound to a certain culture but rather allowed to express itself freely. Indian philosophy is rich enough that it does not lose its essence even when expressed in a foreign language, as evidenced by twentieth-century Indian philosophy in English (Garfield & Bhushan, 2011). Regarding the scepticism of postmodernists and naturalists, such as logical positivists, they themselves face contradictions. Logical positivists struggle to justify how analyticity supports their own principle, i.e., whether their theory is analytic or synthetic. Similarly, the postmodernist claim that truth is an illusion and relative is also self-defeating because when they make such claims themselves, they presuppose truth beforehand. Otherwise, who would trust their ideology? The mediocrity that underlies these sceptical ideologies is that they forget that no deep truth is easily available. David Hume, the great sceptic, also acknowledges this fact while claiming that "if truth be at all within the reach of human capacity, it's certain it must lie very deep and abstruse (Fosl, 2019: 270)." Or, as Jonardan Ganeri cites from Chandogya Upanishad:

Take, for example, a hidden treasure of gold. People who do not know the terrain, even when they pass right over it time and again, would not discover it. In exactly the same way, all these creatures, even though they go there every day, do not discover this world of Brahman, for they are led astray by the false. (Ganeri, 2007: 2; CU 8.3.1–2).

Indian philosophers have argued for these themes right from antiquity to modern times. As we have demonstrated, the centrality of these issues in our composition highlights the intricate connection between Indian metaphysics and spiritual exploration. And those who seek to transition the discourse from spiritualism to rationalism, like Daya Krishna, often seem influenced by a foreign cultural complex. While it is valid to argue that Indian philosophy exhibits logical and argumentative qualities, as Daya Krishna suggests, it is crucial to acknowledge that these tools are employed as means toward certain ends. As we have explored in our composition, these ends are found to be spiritual, not strictly in a mystic sense but in an experiential one. Therefore, it may not be prudent to define the essence of any culture solely through its means. However, it can be argued that in the process, Indian metaphysics employs diverse means, whether epistemology, logic, or argumentation. Yet, its culmination lies in moksha Vidya, i.e., the science of liberation. And one should not feel shy about it because it is the only way to the farewell to eternal suffering. Indian materialism, of course, offers a different connotation in this regard, but even this perspective can be brought into the discourse and dialectics. Without a doubt, the hard problem of consciousness or self will haunt them, too, much like it haunts modern naturalism. Likewise, does materialism truly help us reconcile with the perpetual nature of suffering haunting humanity? Its culmination seems to lead nowhere but to paradox. However, we should aim for synthesis because that is where serenity lies. We would conclude this composition with words from Abhinavagupta's Īśvara Pratyabhijñā Vimarśinī, which also convey the message to practice synthesis (samanvaya):

Not just the effect–cause relationship, or the process of remembering, or the cancellation (exposure of erroneousness) of one cognition by another, which are common to all practices by which ordinary people's lives go on, even various specific practices such as buying and selling (mixed with defilement), or the interaction between religious instruction and an instructed (unmixed with defilement), presuppose the existence of a single knower; for, after all, it is synthesis (samanvaya) which is the life-breath of any practice whatsoever (Īśvara Pratyabhijñā Vimarśinī, 1.7.13–14; Chakrabarti, 2012: 175).

References

Bilimoria, P., & Sherma, R. D. (Eds.). (2020). *Contemplative Studies and Hinduism: Meditation, Devotion, Prayer, and Worship*. India: Taylor & Francis.

Chakrabarti, A. (2012). *Arguing from Synthesis to the Self: Utpaladeva and Abhinavagupta Respond to Buddhist No-selfism*. In Hindu and Buddhist Ideas in Dialogue (1st ed., pp. 18). Routledge.

Chatterjee, M. (1998). *Contemporary Indian Philosophy*. India: Motilal Banarsidass.

Deshpande, S. (Ed.). (2015). *Philosophy in Colonial India*. India: Springer India.

Doniger, W. (2005). *The Rig-Veda*. United Kingdom: Penguin Books Limited.

Fosl, P. S. (2019). *Hume's Scepticism: Pyrrhonian and Academic*. United Kingdom: Edinburgh University Press.

Ganeri, J. (2007). *The Concealed Art of the Soul: Theories of Self and Practices of Truth in Indian Ethics and Epistemology.* United Kingdom: Clarendon Press.

Ganeri, J. (2011). *The Lost Age of Reason: Philosophy in Early Modern India 1450-1700.* United Kingdom: OUP Oxford.

Ganeri, J. (2012). *The Self: Naturalism, Consciousness, and the First-Person Stance.* United Kingdom: OUP Oxford.

Garfield, J. L. (2010). Taking Conventional Truth Seriously: Authority Regarding Deceptive Reality. *Philosophy East and West, 60*(3), 341–354.

Garfield, J. L., & Bhushan, N. (Eds.). (2011). Indian Philosophy in English: From Renaissance to Independence. Oxford University Press, USA

Kalupahana, David J. (1975). *Causality--the central philosophy of Buddhism.* Honolulu: University Press of Hawaii.

Krishnananda, S. (Trans.).(1983). *Brihadaranyaka Upanishad.* The Divine Life Society, Sivananda Ashram, Rishikesh, India. P 204.

Loux, M. J., Crisp, T. M. (2017). *Metaphysics: A Contemporary Introduction.* United States: Taylor & Francis.

Mādhava, & Gough, A. E. (Trans.), & Cowell, E. B. (Trans.). (1996). *The Sarva-darśana-saṃgraha, Or Review of the Different Systems of Hindu Philosophy.* India: Motilal Banarsidass.

Mahadevan, T. M. P. (1976). *The Philosophy of Advaita, with Special Reference to Bhāratītīrtha-Vidyāranya.* India: Arnold-Heinemann Publishers (India).

Matilal, B. K. (1981). *The Central Philosophy of Jainism (anekānta-vāda).* India: L.D. Institute of Indology.

Mohanty, J. N. (1992). *Reason And Tradition in Indian Thought: An Essay on The Nature of Indian Philosophical Thinking.* United Kingdom: Clarendon Press.

Munslow, A. (2018). *Narrative and History*. United Kingdom: Bloomsbury Publishing.

Murti, T.R.V. (1955). *The Central Philosophy of Buddhism: A Study of the Madhyamika System* (1st ed.). Routledge. https://doi.org/10.4324/9780203706701

Murti, T.R.V. (1973). *Saṁvṛti and Paramārtha in Mādhyamika and Advaita Vedanta. In: Sprung, M. (eds) The Problem of 2 Truths in Buddhism and Vedānta*. Springer, Dordrecht. https://doi.org/10.1007/978-94-010-2582-9_2

Nicholson, A. J. (2010). *Unifying Hinduism: Philosophy and Identity in Indian Intellectual History*. United Kingdom: Columbia University Press.

Olivelle, P. (1998). *The Early Upanishads: Annotated Text and Translation*. India: Oxford University Press.

Padhi, B. (2005). *Indian Philosophy and Religion: A Reader S Guide*. India: D K Printworld (P) Limited.

Pahi, B. (2000). *Vaiśeṣikapadārthavyavasthā aspaddhatimulakavimarśa*. In University of Rajasthan (Ed.), Studies in Indian philosophy: 6. Department of Philosophy, University of Rajasthan, Jaipur.

Perrett, R.(1998). *Causation, Indian theories of. In The Routledge Encyclopaedia of Philosophy*. Taylor and Francis. 10.4324/9780415249126-F055-1

Perrett, R.W. (Ed.). (2001). *Philosophy of Religion: Indian Philosophy* (1st ed.). Routledge. https://doi.org/10.4324/9781315053981

Phillips, S. H. (1997). *Classical Indian Metaphysics: Refutations of Realism and the Emergence of "new logic."* India: Motilal Banarsidass.

Radhakrishnan, S. (1989). *Eastern Religions and western Thought.* India: Oxford University Press.

Raghuramaraju, A. (2007). *Debates in Indian Philosophy: Classical, Colonial, and Contemporary*. India: OUP India.

Ram Prasad, C., Kuznetsova, I., & Ganeri, J. (Eds.). (2016). *Hindu and Buddhist Ideas in Dialogue: Self and No-Self.* United Kingdom: Taylor & Francis.

Roberts, G. (Ed.). (2001). *The History and Narrative Reader*. United Kingdom: Routledge.

Russell, B. (2001). *The Problems of Philosophy.* United Kingdom: Oxford University Press.

Śarmā, C. (1996). *The Advaita Tradition in Indian Philosophy: A Study of Advaita in Buddhism, Vedānta and Kāshmīra Shaivism*. India: Motilal Banarsidass Publishers.

Sen, A. (2012). *The Argumentative Indian: Writings on Indian History, Culture, and Identity*. ("The Argumentative Indian: Writings on Indian History, Culture and...") India: Penguin Books.

Sharma, A. (2004). *Advaita Vedānta: An Introduction*. India: Motilal Banarsidass Publishers.

Thakchoe, S. (2023). *The 2 Truths in Indian Buddhism: Reality, Knowledge, and Freedom.* United States: Wisdom Publications.

Tripathi, R. K. (1969). *The Central Problem of Indian Metaphysics. Philosophy East and West, 19*(1), 39–43. https://doi.org/10.2307/1398095

Watson, A. (2017). *Self or No-Self? The Ātman Debate in Classical Indian Philosophy*. In J. Tuske (Ed.), *Indian Epistemology and Metaphysics*. India: Bloomsbury Publishing.

Chapter 4

Indian Literature: Dharma Centric Narrative

Ravinder Singh,
Professor, Department of Punjabi,
Dyal Singh College, University of Delhi, Delhi.
Former Fellow, Indian Institute of Advanced Study, Shimla.

In the Indian context, the word 'literature' has been taken from the sense of the Sanskrit term Sahitya, which is a little different in its etymology. Etymologically, the term "literature" is derived from the Latin term *'litteratura'* which means "learning, writing, grammar," and originally, it was "writing formed with letters (*littera*)." Along with this, the term has also been applied to spoken or sung texts. Literature is often referred to as "writing" or, more poetically, "the craft of writing." Definitions of literature have varied over time. In western Europe before the 18th century, literature generally denoted all books and writing, and it is also used as "oral literature" and "the literature of preliterate culture." The Encyclopaedia Britannica classifies literature as "the best expression of the best thought reduced to writing."

Our approach towards the expression of the word 'literature' is somehow different since '*Sahitya* (साहित्य)' is not confined merely to the expression of thoughts but is more related to the quality of thoughts and its concerns with human life. Etymologically, Sahitya is an abstractive of 'Sa-hit (स-हित)' that means 'together with' or 'inclusive.' It has some built-in quality of thoughts that are concerned and connected to well-being. The concern of literature as Sahitya is located in the well-being of society and human beings as a whole.

It is important to ascertain how we perceive and respond to our social system/order and its relationship with human beings. Sahitya is very much imbibed in this idea of inclusiveness of social order and its relation to humanity. This idea of inclusiveness epitomises our worldview based on unique Indian knowledge traditions. The Indian social order has been defined as a structure under an integrated system of *Dharma* based on a Brahma-centric worldview. According to this view, there is no 'otherness' beyond time and space, and in this time-bound existence, one should treat everyone as self. The social order structured around inclusivism operates as per an evolved, disciplined moral order called *Dharma* (not an organised religion). Therefore, Sahitya (literature) expressed the human concerns within this order, and its purpose is to establish or strengthen the core idea of inclusivism. That is how ancient and medieval Indian literature represented core concerns of humanity and the social system while creating dialogue through an inclusive worldview.

There is another aspect of literature that is connected with the unconscious mind. The unconscious mind is a state in which conscious observations and experiences get settled in the mind to influence our acts later. Consciousness is also constructed through the experience of human life in a particular time and space. In the Indian context, the geo-cultural time and space of Indian civilisation provided the basic abilities of the mind to think, perceive and act according to the evolution of knowledge. The evolution of knowledge means the journey of finding answers to the questions of ultimate reality, about creation and creator. On this journey, the Indian mind, belonging to Indian civilisation, was conditioned by its intellectual practices. All these intellectual practices shaped the Indian knowledge tradition largely based on the commonly accepted idea of *Brahman* as a self-created creator and creation. With this kind of cognitive conditioning, the Indian mind perceives its socio-cultural reality and expresses it accordingly. That way, our societal and human responses are very much on the same ground. This is an important factor that constitutes our mind and its expression in language and literature. So, it is not easy to separate *Chetna* from the expressions.

Modern literature is somehow exclusivist in its nature, and it has impacted the nature of Indian writing and its literary traditions as well. Western literary traditions are rooted in social structures influenced by the *Abrahamic* worldview. The western sociological outlook has evolved with the theocentric perspective of the world and its existence. From this point of view, modern literature and its interpretive, critical theories lack the traditional Indian spirit of Sahitya. It promotes outwardly exclusive elements of society through literary modes of expression without any objective of uniting or creating inclusiveness in the social order. This exclusivist approach to literary writing and critical thinking is creating more conflicts than resolving the existing ones. Highlighting social disorders through literature is perfectly relevant until it provides or suggests establishing some inclusive social and moral order. But only exhibiting the social-cultural conflicts and eulogising separate identities leads us to more conflicting and clashing societies. This character of 'literature' is not similar to Sahitya since it hardly shows any concerns for resolution. In the present times, certain modern western literary-critical thoughts have pitted different social categories against each other. This exclusivist character of literature promotes and strengthens the idea of 'otherness' in society instead of resolving the differences created based on otherness. Thus, the Indian literary tradition, with its creativeness and analytical paradigm, has gone through an unwarranted change with the advent of western modernist ideas in the last century.

The reinterpretation of ancient and medieval Sahitya, according to modern "literary" critical tools, is unjustified since both traditions have different perceptions of creation and expression. For instance, interpreting the *Ram-Katha* characters 'Rama' or 'Sita' from feminist critical ideology cannot do justice to the exposition of actual socio-cultural composition presented in the *Ramayana*. This epic is not a piece of 'literature' but a *Sahitya* presented in a poetic form. Every event and characterisation of various characters complement the narrative flow in the direction where the goal of inclusiveness and establishment of *Dharma* is achieved (*Raj-Dharma* in this context). This goal of achieving *Dharma* is a prime factor in all the ancient and medieval literary narratives. Thus, in *Sahitya*, the purpose of writing is to create harmony, propagate core moral values, and ensure the well-being of society and humanity as a whole from an inclusivist worldview is much more important than merely expressing thoughts.

Indian civilisation is a *Dharma centric* and knowledge-oriented civilisation. Here, the word Dharma stands for a universal moral order operating in the world. It has given rise to 4 major Dharma traditions, namely, Sanatan Dharma, Jainism, Buddhism and Sikhism. The ideas of a permanent, self-dependent, ever-present, ultimate reality (Brahman=ब्रह्म), the impermanent, ever-changing, phenomenal world (Jagat=जगत) and the living beings inhabiting this phenomenal world (Jiva=जीव) are the core concepts representing the world view of this civilisation. Posting a fundamental unity of Jiva and Brahman, it presents a philosophy of life (*Advaita*) in which the realisation of the ultimate reality (moksha=मोक्ष) is the core concern of all beings. This philosophy of life structures the relationship with the cosmos, nature, and human beings harmoniously. Therefore, Indian epistemology is essentially *Brahman*-centric in relation to western epistemology, which is *Abrahamic*. The Indian thought process operates with the core narrative structures of its cosmological, anthropological, and sociological conceptualisations and ideas, which are based on ancient knowledge practices. Ancient knowledge and intellectual practices tried to formulate explanations for pertinent questions about human existence. While exploring the answers to human existence, these intellectual practices arrived at the ultimate conceptualisation for defining creation and the creator as purely a self-sustained system or an order named *Brahman*. The visible world and human existence are nothing but the manifestation of that order in material form. That way, the *Darshan* (philosophy) of this knowledge constructs the consciousness of *samsara* as a *Brahman*-centric *Dharma* order to be experienced as a social system. This whole knowledge has been perceived, memorised, and transmitted in socio-culturally structured language systems. Since abstract concepts are difficult to define without concrete examples, the idea of Brahman was explained in the easily understandable socio-cultural communication systems of language and narrativity.

Literature is an extension of linguistic expression for socio-cultural existence. Literature and society are linked through the language of a particular civilisation based on the epistemological insights of its Darshanik (philosophical) knowledge explaining human existence. Indian literary/narrative tradition dates back to ancient times. Its origin is believed to be from the oral tradition of the Vedic period. Vedic or Veda means knowledge, and that knowledge is articulated in a poetic form. Here, the poetic form was just an expression of intellectual practices related to the exploration of ultimate truth or reality. Oral traditions have successfully stored and transmitted that knowledge from one generation to the next while adding more and more meaning to it. In this sense, the renderings as oral traditions used various forms of poetic expressions to transmit that knowledge to the masses. The knowledge of ultimate truth, e.g., the questions of existence, was conceived as an abstract conceptual idea, and it has always been difficult to express abstract ideas in a concrete language without using prevalent socio-cultural structures and linguistic idioms. This peculiar situation shaped the expression of Vedic knowledge in literary form. Ancient Indian knowledge texts are composed in poetic and other literary genres, making them easy to perceive, memorise and transmit. So, the literary tradition of the Indian sub-continent is rooted in Vedic knowledge practices.

It is very clear now that these Vedic or knowledge practices were fundamental, and literary practices are only the poetic expression of that. This binary relation of knowledge and literature is as old as the evolution of a human being becoming a conscious being. Hence, consciousness is also a repository of the earliest and continuous intellectual practices preserved as memories in the human race of a particular geo-cultural space called civilisation, in this context, the Indian Civilisation. After that, whatever has been expressed about the socio-cultural system is essentially rooted in the knowledge-oriented, geo-culturally evolved civilisational formation.

Indian literary traditions have their literary structures, which operate through the definition and meaning of literature, such as Sahitya. Discussions about the definition of Indian literature and its hallmarks have been going on for a long time. A major idea that emerged about Indian literature is that its scope or definition necessarily includes the literature created by the Indians in the geographical region of India. A renowned poet, Subramaniam Bharati, speaks of the unity of Indian literature to recognise a commonality in the literature of all languages beyond the linguistic variations:

Seppu mozhi padhinettu udayal,
Enil chintanai onrudayal.
(She {India} has 18 languages to speak,
even then the chintana {thinking} is one.)

The commonalities are thoughts born out of Indian civilisation, which has been flowing as a tradition for centuries and has built socio-cultural behaviour. This also illustrates the non-linguistic elements of our literary expressions. Therefore, it is very important to have a proper understanding of Indian civilisation in defining the intrinsic structures of Indian literature. Various civilisations have given the conception of commonality and integrity to the literature only through the continuity of their heritage. Literature creates a dialogue with the core concerns of human life and the inherited experiences of its civilisation. It prepares a response to contemporaneous situations and gives new shape to the understanding through this dialogical process. In the literature, homogeneities are certain to emerge from the underpinning of a common background. On this basis, various languages of India hold themselves together and point to a commonality.

Over time, certain hallmarks of Indian literary identity emerge that define and operate as the basic inspiring factors of contemporary literature. Professor Gokak insists that consistency in terms of the choice of themes and their portrayal, or the writer's discerning understanding of his entire culture, shapes Indianness in Indian literature. Similarly, another suggestion from Shri K. S. Srinivasan also seems to be very appropriate that the theme of karma in every literature, the 4 objectives of life (Dharma, Artha, Kama, and moksha) and belief in rebirth, etc., should be seen as part of our socio-cultural life shaping the consciousness. In this way, we can also grasp the similarities of style and content in our literature. This way, we can easily understand the Indian way of life, which is deeply embedded in the ways of thinking in this vast country. From the preceding discussion, we can conclude that some of the popular philosophical ideas have continued to be a part of our daily life and literature. Like:-

- The fate that governs human life
- Karma, Punya and the cycle of births
- Life is temporary, mortal
- The world's a stage
- The irony of the coexistence of joy and sorrow
- The concept of living and non-living beings
- Ethical ideas include the essential greatness of man, attaining happiness through self-control and domesticity, etc.

All these elements show the commonality between different languages and suggest how Indianness/emotions are shared by all despite differences in region, social class, and language. Another sense of Indian literature is the totality of literature composed in all the languages of the country. The similarity of these literary subtleties can be easily comprehended by considering the India-wide movements of literary ideas. Although the family of languages is different, their literary 'elements' show similarities. Literary ideas of Ramayana, Mahabharata, Puranas, Bhagavata, the classical literature of Sanskrit, i.e., Kalidasa, Bhavabhuti, Bana, Sri Harsha, Amarak, the immortal works of Jayadeva, the literature of Buddhism, Jainism and other religions written in *Pali, Prakrit and Apbhransh* have been inherited by all the languages of India. All the Indian writings have continuously used the contemplative experience of *Upanishads, Shaad-Darshan, Simriti,* etc., in the scriptures and several other poetic works, *Nat-Shastra, Dhavanyaloka, Kavya Prakash, Sahitya Darpana, Ras Gangadhar* etc. Their influence has certainly been extremely synergistic, and a kind of fundamental uniformity has come naturally to the literature inspired by them. Thus, flourishing in a common civilisational geo-cultural space, Indian literature has a continuous and natural phenomenon of commonness.

According to the Indian Knowledge System, Jiva and Jagat are fleeting manifestations of the Creator. This means that everything that comes into existence is considered to be mithya - a reality that is created by humans and believed to be true. Our knowledge traditions do not prescribe organised structures of social construction or practices. Instead, they provide a guiding principle for the betterment of social order, which is known as Dharma. Whenever there is a significant social disorder due to ignorance of Dharma and selfish human behaviour, the importance of upholding Dharma is emphasised. This was evident during the Mahabharata time and later during the Bhakti period when Bhakt and Sikh Gurus highlighted the significance of Dharma.

During medieval times, literary texts were created to interact with the socio-cultural sphere of human activities. They addressed ill practices that deviated from Indian knowledge-based Dharma conducts. Gurbani, for example, is considered to have established the Dharma Order to eradicate socially ill practices that were prevalent at the time. The Bhakti movement was a great social renaissance with a main focus on creating social equality on human grounds. It propagated a non-dualistic Vedic philosophy to create equality and harmony among different classes and castes, recognising that the omnipresent creator cannot be unequal.

The beginning of Indian literature is considered to be from the Vedas, as Prof. Kapil Kapoor says-

कथावेदसेहीआरंभहोतीहैऔरभक्तिकेबीजभीवेदमेंहीहैं।कथाकेधात्वर्थ "कहना" केअनुरूपसर्ववेदको "वेदकथा" हीकहागयाहै।ब्राह्मण, उपनिषदत थाब्रहददेवताआदिमेंजोकथाएँविस्तारसेदीहैंउनकाबीजऋग्वेदकेउनसंहिता केसंवादोंमेंउपलब्धहै, जिनमेंदोयातीनपात्रोंकापरस्परकथोपकथनइनकथाओं काआधारबनजाताहै।[3]

Prof. Kapoor explains that in Indian tradition, storytelling has been the primary method of imparting knowledge. There are various types of narratives in the oral tradition of India, such as Upanishad stories, Buddhist Jatakas in Pali, Jain *Gathas* in Prakrit, sub-narratives of *Mahabharata, Puranic* stories, *Nidarshan* stories in *Panchatantra*, and countless war and love stories in different Indian languages. The main objective of these ancient legends has always been to teach Dharma. Although the stories may differ, the objective remains the same. In the search for Dharma, the Upanishads teach that it lies in knowledge (*Gyan*), while the Buddhist Jatakas suggest that it lies in the act (*Karma*) undertaken for the welfare of others. The *Uttar Purana* states that it lies in devotion (*Bhakti*). The Indian tradition of answering fundamental questions of human existence through dialogues has been a practice for centuries. This knowledge (*Gyan-Chetna*) has been

---

3. प्रोफ.कपिलकपूर, कथापरंपरा, रति-भक्ति: भारतकीकथापरंपरामें, डीकेप्रिंटर, दिल्ली। 2011 (पृष्ठ-51)

present for thousands of years and is still capable of solving basic life questions. The *Bhagavad Gita* is also significant in this context, as Adi Shankaracharya's pronouncement on it is noteworthy, according to Prof. Kapoor:

वैदकिज्ञान, बौद्धकर्मतथापौराणकिभक्तकिोरसमेंबांधाआदशिंकराचा र्यने, जन्हिोंनेभगवतगीताकेदूसरेअध्यायपरटीकाकरतेहुएनरि्णयकयिाकि "ज्ञानयुक्तकर्महीभक्तहि।"[4]

Thus, one thing is clear: the basic nature of Indian literature is knowledge-oriented, and its roots lie in our Vedic heritage. For hundreds of years, the literature of our country, while carrying out the tradition of philosophical contemplation, has been drawing social ethics on the questions of spirituality or self-identity. It is in these philosophical traditions that certain eternal concerns of human life are also ascertained, which are consistent with the consciousness of Vedic knowledge. In this context, Swami Muni Narayan Prasad says:-

"All Upanishads teach *'brahmvidya'* the science of the Absolute, whose ultimate goal is to free the seekers from the tangle of worldly trials and tribulations of the day-to-day life. This freedom is known as 'Mukti' or '*moksha*.'"[4]

We can see that the nature of early Vedic literature was knowledge-oriented. In the stories of the *Upanishads*, religion (*Dharma*) is accepted only in the form of knowledge, and the heroes of these stories, like *Nachiketa*, are inquisitive about knowledge. Even further, the literature that we find is more related to these fundamental questions of human existence. It is from the development of knowledge-centric literature that karma and devotional traditions begin. *Jatakas*, written in Pali, are stories related to the previous births of Bodhisattvas. These literary narratives aim to establish good moral conduct (*Dharmik*) in ordinary life. Bodhisattva means a seeker who practices the virtues of

---

4. प्रोफ. कपिलकपूर, कथापरंपरा, रति-भक्ति: भारतकीकथापरंपरामें, डीकेप्रिंटर, दिल्ली। 2011 (पृष्ठ-51)

knowledge, truth, mercy, etc., and who advances towards enlightenment (*Buddhatava*) through his conduct at every birth. For him, religion is in action, not in knowledge. However, the nature of these stories remains concerned with human existence.

Ramayana and *Mahabharata* are 2 great literary texts whose narratives have become an inseparable part of the Indian folk mind that can be related to every field of life. Both these texts are great examples of Indian literary tradition. Valmiki's *Ramayana* has had a profound impact on the behaviour of Indian society and culture. *Ramayana* not only influenced Indian life and ideology but also influenced literature and became the source of many other scriptures. *Mahabharata* is a great scripture representing Indian civilisation, culture, knowledge, and idealistic narratives. It is also a founding scripture of Indian personality.

The *Puranas* were composed after the *Upanishads*, *Brahmanas* and *Aranakyas*. All these are related to the study of the Vedas, and in this series, the Puranas were also composed in narrative form to bring the knowledge of the Vedas to the understanding of the common people. The narrative tradition comes out in a more distinct form from the Puranic literature. This narrative also forms a part of the socio-cultural expressions of the people's lives, affecting the consciousness of contemporary society. As Dr. Ramsharan Gaur says that:-

पुराणभारतीयसंस्कृतिकीआधारशिलाहैंएवंभारतीयसमाजकेआद
र्शोन्मुखजीवनमूल्योंकीप्रतिष्ठाकरनेवालेहैं।इनकाउदेश्यसत्य, अर्ध-
सत्यऔरकाल्पनिककथा, रूपक, अलंकारऔरअतिशयोक्तिओंकेमाध्यमसे
आध्यात्मिकप्रेरणादेनाहै।[5]

The *Puranas* also contained a tradition of Vedic thoughts and cognition, and they also developed elements of narrative creation. Coming from

---

5. Introduction, Page-1, Katha Upanishad, Swami Muni Narayan Prasad, D. K. Print World, New Delhi 1998.

the tradition of Vedic literature, their nature is also related to religion (*Dharma*) and philosophy (*Darshan*).

Likewise, the *Kathasaritsagara* is a very complex narrative and is interwoven with one another like a web. Even though it is an example of pure narrative, the motivational elements that are seen working behind the depth of the subjects are directly or indirectly connected to the same Indian tradition of knowledge, which is related to the narratives available before it. Broadly, the topics related to worldly pleasures and power acquisitions have only appeared in these narratives. Hence, it is associated with the meaning of the 4 *Purusharth*. The stories of the *Panchatantra* are an attempt to establish the moral values of social conduct through the narratives of animals. The purity of deeds has been the basis of these stories. Although the stories of *Panchatantra* are related to animals, according to their structure, even if human characters are replaced by animal characters, they will give the same meaning as animal characters. This means that these stories express the concerns of human life through animals.

It is very evident from the above discussion that the Indian literature term, Sahitya, has some definitive and qualitative differences from that of literature. Its internal and external binary is essentially structured within the Indian civilisational context, which defines the socio-cultural order established in *Dharma*, the righteous way of living. *Dharma* is an ethical and moral order of conduct as well as the goal of all human activities.

References

Dr. Ramsharan Gaur, *Purana evam Dharamshastra*, Bhartiye Sanskriti ke Adhar Srotra, Swaraj Prkn, Delhi. 1998. P-103

Introduction, Page-1, Katha Upanishad, Swami Muni Narayan Prasad, D. K. Print World, New Delhi 1998.

प्रोफ. कपिल कपूर, कथा परंपरा, रति-भक्ति: भारतकी कथा परंपरामें, डी के प्रिंटर, दिल्ली। 2011 (पृष्ठ-51)

प्रोफ. कपिल कपूर, कथा परंपरा, रति-भक्ति: भारतकी कथा परंपरामें, डीकेप्रिंटर, दिल्ली। 2011 (पृष्ठ-8)

Chapter 5

Exploring Ethical Leadership and Personal Development: Insights from the Bhagavad Gita

Seema Sharma,
Assistant Professor, Department of English,
Maharaja Ganga Singh University, Bikaner, Rajashtan.

The Bhagavad Gita, often revered as a timeless guide to righteous living, presents profound insights into ethical leadership and personal development. Rooted in the dialogue between Prince Arjuna and Lord Krishna during the Kurukshetra battle, the Gita imparts wisdom that goes beyond its original setting, offering universal principles for effective leadership in various environments. This study seeks to explore the significance of the Gita's lessons in modern leadership scenarios, emphasising its moral guidelines and strategies for personal development.

Ethical Leadership:

The Bhagavad Gita emphasises ethical conduct as a cornerstone of effective leadership. Central to this ethos is the *Dharma,* or duty, which guides individuals to act with integrity and righteousness. Through the character of Lord Krishna, the Gita illustrates the importance of upholding moral principles in times of adversity. Gita propels us to forsake our responsibilities under the false assumption that they are flawed, and instead assume the unsuitable duties of others, we find ourselves in direct opposition to our inherent inclinations. This was precisely the predicament Arjun faced. As a Kshatriya, his natural inclination was towards military and administrative pursuits. However, circumstances compelled him to partake in a righteous war. Krishna says to Arjuna about Dharma:

श्रेयान्स्वधर्मोविगुण: परधर्मात्स्वनुष्ठितात् |
स्वभावनियतंकर्मकुर्वन्नाप्रोतिकिल्बिषम् ||18.47||

It is better to do one's own *Dharma*, even though imperfectly, than to do another's *Dharma*, even though perfectly. By doing one's innate duties, a person does not incur sin.

The quality that empowers an individual to fulfil their responsibilities effectively and efficiently is their conscience, which originates from within. In this context, the valuable counsel of Bhagawan Krishna persuades and directs Arjuna to fulfil his obligations towards the state without excessive contemplation of opposition. This also sheds light on the adherence to following one's own duties and fulfilling them regardless of the challenges encountered. On the contrary, Leaders should be urged to adhere to their duties while transcending selfish desires, thereby fostering trust and respect among their followers. Moreover, the Gita advocates for a leadership style characterised by compassion, empathy, and fairness, emphasising the well-being of all.

Karma Yoga:

The practicality that surrounds the Bhagavad Gita is that it discusses *Karma Yoga* - selflessness and dedication to the improvement of humanity - as extensively as it does. All of this is accomplished through logical reasoning and validation. Lord Krishna, who introduced the concept of altruism, emphasised working for the greater good by unconditionally helping others. He prophesied that this is the most effective form of devotion, as it allows individuals to connect with the Supreme and attain spirituality, ultimately leading to inner peace and wisdom. Altruism brings about grace, thus paving the path to faith. Faith is the base of truth, and therefore, altruism enables us to perceive what is true in our lives. When one assists others, it empowers them to strive for perfection in life. Setting examples for others by practising what one preaches is a quality that distinguishes true leaders and is something they should aspire to. Selfless service sets genuine leaders apart from those who merely make empty promises.

यज्ञार्थात्कर्मणोऽन्यत्र लोकोऽयं कर्मबन्धन: |
तदर्थं कर्म कौन्तेय मुक्तसङ्ग: समाचर || 3.9||

Work must be done as a yajna to the Supreme Lord; otherwise, work causes bondage in this material world. Therefore, O son of Kunti, for the satisfaction of God, perform your prescribed duties without being attached to the results.

Importance of Self-Awareness

The Bhagavad Gita emphasises the significance of self-awareness for effective leadership. This self-awareness goes beyond just understanding our physical and psychological aspects, delving into the depths of our consciousness. In ancient Vedic teachings, human consciousness is believed to transcend beyond the psychological and physical realms. Krishna, in Bhagavad Gita 3.22, says, "hear voices and see colours, but these perceptions are not tied to our physical senses." The Bhagavad Gita suggests the practice of meditation to establish a connection with our authentic selves.

प्रशान्तमनसं ह्येनं योगिनं सुखमुत्तमम् |
उपैति शान्तरजसं ब्रह्मभूतमकल्मषम् || 6.27||

Great transcendental happiness comes to the yogi whose mind is calm, whose passions are subdued, who is without sin, and who sees everything in connection with God.

Through meditation, one achieves a state of inner peace irrespective of external circumstances. This practice allows individuals to access a profound source of energy by delving into the core of their being.

Building Strong Character through Meditation:

The Bhagavad Gita emphasises the importance of cultivating good discipline and developing a strong character to achieve true meditation. Essentially, realising one's true potential and purpose is contingent upon possessing these qualities. This is particularly relevant in the contemporary world, where leadership is often marred by unethical and immoral behaviour.

Qualities of Effective Leadership:

In *the Bhagavad Gita*, Krishna outlines 3 distinct disciplines that are essential for effective leadership: the discipline of acquiring knowledge, the discipline of effective communication, and the discipline of maintaining composure. All these disciplines play a crucial role in fostering effective leadership.

यद्यदाचरतिश्रेष्ठस्तत्तदेवेतरोजनः।सयत्प्रमाणंकुरुतेलोकस्तदनुवर्तते ।।3.21।।

(3.21. Therefore, Krishna warns Arjuna that he needs to lead by example. Viewed from the perspective that leaders' hands are tied, they lose the degrees of freedom, and the whole world will keenly watch the leaders' actions and blindly follow them leaders) further, he says the sense of accomplishing the task wholeheartedly is necessary in the following lines:

यदि ह्यहं न वर्तेयं जातु कर्मण्यतन्द्रितः ।
मम वर्त्मानुवर्तन्ते मनुष्याः पार्थ सर्वशः ।।3.23।।

Waging war is the natural task of a ksatriya. It is his bounden duty to fight to the finish. He must undertake this assigned task with a sense of pride and privilege, as well as a sense of service and sacrifice (yajna bhavana).

Drawing from the Bhagavad Gita, several qualities essential to effective leadership emerge. Foremost among these is self-awareness, the foundation upon which other leadership traits are built. By understanding one's strengths, weaknesses, and motivations, leaders can make informed decisions and inspire trust in others. Additionally, the Gita extols virtues such as courage, resilience, and equanimity, which empower leaders to navigate challenges with grace and fortitude. Furthermore, the text emphasises the value of humility and service-oriented leadership, wherein leaders prioritise the well-being and happiness of their team members above personal gain.

Leading by Example:

The Gita stresses the gravity of actions over words. It states, "Whatever action is performed by a great person, common people follow in their footsteps, and whatever standards they set by exemplary acts, the world pursues." As a leader, your impact is significant. By setting a noble example, you motivate others to follow suit.

Krishna recommends that individuals strive to serve the well-being of the world through selfless actions. By dedicating oneself to work without selfish motives, one can achieve the ultimate purpose of life. The action of leading transforms into a spiritual journey when one's efforts not only fulfil immediate objectives but also foster spiritual growth on a larger scale.

Performing actions without being attached to the outcome can be a challenging lesson to grasp. It is crucial to work diligently without anticipating any form of reward. Individuals should aim to act selflessly, remaining unfazed by both success and failure. Nurturing a feeling of equanimity entails doing what is morally correct without seeking acknowledgement or recompense. Developing a state of equanimity allows individuals to effectively navigate the external world by effectively managing their internal world. In this manner, Lord Krishna imparts valuable lessons on self-management while actively participating in various endeavours. (Madavan 14).

Personal Development and Self-Realisation:

Beyond its insights into ethical leadership, the Bhagavad Gita offers profound wisdom on personal development and self-realisation. Through the teachings of Karma Yoga, Bhakti yoga, and Jnana yoga, the Gita presents diverse paths for individuals to attain spiritual enlightenment and fulfilment. By engaging in selfless action, cultivating devotion, and seeking knowledge, individuals can transcend egoic limitations and realise their true nature. Moreover, the Gita emphasises the integration of mind, body, and spirit, advocating for a holistic approach to personal growth that encompasses physical, emotional, and spiritual well-being.

Continuous learning:

Krishna imparts wisdom to Arjuna, emphasising the significance of continuous learning. To thrive in ever-changing environments, leaders must also embrace lifelong learning and constantly acquire new knowledge.

Inclusiveness:

The Gita surpasses limitations. Leaders who adopt diversity and inclusiveness foster harmonious work settings.

Conflict Resolution:

Krishna navigates Arjuna through internal strife. Leaders' ought to resolve conflicts with sagacity, compassion, and impartiality. "The fighter Arjuna's battleground is his own self. There are a million mutinies going on inside the self: the fight between reason and emotion, between the head and the heart, between what one is and what one can be. In contrast, Krishna, the warrior, finished the fight by himself. The true warrior does not deplete his energy in the emotional drama that binds him to self-defeating patterns of fear and guilt. He pierces through his self-created enemies with the sword of Self-awareness and the shield of sharp discrimination." (Chatterjee 2).

Empowerment:

Krishna enables Arjuna to accomplish his mission. Leaders must empower their teams, fostering a feeling of ownership and a shared vision. Empowerment encompasses the cultivation of wisdom and discernment. The Gita highlights the significance of spiritual knowledge (Jnana yoga) in effectively navigating the trials of life and making well-informed choices. Through the pursuit of wisdom and discernment, individuals can equip themselves to surmount obstacles and accomplish their aspirations. Fulfilling one's duty (Dharma) without being attached to outcomes is closely linked to empowerment. The Gita stresses the significance of carrying out one's responsibilities with commitment and honesty, irrespective of the situation. Embracing one's Dharma enables individuals to feel empowered by their actions, as they are in harmony with a greater purpose.

Communication Skills:

According to Krishna, the fundamental aspect of communication lies in conveying messages honestly and respectfully to others. Leadership cannot achieve effectiveness without proficient communication skills. For leaders to be successful, they must possess the ability to inspire their followers through their words, thereby directing them towards a shared vision and objectives. Renowned leaders such as Gandhi, Dr. King, and Kennedy gained recognition for their effectiveness primarily due to their eloquent communication skills.

Application in Contemporary Leadership:

In today's complex and rapidly evolving world, the principles elucidated in the Bhagavad Gita hold relevance for leaders across various domains. By embodying ethical conduct, cultivating essential leadership qualities, and fostering personal development, individuals can create a positive impact and inspire meaningful change in their organisations and communities.

Furthermore, the Gita's emphasis on interconnectedness and universal principles underscores the importance of inclusive and compassionate leadership in addressing global challenges. In modern times, one must convert efforts into endeavour, efficiency, effectiveness, and, finally, excellence. As Gita puts it, efficiency in action (karmasu kausala) is yoga (the ultimate perfection). (Jayamani 62.) The context of the *Shrimad Bhagavad Gita* is a battlefield, which is often considered a metaphor for the challenges and stresses of daily life. The Shrimad Bhagavad Gita's teachings on managing one's mind and emotions and focusing on the present can be effective in managing stress in the corporate environment. (Dubey, et al. 2024).

The ultimate challenge in leadership lies in renunciation. The eighteenth chapter of the Bhagavad Gita imparts a crucial lesson on effective leadership, emphasising the importance of renunciation. Renunciation, as defined in the Gita, involves refraining from selfish actions (*sanyasa* in Sanskrit) and letting go of attachment to the outcomes of one's actions (*tyaga* in Sanskrit). Krishna highlights key areas where genuine renunciation should be practised, including:

1. Letting go of negative thoughts, words, and deeds
2. Rejecting inequality and advocating for equality
3. Abandoning selfish desires in favour of selfless service
4. Discarding indiscipline, dishonesty, and laziness in favour of integrity and proactivity
5. Overcoming arrogance and ignorance by embracing an open-minded approach
6. Moving away from fleeting happiness derived from self-centred behaviours and seeking enduring happiness that benefits all.

According to the Bhagavad Gita, renunciation in leadership entails selfless giving and working towards the common good. This notion stands in stark contrast to the prevalent deceit, dishonesty, and self-serving behaviours often associated with leadership today. Genuine renunciation involves leaders sacrificing their power, position, and personal gains for the betterment of their people, a rare sight in contemporary leadership. Many leaders make grand promises to their followers only to forget about them once they attain leadership roles, losing sight of the well-being of those they are meant to serve.

Practising renunciation demands a focus on people and a display of compassion towards them. Servitude and compassion are the main elements that promote both renunciation and effective leadership.

In the Bhagavad Gita, Krishna expounds on the fundamental nature of genuine renunciation, underscoring the necessity of bravery and disengagement from self-centred cravings. Genuine renunciation entails recognising one's obligations and earnestly endeavouring to fulfil them. Nurturing others empowers us to contemplate collective welfare and contemplate ways to contribute to society. (Dhamija 9) Bhagavad Gita offers some of the finest lessons of leadership values, following which leaders can transform their character and change the world outside. A transformation outside is, in fact, the extension of the transformation within. (Nayak, 14).

Conclusion:

The Bhagavad Gita serves as a timeless source of wisdom for those seeking to cultivate ethical leadership and personal development. Through its teachings on Dharma, leadership qualities, and paths to self-realisation, the Gita offers valuable insights that transcend cultural and temporal boundaries. By fusing these principles into their leadership practices, individuals can nurture thriving organisations and contribute to an equitable, truthful, and harmonious world. *The*

Bhagavad Gita provides timeless insights that transcend cultural and religious barriers. Its teachings offer practical guidance for navigating life's challenges and finding purpose and significance in our actions. By embracing our duties, cultivating detachment, overcoming self-doubt, seeking knowledge, and practising mindfulness, we can apply the Gita's lessons to our modern lives. Serving as a beacon of light, the Gita directs us towards a more balanced, fulfilling, and spiritually aligned existence.

References:

Chatterjee, Debashis. *Timeless leadership: 18 leadership sutras from the Bhagavad Gita*. John Wiley & Sons, 2012.

Dhamija, Aruna, et al. "The Management Mantra of the Bhagavad Gita: Key to Organizational Excellence." *Psychological Studies* 68.1 (2023): 1-12.

Dubey, Pushkar, Amit Joshi, and Ramesh Chandra Mishra. "Blending tradition and technology: Artificial intelligence-enhanced insights into the scholarly research on the Shrimad Bhagavad Gita." *AIP Conference Proceedings*. Vol. 3072. No. 1. AIP Publishing, 2024.

Jayamani, C. V. "Bhagavad Gita and Management." *Commerce Spectrum* 3.1 (2013): 60-6.

Mahadevan, B. "Leadership lessons from Bhagavad Gita." (2012).

Nayak, Akhaya Kumar. "Effective leadership traits from Bhagavad Gita." *International Journal of Indian Culture and Business Management* 16.1 (2018): 1-18.

Tapasyananda, Swami. *Srimad Bhagavad Gita-The Scripture of Mankind*. Sri Ramakrishna Math, 2024.

Chapter 6

Propagation of Traditional Values and Indian Literature in English

Mantha Padmabandhavi Prakashrao,
Associate Professor and Head, Department of English,
Swami Vivekanand Mahavidyalay, Shirur Tajband, Tq. Ahmedpur,
Dist. Latur, Maharashtra.

Ancient India was enriched with great traditional knowledge and values, and it was aimed at the welfare of Indians as well as the world. From Indian languages to commerce, from medicine to astronomy, and in different disciplines, India excelled in knowledge and implementation. The traditional Indian knowledge also encompasses philosophy, Indian literature, environmental conservation, and life sciences, including Ayurveda and medical tradition. Similarly, mathematics, Agriculture, Architecture, Arts and dance forms, education systems and other technologies are also unique in their own way. In addition, the morals and ethics were of highly substantial knowledge traditions in India.

The Indian traditional values essentially include ethics, values, beliefs, and rules of conduct, as well as culture and socio-political and economic organisation patterns. Traditional values also include faith, duty, respect, and integrity. Besides, Indian culture is the oldest of all cultures in the world. Culture refers to a pattern of thoughts and behaviour of people of that country, state, or community. Indian tradition and its values can be apprehended through the scriptures and Vedas as they encompass the traditional values of India. "Traditional values are the moral and ethical principles which are held to promote the sound functioning of the family and to strengthen the fabric of society." (Verity folkschool).

India is conferred with superfluity of value-based living conditions in the form of scriptures, culture, heritage and even saints. The Vedas are the integral values of India. The influence of Vedas on Indian culture and its heritage is immense. Even today, these Vedas are respected by Indians. Rig Ved and Atharva Ved mention truthfulness, modesty, honesty, non-violence, and purity of heart. But these are considered divine qualities in some scriptures, like *Bhagavad Gita.* Similarly, family values, community involvement, personal responsibility, and education are also some of the traditional values in India. The Holy Scriptures, like *Srimad Bhagawat* and *Bhagawat Gita*, are the depositories of human values. The satvik values such as non-violence (Ahimsa), Shanti (peace), Daya (compassion), Satyam (truth), Sthairyam (steadfastness), Kshama (forgiveness) and Danam (charity) are some of the divine and universal values, which divulge the humanity, throughout the world.

Religion and culture also play a significant role in sustaining India's traditional religious and cultural values. Bhagawat Gita is a priceless gift for the human beings. It describes the primary principles that help people to lead a higher way of life with larger goals. Similarly, the 5 precepts of Panchashila are unique, and they have several morals and ethics applicable to human values. It is rightly said, "The cultural ethics in ancient India are deeply influenced by the teachings of Hinduism and Buddhism. These teachings emphasised moral values, selflessness, and the importance of fulfilling one's duty. In addition, Dharma is not saved by persuasion; it is not by following the scriptures; it is saved by destroying oneself, and hence one should learn to sacrifice one's life for justice, truth, and Dharma (Duty)." (Singh, p.159).

The Indian saints are like masters, and their principles are sources of virtues and values that lead to moksha or liberation. Jayaram pertinently points out the significance of a spiritual master or a guide in one's life. "As all the rivers must eventually lead to the sea, there are many spiritual paths leading to the same destination. Some paths are shorter than others: some are difficult to navigate, and the path may not always be visible. A guide, in the form of Guru (spiritual master), is needed to this path, someone who holds the person and shows them the way." (Jayaram, p.777)

Almost in every religion, the spiritual aspect is quite similar, as the emphasis is placed on moral conduct. Family, culture, and values are propagated to generations through literature and to the world through Indian English literature. India is valued throughout the world for its cultural diversity and integrity. Despite many religions and cultures, India has sustained its values and traditions by preserving them in the form of Vedic culture. C. A. Conrad, in his book Business Ethics - A Philosophical and Behavioural Approach, writes, "Ethics answers the question of how we should behave properly. It is also called practical philosophy. So, ultimately, it is no more and no less than the meaning of life and the meaning of our existence as human beings.... The term ethos is used when the individual chooses a part of morality as a basis for action. Virtues, on the other hand, are practised and internalised dispositions of inner attitudes, to do good, to behave ethically." (Conrad, 2018).

Linguistic factors are also significant in the promulgation of traditional values in the form of literature in the regional languages. Sanskrit was the old and traditional language which enriched the traditional value system in India. Indian traditional values, culture and heritage have been passed on to generations through folklore, oral storytelling, and folk tales. And Indian English literature is instrumental in spreading Indian traditional values to the world. The Ancient Indian philosophical texts like Vedas, Upanishads, Buddhist scriptures, Bhagavad Gita and Bhagawat have played a significant role in the dissemination of Indian philosophical, spiritual, religious, and traditional values to the world. The translations of Vedas into English helped the contributors disseminate Indian philosophy and its values globally. The Modern English translations of the Rig-Veda Samhitaa into volumes by Prasanna C Gautam are unique in their own way. Rajaram Mohan Roy's Translation of Aitareya Upanishad disseminates the values to the world. A. C. Bhaktivedanta Swami Prabhupada, a Vedic Scholar, translated *The Bhagawat Gita* into English, a crown jewel of India's spiritual wisdom. It includes the concepts such as karma (Action) and Dharma (duties and responsibilities). Likewise, Indian mythology and folklore, as depicted in the scriptures like Ramayana and Mahabharata, which were originally written in Sanskrit, have a philosophical impact on the world. Manmatha Nathan Dutt translated Ramayana into English after T. H. Griffith. A poet, P. Lali translated the entire *Mahabharata* into English and disseminated Indian traditional values to the world. The ideal narratives provided a rich tapestry featuring gods, goddesses and all the mythical creatures that have influenced humans and their approach towards society and nature. The heroic and archetypal characters like Rama and his brother Laxmana are ideal figures whose manners have a great influence on Indians and people across the world. The qualities of Rama, such as respect for elders, integrity, tolerance, truth, morals, Dharma, and modesty, are significant qualities of Ramana and have a great impact on the people. The concept of Ramarajya, or peaceful society, is popular in the name of Lord Rama. Moreover, the courage, valour of Arjuna, and righteousness of Lord Krishna broaden the perspective of humans on their lives globally.

Indian poetry and verses written in Sanskrit contain traditional values and philosophical insights. The poetry written in regional languages such as Bengali, Sanskrit, Tamil, Marathi, and Telugu has proliferated the traditional Indian values and ethics. The poetry in Sanskrit by renowned poets like Kalidasa's *Abhignana Shakuntalam* was translated into English by Arthur Franklin and later translated into English by Indian English writers. *Raghuvamsam* and *Kumarasambhavam* are the 2 epics of Kalidasa. Similarly, Ved Vyas, Valmiki, Bhavabhuti, Bharavi, Magha and Harshavardhana are some

Sanskrit poets. Their writings are later translated into English, thereby helping the propagation of India's values, culture, and heritage to the world. Additionally, the verses written by the Indian saints and their translations into English helped readers worldwide understand spiritual life and its importance. Mirabais' love for Lord Krishna, her spiritual verses, and her hymns are translated into English by Alston and Subramaniam. Saint Tulasidas's admiration for Ram and the translation of his Vinai Patrika into English by Ajai Kumar and Ramcharita Manas into English propagates the ideal of the soul's eternal yearning for peace and salvation. Saint Dnyaneshwar's verses capture the spiritual culture that contributes to the peace, mental health, and harmony of mankind, thereby increasing understanding among humans. *Panchatantras* by a sage, Vishnu Sharma, encompass the important lessons of life in the form of tales.

Bhanabhatta's fiction, like *Kadambari, Harsha Charita and Parvati Parinaya*, depicts indigenous culture. Sanskrit poetry is an infinite treasure of knowledge that gives immense information about ancient thoughts and principles. In addition, Sanskrit dramas are a literary treasure of traditional values and ethics. Asvaghosa's works encompass Buddhist doctrines and principles. His famous work *Mahayana- Sraddhotpada Sastra* is about the awakening of faith in Mahayana. The English translations of these fictions contributed to spreading knowledge to generations.

In pre-independent India, the representation of traditional values through Indian English literature is noteworthy. During this era, literature was a powerful medium for awakening and creating social awareness. Early poetry in the nineteenth century mainly dealt with Indian or oriental themes. Great writers like Derozio and M. M. Dutt wrote poetry, though they imitated English poetry. Similarly, Bankin Chandra Chaterjee's *Rajmohan's Wife* is the first Indian novel in English, and *Anandmath* was the second novel. Similarly, Krishna Panth's *Bay of Bengal, Kandan* and Toru Dutt's *Bianca,* Jogendra

Singh's *Nur Jahan,* and Madhusudan Dutt's *Kamarupa and Kamalata* are noteworthy. Similarly, Madhusudan Dutt's play, *Is This Civilisation,* and Ramkinoo Dutt's *Manipur Tragedy* (1893) are quite remarkable in depicting Indian traditions in literature.

Rabindranath Tagore was a bilingual writer who translated his own works in Bengali into English, and his works are noteworthy for depicting the philosophical and traditional values of India. Tagore's works, such as *The Post Office, Chitra, Sacrifice* and other plays, all represent the traditional values of humanity, faith, trust, devotion and so on. Similarly, Mulkraj Anand and R. K. Narayan's love for ancient Indian culture and tradition is evident through their writings. Writers like Arundhati Roy infused their works with Indian culture and mythological elements. The incorporation of Indian traditions like rituals, customs and values offers a deeper understanding of Indian traditional values on a global platform.

Post-colonial Indian English literature placed emphasis on national and cultural heritage, human relations, and values. Post-modern Indian English writings were mostly diasporic. The writings of Anita Desai, Chitra Banerjee Divakaruni, Gita Mehta, Namita Gokhale, and Jhumpa Lahiri's deal with displacement and disintegration of cultures. Their writings also portray their longing for Indian culture, tradition, and values, including the cuisine, clothing, and mannerisms of their homeland.

The Indian writings in English, from ancient translations into Indian English to post-modern writings, all reverberate with Indian culture and propagate traditional values at the global level. The narrative style and techniques of Indian writers and their unique experiences also provide an insight into mythology folklore, incorporating customs, traditions, values, and ethics that are purely Indian. The changing socio-cultural aspects of contemporary Indian society also shed light on the changing socio-cultural and ethical perspective of the writer.

References

Conrad, C. A. (2018) *Business Ethics - A Philosophical and Behavioural Approach Business Ethics*, doi: 10.1007/978-3-319-91575-3. https://verityfolkschool.com>a-series.

Jayaram V. *Purusharthas and other 4 Aims of Human Life.* Retrieved April 4, 2024. From (http://www.hinduwebsite.com/hinduism/h-aims.asp)

Prabhupada, A.C. Bhaktivedanta Swami (1972). Bhagawat Gita As it is. Bhakti Vedanta Book Trust. Mumbai. 2010.

Singh, Bhagwan, *Pracheen Bharat Ke Itihas*, Sastra Sahitya Mandal, Delhi, New 2011.

Chapter 7

Indian Knowledge Tradition and Literature of Gorakhnath

Amod Kumar Rai,
Associate Professor, Department of English,
DDU Gorakhpur University, Gorakhpur, Uttar Pradesh.

Indian knowledge tradition is like the eternal flow of Ganga. It is a wonderful coincidence that Indian saints and seers chose the metaphor of 'river' for knowledge and life. Just like the river continuously flows in its original form, Indian knowledge traditions are flourishing in their original form. Anything which is constant is eternal. It never changes its original form, and that original form is of Indianness, which is eternal. If we explain that with the help of the metaphor of a river, then we can say that Rig-Veda is our Gomukh - the source of knowledge, which is like the beginning of the day for us; that is, from here, our knowledge begins. The sun rises.

Devaprayag is our Upanishad. Haridwar, where Sapt Rishi or Ganga flows in 7 ways, is where all the scriptures of our knowledge tradition come from. In the end, comes where the river water spreads and different rivers meet each other, which is our holy confluence. It is the place where various branches of knowledge, such as new knowledge of Jain, Buddhism, etc., emerge. A few centuries before Christ, Indian knowledge spread throughout India. While travelling, it established its roots in the form of Sangam literature in southern Tamil Nadu. Subsequently, with time, this centre of the South also became the centre of the emergence of Bhakti through Kannada, from where 'Alwar' and 'Nayanmar' saints were born. Bhakti arose in Dravid (South), and it was spread in the north by Ramanand.

Bhakti was first established in Tamil Nadu itself. The poetess' Andal' became prominent at that time. Andal's hymn '*Tirumalai*' is still sung in the temples of Tamil Nadu. Saint Gyaneshwar and Namdev, etc., developed this trend of devotion in Maharashtra and Shankardev, etc. in Assam. Shankar established the Indian knowledge tradition in the eighth century. Through his travels and discourses throughout India, he gave a new dimension to Advaita Vedanta, which comes to us in the form of philosophy. The ninth century is the period of Indian history from which Indian knowledge started being written in folk languages. In a way, we can say that from here, '*Vernacularising*' (nativisation) of Indian knowledge begins. Creating knowledge in native languages put Acharya Hazari Prasad Dwivedi's conclusion in this context is that - ..". Indian Buddhist sect accepted the supremacy of public opinion from the beginning of the year AD, till the end and disappeared after it became part of the public discourse. "This state continued till 1000 years after AD for many sects. It has no contact with the Muslim community. Coming down from the high seat of scholars and pundits, our real ground of prestige is towards public opinion, which began a thousand years ago. Hindi literature is the embodiment of that natural result" (Dwivedi, 74). Gorakhnath and other saints belong to this school of consciousness. His literature is available in both Sanskrit and vernacular languages. Later, through the Bhakti movement, the Indian knowledge tradition would sing praises at the all-India level, which is reflected within this tradition itself in the form of Saint Kabirdas, Jayasi, Mahatma Surdas and great saints like Goswami Tulsidas, etc. Adi Shankaracharya, Guru Gorakhnath, Saint Gyaneshwar, Vasavanna, Mirabai, Shah Hussain, Kabir, Tulsidas, Jaidev and Shankar Dev etc. These sages worked ceaselessly to awaken the Indian consciousness.

In the west, knowledge has been seen as an influential centre of power – Knowledge is considered the Supreme power, in fact. But in India, knowledge has been accepted as the best medium for the purification of human consciousness. Here, knowledge is seen as a "purifier." Even fire may not be able to purify us as much as knowledge purifies and refines us and our consciousness. The religion of the west is God-centric, but our religion is man-centric. Our entire scriptures focus on the purification and refinement of the human mind. The proclamation "Neither man is the best nor even the slightest" was popularised thousands of years ago. In the medieval period, Goswami Tulsidas gave a serious indication towards the importance of human life by saying, "Bade bhaagmanush tan paava, sur durlabh sab grantahingava." Similarly, in the 18 Puranas, Maharishi Ved Vyas accepted charity as the greatest virtue and sadism as the greatest sin –

अष्टादसपुराणेषुव्यासस्यवचनद्वयम |
परोपकारःपुण्यायपापायपरपीडनम || (Web 1)

(*Two statements of Vyasa in the 18 Puranas. Altruism is for the sake of virtue and oppression of others for the sake of sin*)

'Goswami Tulsidas further expressed this point in '*Parhit Saras Dharam Nahi Bhai*' *Pain* is not equal to pain, said Aghamai. There is a bigger message than this to human society from the level of religion: what can happen, and what can be done? Our religion should be to follow the path of charity and avoid sadism. It is a path, the teachings of which have been given to us from time to time by our sages. That's why Indian knowledge and its traditions are eternal: because they are human-centric, people- and society-oriented. The proof of the scriptures here is not the scriptures but the people only because what is there in the people's knowledge is constantly flowing, and the knowledge of the scriptures is bound and stagnant. That's why, in India, a large part of the knowledge tradition is oral and resides in the hearts of the people. Because of this, if one does not understand the oral tradition of India, he also does not understand the life tradition of this country as a whole. That is why Sanatana is not a religion in Indian society but a form of religion. It has a special quality which always remains new. The knowledge accumulated among the people is also proof of this. That is why religion has been established here as the discriminating power of man, and it is also reputed in our knowledge tradition-

आहार निद्रा भयमैथुनं च सामान्यमेततपशुभिर्निराणाम |
धर्मो हि तेषामधिकोविशेषःधर्मेणहीनाःपशुभिः समानाःसमाना || (Web, 2)

(*Food, sleep, fear, and sexual intercourse are common to animals and humans. Righteousness is their greatest distinction)'*

Without righteousness, they are like animals. Religion has been seen in a very dynamic form by the sage tradition of India. The 10 characteristics that have been mentioned are important; the values inherent in them are worth considering for society and the world. When the Mahabharatakar said:

धृतिः, क्षमा, दमों, अस्तेयं शौचमिनिन्द्रयनिग्रह धिविर्धः
सत्यमक्रोधः दशकं धर्म लक्षणं । (Web 3)

(*Patience, forgiveness, restraint, stealth, purity, restraint of the senses, patience, knowledge, truthfulness, and anger are the 10 characteristics of religion.)*

So, it has also been defined as the basic consciousness of religion. This is what Goswami Tulsidas has put before society in his book *'Ramacharitmanas'* in the form of Dharmaratha. A 'chariot of righteousness, in which is the wheel of solar and patience. The banner on that chariot is one of truth and the other of the firmness of virtue. The horses shod in this chariot are of power, discrimination, restraint of the senses and altruism and are bound by the ropes of forgiveness, grace and equality. *Stuti* is the charioteer on this chariot. Here, renunciation is the shield, and contentment is the sword. Charity is the axe and wisdom is the mighty power, the best science is the hard bow. A steady mind free from sin is like a tarkas, *Shama* means being in control of the mind, Yama means the sense of non-violence, and the purity of the rules (toilet, etc.) are the many arrows of this religion. The service of the Brahmin and the Guru is the impenetrable shield of this war. There is no other way for humanity to triumph like it.' What has Goswami said through this metaphor now? That the fulfilment of the best human values is the greatest victory of man in the struggle of life-

सौरजधीरजतेहिरथचाका | सत्यशील दृढ ध्वजपताका |
बल बिबेकदमपरहितघोरे | क्षमाकृपासमतारजुजोरे || (web 4)

(Strength, discrimination, restraint, and the welfare of others. Forgiveness, grace, and equality are the greatest virtues)

This consciousness of religion is the basic premise of our tradition of knowledge, which not only separates man from the animal but also elevates him above it. It connects the human to the non-human world. It has a worldview that considers the whole earth as a family. By adopting these values, unity can be established throughout the creation. It is the wisdom of our sages, on which the whole creation stands together as a family, above all humanly appropriate narrowness and weakness-

अयंनिजःपरमवेत्तिगणनालघुचेतसाम् |
उदारचरितानामतुवसुधैवकुटुम्बकम || (Web 5)

(This is the counting of the light-minded as their own and the other's. But the earth is the family of the generous)

India's knowledge tradition is extremely vast, which includes the entire history of ancient India. The knowledge gets absorbed. Astrology, Mathematics, Yogashastra, Metallurgy, Vastushastra, Sculpture, Science, Indian musical instruments, and water management, as well as Vedas, Vedanga, Indian philosophy, literature, Rhymes, grammar, education etc., are all included. This rich tradition of knowledge is thousands of years old. In this, along with the management of modern science, there is a wonderful treasure for various walks of life. Its scope is very wide, and the combination of these gives us insight into our culture and preserves our identity, increases the attitude toward learning, saves the environment, and promotes Shivatva, which shows the way to the future. By passing this knowledge from generation to generation, today is also part of our cultural and spiritual knowledge, the realisation of which is central to our being Indian and awakens in us a sense of pride. That is why the glory of knowledge is paramount here. Knowledge divine is seen as a light. This is why scholarship and knowledge in the Indian tradition are 2 different things. The study of various texts can make us a scholar, but the knowledgeable one is one whose soul is awakened. When we see ourselves in others and others in ourselves, we are on the path of 'Atmanahpratikulanipareshamnasamacharet,' when within us, the feeling of 'Aa no bhadraḥkratavoyantuvisvataḥ' prevails, then true knowledge is born within us, which our Manisha has termed as 'Sadhumat.' Wherever your wishes and aspirations end and, we find cessation of mere mortal suffering as the most important part of the path of life. Mahavir Swami, Mahatma Buddha, Shankaracharya, Guru Gorakhnath, Gurunanak, Saint Kabirdas, Mahatma Surdas, and Goswami Tulsidas are the biggest examples of this 'Sadhumat,' whose entire life is dedicated to public welfare. Real excitement within us comes only when we start living for others and keep altruistic thoughts in our minds. Only that one is called truly happy. It was from this very plane that our seer sages made this appeal.

नत्वम् कामयेराज्यंनस्वर्गम न पुनर्भवं |
कामयेदुःखतप्तानामप्राणिनामआर्तिनाश्रम || (Web 6)

(I do not desire a kingdom, nor heaven, nor rebirth. I desire the destruction of the enemies of the creatures who are suffering)

In India, knowledge is said to be eternal, and life is said to be eternal. The meaning of life lies in the meaningful discharge of values. Many of our talents go to waste due to a lack of values. Hazari Prasad Dwivedi has made a big distinction between success and accomplishment. His view is, "There is a difference between success and fulfilment. Through the accumulation of weapons and an abundance of external equipment, man can achieve that thing, which he has pompously named as success. But man's fulfillment lies in love, is in friendship, is in sacrifice. It lies in giving oneself selflessly for the well-being of all." Today, many people are living successful but meaningless lives. Life becomes meaningful through sacrifice, love, and the implementation of truth and non-violence in one's conduct and just living. While describing the glory of renunciation, it is said in *Ishaavashyopanishad* –

इशावास्यमिदम सर्वं यात्किंच्याम जगत्यांजगत |
तेनत्यक्तेनभुंजीथामागृधःकश्यस्वदधनं || (Web 7)

(Everything in this world belongs to the Supreme Personality of God. Enjoy whatever He has given you. Do not covet anyone's wealth.)

Here, the first line literally signifies that God is present everywhere, but the second line, about enjoyment and sacrifice, is amazing. This is the path on which we can protect ourselves as well as the rest of the universe. In the absence of sacrifice, our love also becomes lifeless. That is why our saints have described renunciation as the root of religion and have accepted non-violence as the greatest religion. Mahatma Gandhi, while describing the glory of non-violence, said, "The sages who invented the word non-violence in moments of terrible violence were ahead of Newton in their intelligence and even ahead of Wellington in their strength. I myself know the depth of this word. Couldn't measure." It is worth noting here that Wellington is the same one who defeated Napoleon Bonaparte in the 'Battle of Waterloo.' In 'Mahabharata,' non-violence has been established as the greatest religion, as the greatest penance, as the greatest truth and has been described as the medium of religious practice –

अहिंसापरमोधर्मस्तथाहिंसापरंतपः |
अहिंसापरमंसत्यंयतोधर्मःप्रवर्तते। (Web 8)

(Non-violence is the Supreme religion, and violence is the Supreme austerity)

Non-violence is the Supreme truth because it is Nirgun in itself, and Sagun only happens when wearing the garment of truth. We have 2 things here: talent and intelligence. Our sages were wise and were called seers. In the absence of wisdom, even a talented person's life becomes meaningless. The journey from talent to wisdom is what makes human life meaningful and makes it humane. That is why the Indian sage tradition has advised a talented person to be very alert and cautious. If talent is not channelled towards wisdom, then sooner or later, there is a great danger of it turning into power. Be it technology, politics, literature, society, economics, philosophy, etc., talent turns into power in the absence of intelligence. Talent can be converted into wisdom only when we have the strength to follow the truth. There should be a feeling of loyalty towards the truth. Truth is the soul of Indian culture, which is realised only by wearing non-violent clothes. Mahatma Gandhi considered truth as God. In his eyes, 'Truth is God.' Our culture is of 'Asato Maa Sadgamayah Tamso Maa Jyotirgamaya.' That is why man must answer for his deeds.

We should be very alert towards nature because nature is the witness of all our actions. It is said in Mahabharata-

आदित्याचान्द्ररवानलिान्लौचद्वौभूमरिपोहृदयंयमश्च |
अहश्च रात्ररिश्च उभेचसंध्येधर्मस्य जानातनिरस्यवृत्तम | (Web 9)

(The sun, moon, forest, air, and fire are the 2 elements: the earth, water, the heart, and Yama raja. He knows the conduct

of a man in the day and night, both in the twilight and in the evening.)

The knowledge that Indian Manisha has inculcated in us through tradition is based on some basic values – love, sacrifice, tolerance, dutifulness, forgiveness, affection, kindness, compassion, modesty, attitude, and justice. These are the values which brighten our souls and make us less sad and sensitive. When Hazari Prasad Dwivedi, in one of his essays **'Man is the Aim of literature,'** defines the aim of literature as 'human being,' then he raises this point from within the Indian knowledge tradition, "I want to look at literature from the human point of view. I am biased. I hesitate to call that which cannot save a human being from misery, inferiority, and hopelessness, which cannot make his soul bright, which cannot make his heart more sorrowful and sensitive. These lines of Acharya Dwivedi not only clarify the purpose of literature, its goal and its huge human aspect but also reveal the huge goal of Indian knowledge tradition. They hesitate to call that literature, which does not expand man's humanity, as literature. Expanding human sensitivity is also an accepted and established religion of our knowledge tradition."

Hindi literature is generally considered to have started in the eleventh century, the credit for giving birth to which goes to the Buddhist-Siddhas, Nath-Yogis and Jain monks who were detached from society and the world. The creativity of these recluses proved that, in reality, understanding the pain and suffering of society and paving the way for its solution is the best definition of being a Saint. The words of these saints not only reveal the social, religious, and political conditions of that time, but this literature also reveals in its consciousness the foolishness of those disinterested saints and the fire within them. It is true that the work of philosophy is to understand the world, and the work of politics is to change it but to create another world parallel to it is the work of literature. Literature is, in a way, a reconstruction of the world. The literature of saints also creates a new world in one's consciousness. The literature of Gorakhnath, Kabir, Sur, Tulsi and Jayasi is like this. Gorakhnath is a Saint of the Indian knowledge tradition whose literature attacks many myths, prevalent evils, and religious rituals of his time and shows the path to the wandering society. In this form, he creates a new world. A world free from all forms of inequality and against inhumanity. Caste, religion, sect, and above all, a world of love and brotherhood. Any literature also evolves from its earlier tradition and is influenced by its contemporary and later literature. Gorakhnath's literature also follows the tradition of the Siddhas prevalent before him. Taking it forward, on one hand, it echoes the medieval consciousness, and on the other hand, it is a source of time. The life stream of the vibrant society also flows in it. The best tradition of Indian knowledge contained in scriptures and the tradition of folk language in the form of Apabhransha in ancient literature of Hindi and Sanskrit were inherited during this period. Sanskrit and Apabhransa literature were parallel to Hindi literature. Gorakhnath's literature is best written on this sandhi-bela of Sanskrit and Apabhransha. It is the literature of the Indian knowledge tradition, pointing towards his pan-Indian personality about which Acharya Hazari Prasad Dwivedi writes - "In the tenth century of Vikram Samvat, the great Guru Gorakhnath appeared. So influential and so glorified after Shankaracharya that there is no second great man in India. Even today, his followers are found in every corner of India. The most powerful religious movement before the Bhakti movement was the Yogamarga of Gorakhnath. It was the same. Gorakhnath was the greatest leader of his era."

When Hazariprasad Dwivedi declared Gorakhnath as the second most influential man after Shankaracharya, he simultaneously pointed towards many dimensions of Gorakhnath's personality. Shankaracharya was a great Shaiva by whom the unorganised Shaiva ascetics were organised all over India. It was Gorakhnath who did the work of uniting the remaining Shaivite followers. During his time, followers of Shaivism were associated with various monasteries and temples. There were as many sects as there were thrones. In fact, in the absence of an influential great man, unity was not being maintained among them. Gorakhnath was such an influential and great man. The influence of Shankaracharya in the field of Indian philosophy and spirituality is so strong that without discussing him, progress in this field cannot be made. Similarly, the discussion of pre-medieval religious and spiritual history remains incomplete without Gorakhnath. Gorakhnath also propagated his views by travelling all over India and got recognised, pointing to the famous scholar Bachchan Singh, who is of the opinion that "Mahatmas of that period had the amazing power of travelling, whether they were Shankaracharya or Gorakhnath. Gorakh travelled to Punjab, Gujarat, Uttar Pradesh, Assam, Orissa etc. His influence crossed the borders of these states. The personality of Gorakhnath is very important from the point of view that he played an important role in establishing coordination between different religions. Buddhists, Siddhas, Jains, and followers of all sects like Shaiva, Shakta, and Vaishnav were involved in the religious worship of Gorakhnath. His hold within society and public life was very deep and profound, as well as on social and religious organisations" (Bacchan, 79). Gorakhnath was established as a folk hero, and the Siddhas were protected from the vile tantric trades. He provided security to the public. He advocated the practice of restraint, good conduct, non-attachment, and continuous yoga in life. This was the biggest mantra of his solitary meditation. Maybe that's why his influence is so widespread. It was on India, pointing towards which Bachchan Singh says, "The question arises: Why did Gorakhnath have a nationwide impact? Is it just because they have abandoned the system? Adopted the path of yoga. He might have also been a Tantrik, yes, their system is the hideous system of the Buddhists. He also performed miracles, but his miracles were due to yoga. It is certain that he freed the people from fear due to the nefarious trades generated by the system. They practice celibacy and yoga. But he used to give exclusive emphasis (83)." This is the reason that Gorakhnath ignored all the logical arguments of Shankaracharya.

And despite its thoughtful and serious analytical nature, it makes it special.

The ninth century was a period in which Indian knowledge tradition started expanding through folk languages (indigenous languages). Maithil poet Vidyapati expressed his loyalty towards the native language by saying, "*Desilbaynasabjanmitha.*" When Goswami Tulsidas said

"Nana Purannigamagam Sammatanyad Ramayane Nigditam Kvachidnyatoapi| Swantahsukhay Tulsi Raghunathgatha Bhashananibandhamatimanjulamnoti."

He talked about composing the Indian knowledge tradition in a beautiful and charming language. The literature of Kabir and Sur is also the literature of Indian knowledge philosophy written in the folk language. The foundation of this tradition was laid in the ninth and tenth centuries, in which Gorakhnath was at the forefront. He wrote in both Sanskrit and the indigenous language and laid great emphasis on the discipline of disciplined yoga and cultured practical life inherent in the Indian knowledge tradition. The restrained yoga practice and practical way of life he practised is seen as having a wide and inspiring influence not only for many centuries to come but even today. This is another aspect of his uniqueness. He not only countered the misguided Vamachar and Panch Makar practices of the then Buddhist Siddhas but also travelled across the country and debated with Acharyas of different sects, and by defeating them, he spread the practice of Indian knowledge within the world in the form of Nath Panth. This was a very important work done by him. He is the first Saint to take the Indian knowledge tradition into folk language. He accepted whatever was sattvik in the various sects prevalent in his time. For this reason, he received immense public respect, which gave a very high status to his personality. Drawing attention towards his very wisdom, Bachchan Singh says - "Like Shankaracharya, Gorakh not only travelled but also had debates with teachers of different sects. He was an extremely brilliant and top scholar. He gained people's attention only by defeating his rivals. He might have been attracted towards Nath sect. His struggle with the Kaula sect, Kalamukh, Pashupat, Shakta sect etc. is well known."

At the time Gorakhnath emerged, the country was experiencing an atmosphere of social, political, and religious instability. Politically, the nation was divided into different parts, and religiously, many sects were prevalent, and at the social level, the society was stuck in narrow-mindedness. Gorakhnath rose above all narrow-mindedness and did the important work of establishing religious unity in the country. Personally, he also helped the weak and helpless people in society. In this form, his popularity was very high. At a time when Vaamachara was at its peak in the field of religion and religious practice was being considered a means to fulfil man's corrupt desires, at that time, the purity of practice, purity of conduct, the importance of a restrained life and the power of a life without ostentation were emphasised. The first announcement was made by Guru Gorakhnath. The biggest reason for this is that Gorakhnath knew the Indian knowledge practice tradition very well and its gradual development and importance. At that time, in order to protect the ancient Indian knowledge tradition, it was also necessary to make people well acquainted with the knowledge glory of India. Awareness of one's knowledge tradition was necessary for the renovation of society. This was also very important to protect the ancient religious practice. Gorakhnath re-established the basic principles of Indian spiritual practice, the rules of Gurushishya tradition, initiation, and authority distinction in the Shaiva sect. There was a gross irregularity in the observance of these rules and principles in the then Buddhist-Siddha tradition. Due to their violation, the method of meditation had gone astray. The principles and values of Indian spiritual practice and knowledge tradition can be seen in abundance in Gorakhnath's Sanskrit and Apabhransha-based Hindi works.

Gorakhnath played an important role in keeping the values of Indian knowledge tradition alive. In our thinking tradition, 'patience' has been seen as parallel to 'religion.' Religion cannot be followed without patience. Patience has been kept as the first characteristic of Dharma' *Dhritih, Kshama, Damo, Asteyam...' Tulsidas has also said, 'Dheeraj, Dharam Mitra and Nari...'* While explaining the importance of patience, Gorakhnath has simultaneously distinguished the ease, simplicity and ego-lessness of life as the greatest values. This famous verse of his is an example of this –

हबकि नबोलिबाठबकिनचलिबाधीरेधरिबापाँव।
सहजैरहिबागरबनकरिबाभणतगोरखरांव ॥ (Web 10)

(Don't stutter, don't stutter, don't walk, hold your feet slowly.)

There is also an excellent description of 'Guru-Mahima' in the Indian knowledge tradition. In fact, in our ancient education system, it has also been said to educate the student. India's Guru-disciple tradition is an example of this. This is a very sacred belief. Without a Guru, knowledge is said to be useless. Guru is the light from where the light of knowledge flows within the seeker. Our seers give a higher place to Guru than God. The literature of medieval saints is also good proof of this. Gorakhnath's thoughts also reveal great reverence and respect for the Guru. In his view, all the worldly seekers who are deluded by illusion should make themselves a Guru because without a Guru, there cannot be spiritual realisation-

गुरुकीजैगहिला निगुरा न रहिला,,
गुरुबिनज्ञाननपायिलारेभईया । (Web, 11)

(Without Guru, one remains a fool; without Guru, one cannot get knowledge, brother.)

The sect of Gorakhnath is popularly known as 'Nath Panth,' which is also known as 'Siddhamat,' 'Siddha Marg,' 'Yogamarg,' 'yoga

Sampradaya,' 'Avadhut Mat' and other names. Dr Bachchan Singh, in his *'Second History of Hindi Literature'* says that the Siddhas mentioned by Goswami Tulsidas at the beginning of 'Ramacharitmanas' as *'Yabhyambinanapasyantisiddhahsvantasthamisvaram'* were the Nath-Siddhas. Tulsi is angry with the persecution of the society and says directly, 'Where is the Dhoot, where is the Avdhut, where is the Julhah, say someone... This can also give an idea of the social status of this sect. Saint Kabirdas has remembered Gorakh with great devotion. Kabirdas also mentions his calculations with Gorakhnath, Bhartrihari and Gopichand:'

गोराभरथरिगोपीचंदा | सामनसोमिलिकरैअनंदा
अकिलनिरंजनसकलसरीरा |तामनसोमिलिरहाकबीरा || (Web 12)

All the above-mentioned 3 were devotees of Nath Panth, whose names have been taken with great respect by Kabir. These lines of Kabir present a living proof of the prevalence and spread of Indian knowledge stream among the people. Kabir himself is a strong link of the same tradition after Gorakhnath. Gorakh and his Nath Panth is its starting point, from where the knowledge written in Sanskrit texts spreads in folk languages. The Saint literature of the medieval period is in the tradition of Gorakh.

It is the literature of the best Indian school of thought. Kabirdas has used the word 'Avadhu' in many places. 'Avadhu Gagan Mandal Ghar Ki Jai,' 'Avadhu, Mera Man Matwara etc. At Kabir's place, the use of Ida and Pingla Nadis is also because of the influence of the Gorakhnath and Nath sects. He has used Gorakh and his yoga practice in a very original way. The major speciality of Indian culture is 'self-purification.' Whenever distortion arises within the religion, new religious movements try to remove those distortions and create a healthy environment within the society. History is a witness to the fact that whenever the Vedic religion faced any distortion, it played an important role in creating an ambience of inclusion and harmony.

Buddhism and Jainism emerged against it. When Buddhism, too, started to face distortions in its religious fabric, Bajrayani Siddho created a new sect to fight against the distortions. Due to the woman-centric approach in Sadhana of Siddhas, wrong propagation of Indian religious practice started in the society. This was because the Nath sect was born from within the Siddha Path, Matsyendranath Gorakhnath, etc. The Saint was also among the 84 Siddhas. Gorakhnath was the originator of Nathpanth. He considered this sect as Indian. A vast and healthy form of religious practice was put forward. This was during the period of medieval religious practice. It was such a work that protected not only Indian religious practice but also Indian culture. Almost 500 years of Indian history are covered with the influence of Gorakhnath. That's why after Shankaracharya, he was hailed as the second most influential personality, whose influence was all over India.

References:

Akhilesh Kumar's article on Hdjaincollege.org - "Impact and relevance of Buddhist philosophy on Hindi literature."

Dwivedi, Hazari Prasad- www.hindisamay.com- 'Why do nails grow?' Essay

Dwivedi, Hazari Prasad, *'Ashoka Ke Phool'* LokbhartiPrakashan, Third Paperback Edition 2014, Page-143.

Singh, Bachchan, *Hindi Sahitya Ka Dusra Itihas*, Radhakrishna Publications, First Edition 1996, Page-34.

Radhakrishnan, *Some Thoughts on Indian Culture*, Rajpal and Sons, Edition 2012, Page-88.

Tiwari, Vishwanath Prasad, on Gandhiji in Seminar-"Gandhi in Indian Literature" at Sahitya Akademi on 31st January 2019 (Also available on YouTube) |

Tiwari, Vishwanath Prasad, Asti aur Bhavati, Publication-National Book
Trust, New Delhi, Edition 2014.

Poems Quoted

1. Sanskritwisdom.com In the 18 Puranas of Vyasa

2. wiki.ekvastra.in Food Sleep [Ekvastra]

3. wiki.ekvastra.in patience forgiveness [Ekvastra]

4. Blogger http://businessachivers.blogpost.com

   www.hi.m.wikipedia.org Vasudeva Kutumbkam - VI.

   wiki.ekvastra.in I don't want [Ekvastra]

   Internet Archive https://archive.org-Ishavasyopanisad

5. hindijankariblog.com Non-violence is the Supreme religion verse

6. www.egyankosh.ac.in unit-4Page-4.

Chapter 8

An Exploration into the Contribution of Select Tamil Philosophers to Indian Literary and Knowledge Arena

P. Harshini,

Assistant Professor, PG and Research Department of English,
Ethiraj College for Women, Chennai, Tamil Nadu.

Introduction

The contributions of Philosophers in Tamil literature have no doubt enriched the Indian knowledge system in varied areas such as literature, philosophy, linguistics, history, and culture. Great poets like Thiruvalluvar, Avvaiyar, and others who lived during the Sangam era were adorned with works that were highly philosophic and morally insightful. The Thirukkural, written by Thiruvalluvar, is a classic Tamil text that pericarps moral teaching and ethical principles that are useful today. The book has themes that cover virtuousness, righteousness, governance, and personal and social relationships that contribute to the wider ideological discourse in India. At the forefront of the development and evolution of Tamil language and grammar, Tamil literature stands as a significant force. According to Sascha Ebeling on the significance of Tamil language opined thus, "Tamil was found to be a second "classical" language besides Sanskrit, and the only living Indian language which has a continuously documented tradition of more than 2 thousand years. The antiquity of Tamil literature was soon deployed in a systemic fashion to combat the hegemonic position and linguistic elitism of Sanskrit and, with it, North Indian culture. Ancient Tamil tradition could now be used as a safe "proof" of cultural uniqueness and, therefore, the right and necessity to form an independent nation. Thus, what was initially only a literary discovery became highly consequential in the wider socio-political sphere (23)." Tolkappiyam, an ancient Tamil grammatical text, has crucially provided foundational recognition of Tamil grammar and syntax. The Indian sub-continent's language evolution and linguistic diversity need special attention, especially from scholars. Needless to say, Tamil literature and Language have contributed richly to comparative linguistics, helping to meet the demands. Undubitably, Tamil literature has evolved to be a storehouse of Tamil culture, with its rich history and distinguished identity.

The Sangam literature delves deeper into the social, political, and cultural life of the antediluvian Tamil community. The great epics like Chilapathikaram and Manimekalai offer rich delineations of Tamil culture, practices, and traditional boundaries, thus fostering a unique feeling of profoundness and belonging among Tamil-speaking groups. A variety of genres like poetry, epic, drama, and prose adorn Tamil literature's rich and diverse tradition, which in turn have influenced literary traditions across India. The poetic conventions, literary devices and aesthetic sensibilities evoke a feeling of oneness and unity among Indians. The literary works of Tamil have long served as inspiration to many poets, writers, and artists belonging to other Indian languages, thus adorning the vivacious medley of Indian literature.

The Tamil Sangam literature mainly gains reference from ancient Tamil literature created by the Tamil Sangam which was gatherings of outstanding Tamil scholars and poets who were quite popular in antediluvian south India. This literary assembly was believed to have shown existence for many centuries. The earliest idea about Sangam literature was believed to be held around 300 BCE though accurateness is still unconfirmed.

The Sangam literature is composed of 2 major categories: the Ten Idylls (Pattupattu) and the Eight Anthologies (Ettuttokai). These 2 contributions are said to be the oldest surviving literature in the Tamil language and are priceless in comprehending the cultural, societal, and linguistic ethos of antediluvian Tamil Society. The diverse themes of Sangam literature make it an interesting read and cover topics such as love, war, nature, ethics, and governance. Each of its lines is defined by its intense imagery, loaded symbolisation and deeper emotional thoughts. The poets of the Sangam period made invaluable attempts at the grammar of the language and deeper literary study, thus contributing to the growth and development of the Tamil language.

The most popular works of Sangam literature are "Purananuru," "Ainkurunuru," "Kuruntokai," and "Natrinai." The texts no doubt render invaluable contributions into the lives, ethics, and principles of the folks of ancient Tamilakam together with their deeper communication with natural surroundings. For gaining literary excellence and cultural vitality, Sangam literature should be studied and also celebrated.

In the growth and development of religious and spiritual traditions, the instrumentality of Tamil literature cannot be gainsaid. The saints of the Bhakti movement, the Alvars and Nayanars, with their devotional poetry, have expressed thoughtful spiritual experiences and devotion to gods like Vishnu and Shiva. It would be an understatement to say that their knowledge and wisdom have shaped the spiritual growth of south India and influenced deeper religious customs and notions throughout the nation. Various historical sagas and records that deliver insights into the traditional customs and beliefs of Tamil Nadu and communications with other regions across the nation can also be seen belonging to Tamil literature. The living conditions of the Nayanars and their contributions to the Tamil community can be found carved in epics like Periya Puranam. Likewise, the other significant texts shed light on dynastic rule, trade, business, and cultural exchanges in ancient south India.

Through the dissemination and growth of divine religious traditions, Tamil literature occupies a foremost and significant place. The worshipful poems of the Alvars and Nayanars, who were devoted preachers of the Bhakti movement, shed light on their abysmal fondness for gods such as Vishnu and Shiva. Their contributions have no doubt sharpened the spiritual atmosphere of south India and played a crucial role in influencing spiritual practices and customs throughout the countryside. Tamil literature carries a wealth of historical chronicles and narrations that shed knowledge on traditional Tamil Nadu's historical perspectives and interactions with other parts of the Indian sub-continent. Epical narratives such as Periya Puranam talk about the life of Nayanars and their invaluable efforts to the Tamil community, whereas other narratives show light on the rulings, business, and ethnic dealings in conventional south India. The endeavour on the part of Tamil literature to the rich tapestry of the Indian knowledge system is far-fetched and awe-inspiring. It reflects the rich and diverse Tamil culture and rational acquisition. Through its literary, philosophical, linguistic, and cultural expressions, Tamil literature continues to shape and enrich India's broader intellectual discourse and heritage.

Avvaiyar is popular for her wealth of knowledge of Sangam poems. She particularly focused on the Aham genre, which is known for its focus on individualised and subjective content like love, wisdom, and morality. Her lines are defined by simple terms, clear structure, and a thoughtful vision of human nature. Geetha Gopalakrishnan, in her book, introduces Avvaiyar thus: "Avvaiyar literally means 'respectable woman.' She is often depicted as an old and intelligent lady. There is a statue of Avvaiyar in the village of Muppandai in the Kanyakumari district of modern-day Tamil Nadu. Legend has it that she left the earth from that place. An Avvai festival is organised every year in Nagapattinam district to commemorate her literary contributions. Folklore has it that at the festival venue, a conversation took place between Avvaiyar and Lord Muruga, the guardian deity of Tamilians, when Avvai contemplated retiring from her Tamil literary pursuits, believing that she had accomplished whatever there was to be accomplished. At that point, Lord Muruga appeared before her and jousted with her on an intellectual level. Later, he revealed his true identity and encouraged her to continue her teachings, which she did (13)." Avvaiyar's poems are characterised by moral preachings and pragmatic knowledge in order to lead a rightful and impeccant life. Her verses offer proper direction on diverse facets of life that include ethical conduct, social kinship, and familial virtues. Avvaiyar is conventionally attributed to a variety of works, though accurate authorship of certain texts is still debated. One of her popular works is "Aathichoodi," an accumulation of ethical maxims and adages that are targeted towards transmitting moral integrity in children. The text is studied far and wide, mainly across the country and is known for its ease of understanding and deep sense of knowledge. C. Rajagopalachari explores thus "Avvaiyar, arguably one of the most important female poets in Tamil's two-thousand-and-five-hundred years of literary history, and certainly one of the best known, of any gender. Although people across the state of Tamil Nadu know many of her works by heart, she has received little attention outside India, owing largely to the lack of decent translations."

The other literary contributions of Avvaiyar include "Konraiventhan," an edifying collection of verses that offers guidance and direction to a king and "Vinayagar Agaval," which sings praises of Lord Ganesha. The contribution of Avvaiyar to Tamil literature has had an everlasting effect on the literary and ethical standpoint of Tamil Nadu. Her words are still revered as symbolic of knowledge, virtue, and maternal bond. She is not just respected as a literary genius but as a cultural figure and a paragon, too. Often portrayed as a senior most and intellectual woman, her teachings have a great influence on society. Her life and practical wisdom personify the values of compassion, humility and deep knowledge that are cherished in Tamilian culture.

Thiruvalluvar, one of the most celebrated poets and philosophers, is well known for his masterpiece, the Tirukkural. He is known to have lived in the I century BCE or I century CE, which is now Tamil Nadu, India. Even though much of his life remains covered in mystery, and his identity and background are still debated among scholars, the influence and contribution that he has made to Tamil literature and philosophy is immense. His significant work, The Tirukkural, stands as a living testimony to his deep wisdom and thoughtfulness. George Pope & M. Varadarajan, in their praise for the Tamil Classic, state thus, "The real greatness of Tirukkural is its survival, even after the onslaughts of many heterogeneous creeds. In the last 2 thousand years, it never failed to attract any scholar or lover of wisdom. They have glorified Valluvar and his monumental magnum opus, "The Kural," with scintillating tributes. It is true that the great poet of modern times, Mahakavi Subramaniya Bharathi, aptly said, "Tamilnadu gave Valluvar to the world! And thereby gained the everlasting fame!"

The Tirukkural most often named kural is a magnum opus in Tamil literature and one among the most respected literary texts in the universe. The kural comprises of 1330 couplets (kurals) each having a division of 133 chapters, the topics include ethics, morality, governance, friendship, love and spirituality. Thriuvalluvar's profound ability lies in his power to instil thoughtful ideological truths into succinct and soul rending verses.

The Tirukkural is composed of 3 books, each touching upon life's particular aspects. In the first book, Aram, ethical and moral virtues that emphasise honesty, integrity, morality, and empathy are discussed. Thiruvalluvar most importantly stresses the significance of leading a life of virtue to obtain fulfilment in personal life together with societal concordance. In the second book, Porul, Valluvar sets out to explore the percepts of wealth and economic prosperity. He sets out to discuss topics such as cultivation, commerce, establishment, and the duties of monarchs to their people. Valluvar expostulates an impartial and fair administration that gives precedence to the well-being of its people. In the third book, Inbam, Valluvar stresses the complexity of human relationships, especially love and fellowship. His lines on love, marriage, friendship, and thick family bonds portray his deeper sense of understanding of human nature and the intricacies of interpersonal bonds.

The Tirukkural has no doubt served as a significant influence on Tamil culture, literature, and the nation for centuries. It is respected not just in terms of excellence in the literature world but together for its wisdom across time and ages and pragmatic guidance. Valluvar's preachings will always continue to inspire generations, people of all backgrounds, irrespective of religion, caste or creed and transcend geographical and cultural extremities. It is to be noted that the Tirukkural has been translated into numerous languages and remains a great inspirational read for millions and millions across the universe. The legacy of Thiruvalluvar as a philosopher, poet, and martinet cuts through the imperishable relevancy of the Tirukkural, which serves as a lighthouse of knowledge and enlightenment for humanity.

Advaita Siddhanta, also called Advaita Vedanta, is a popular school of Hindu Philosophy that occurred in antediluvian India and is specifically linked with the preachings of Aadi Shankaracharya (788-820 CE).

Aadi Shankaracharya's key role lay in the revival of the study and practice of Vedanta, particularly the Advaita Vedanta. He was the master craftsman in systematising and elucidating the preachings of Upanishads, Brahma Sutras and Bhagavad Gita, thus rendering understandability and coherency to the Advaita tradition. His statements and ideas were crucial in shaping the foundational texts for the Vedanta studies. Saurabh Singh Chauhan opines thus: "Adi Shankaracharya's prolific writings are a testament to his profound understanding of the scriptures and his dedication to elucidating the intricacies of Advaita Vedanta. His commentaries on ancient Hindu texts remain foundational works in Indian philosophy and spirituality. Driven by a deep sense of devotion and desire to make the profound teachings of the Upanishads, Bhagavad Gita, and Brahma Sutras accessible to all, Shankara embarked on a remarkable journey of literary creation."

Being an excellent philosopher, he laid emphasis on the significance of spiritual practice (sadhana) as a way of realising the facts as stated in the Vedanta. He followed stern principles namely meditaion, self-inquiry, devotion, and renouncement as firm roads to realising of the self and gaining liberation. Shankara's preachings served as a great inspiration to numerous people to follow the life of rumination and inner transformation.

Another profound philosopher, Ramanujacharya, also known as Ramanuja, through his contributions to Vishishtadvaita Vedanta, combined elements of non-dualism and dualism, thus placing emphasis on the close kinship between the individual soul and the Supreme corporeality. Through his knowledgeable commentaries on the principal Upanishads, Brahma Sutras and the Bhagavad Gita, Ramanuja rendered systematised interpretations and firmly rooted his authority in the circle of Sri Vaishnavism tradition. His preachings on Bhakti (devotion) are a sure means of obtaining spiritual liberation and support for social inclusivity and equivalence, brought in a big change in the popularising of spiritual practices and nourished a more inclusive religious society. His philosophical combination and promotion of an ethical life have continued to serve as a great inspiration for seekers and students, thus shaping the intellectual and religious standpoint of India.

Though there are many more popular philosophers who have enriched and enlightened the literary pathway of India and contributed to the rich Indian knowledge system, this study is confined to a few very important philosophers as stated above. This can serve as an itinerary for future researchers to explore more on the field and bring in a much more elaborate study thus widening the need and scope for such a diverse area of this kind.

References

Ebeling Sascha, Colonising the Realm of Words: The Transformation of Tamil Literature in Nineteenth-Century South India. State University of New York Press, Albany. 2010.

TIRUVALLUVAR, TAMIL POET. Tirukkural: Translation in English with Tamil Commentary. N.P., CreateSpace Independent Publishing Platform, 2015.

Give, Eat, and Live: Poems of Avvaiyar. United States, Red Hen Press, 2009.

Gopalakrishnan, Geeta. My Grandmother's Tweets: Stories Inspired by Avvaiyar's Ancient Wisdom. India, Harper India, 2018.

KNOW ABOUT "ADI SHANKARACHARYA": A Great Indian Philosopher, Theologian, & Reformer. N.P., Saurabh Singh Chauhan, 2022.

Chapter 9

Service to Humanity: Jainism and Jain Tirthankara's Contribution to Indian Knowledge System

Pratik Surana,
Chief Mentor and Founder,
Quantum Infotrainers & Consultants Pvt. Ltd. Pune, Maharashtra.

The cultural and intellectual fabric of India is embellished with the profound insights of innumerable spiritual giants who have guided successive generations towards enlightenment. The Jain Tirthankaras, esteemed individuals, are regarded as spiritual Gurus who exemplify the values of wisdom, compassion, and non-violence. Their profound understanding of the essence of existence and human consciousness has had a lasting impact on the Indian scholarly framework, shaping philosophy, ethics, and spirituality for thousands of years.

In the context of Jainism, the Tirthankaras hold a cherished status as enlightened entities who have achieved moksha, or liberation, by engaging in rigorous asceticism and demonstrating unshakeable dedication to non-violence, known as ahimsa. The title "Tirthankara" can be translated as "ford-maker," denoting their function as spiritual mentors who assist individuals in traversing the vast expanse of life. According to Jain tradition, it is believed that there has been a total of 24 Tirthankaras in each cosmic era. The most recent Tirthankara in the present era is Lord Mahavira, who is considered the 24th Tirthankara.

The Involvement in the Indian Knowledge System:

1. The fundamental principle of Jain philosophy is ahimsa, which goes beyond simply refraining from bodily injury and includes thoughts, words, and actions. The Tirthankaras expounded upon the intrinsic importance of ahimsa in cultivating societal peace and compassion. Their doctrines not only served as a source of inspiration for Jainism but also exerted a tremendous influence on other Indian intellectual schools, such as Buddhism and Hinduism.

2. Jainism presents a sophisticated interpretation of karma, which is the principle of cause and effect that governs the process of birth and death. The Tirthankaras explained the complexities of karma, highlighting the significance of intention (bhava) and the nuances of karmic slavery. The scholarly contributions of their work on karma theory have significantly enhanced the Indian philosophical conversation, providing deep contemplations on the essence of ethical accountability and the attainment of spiritual emancipation.

3. Ethical Conduct (Righteousness): The Tirthankaras demonstrated a commendable adherence to ethical norms, promoting values such as veracity (satya), abstention from theft (asteya), purity (brahmacharya), and non-avarice (aparigraha). Their moral precepts served as a guiding principle for individuals and communities, directing them towards virtuous existence and spiritual advancement.

Anekantavada, also known as the doctrine of non-absolutism, is a fundamental principle of Jain philosophy that has been expounded upon by the Tirthankaras. According to this philosophy, it is posited that reality possesses inherent complexity and cannot be comprehensively understood by a solitary viewpoint. Through its embrace of the intricate nature of life, anekantavada cultivates qualities such as tolerance, humility, and intellectual openness, thereby enhancing the Indian intellectual tradition using a dialectical methodology in the pursuit of truth.

The Jain tradition, one of the most ancient extant religions, holds in high regard 24 Tirthankaras as spiritual mentors who have undergone the journey of enlightenment and achieved liberation from the pattern of reincarnation. The teachings and exemplary lives of each Tirthankara have had a major impact on the Indian knowledge system, influencing the development of philosophy, ethics, and spirituality. Let us explore the unique contributions made by each Tirthankara and their lasting influence on Indian intellectual tradition.

Rishabhanatha (Adinatha) is considered the inaugural Tirthankara and is highly respected for establishing the fundamental principles of Jainism. The individual in question presented the fundamental principles of non-violence (ahimsa), truthfulness (satya), and austerity (tapas), so establishing the ethical foundation that would consistently shape Jain philosophy over an extended period of time. Rishabhanatha's teachings prioritised the significance of self-control and the pursuit of spiritual growth, establishing the foundation for future Tirthankaras to elaborate on.

Ajitanatha, the second Tirthankara, made significant contributions to the Indian knowledge system through his extensive expounded explanations of the ideals of non-violence and compassion. He stressed the interdependence of all living beings and promoted the adoption of ahimsa as a method to reduce suffering and achieve spiritual freedom. Ajitanatha's teachings emphasised the inherent worth of all conscious beings, cultivating empathy and respect for life.

Sambhavanatha, the third Tirthankara, enhanced the Indian knowledge system by imparting profound lessons on ethical behaviour and virtuous existence. He preached the merits of veracity, uprightness, and self-control, directing persons towards a life of ethical uprightness and spiritual development. Sambhavanatha's focus on ethical behaviour established the foundation for the evolution of Jain ethics, which still exerts a significant impact on Indian society in the present era.

Abhinandananatha, the fourth Tirthankara, made noteworthy contributions to the field of Indian philosophy by imparting teachings on meditation and the quest for inner purification. The author expounded upon the concept of introspection (anupreksha) as a method for fostering self-awareness and spiritual enlightenment. The focus on contemplative activities by Abhinandananatha had a significant role in the advancement of Jain meditation techniques, facilitating the cultivation of inner tranquillity and spiritual enlightenment.

Sumatinatha, the fifth Tirthankara, made significant contributions to the Indian knowledge system through his detailed explanation of the idea of karma and its profound consequences for spiritual development. The individual elaborated on the complexities of karmic bondage and the significance of intention (bhava) in influencing subsequent experiences. The teachings of Sumatinatha enhanced comprehension of karma theory, offering valuable insights into the mechanics of causality that control the cosmic order.

Padmaprabha, the sixth Tirthankara, enhanced the Indian knowledge system by imparting lessons on non-attachment and detachment. The individual highlighted the impermanent quality of physical existence and promoted the development of detachment (vairagya) as a method to surpass worldly anguish. The teachings of Padmaprabha have served as a source of inspiration for successive generations of individuals who have sought to abandon earthly gratifications and embark on the journey towards spiritual emancipation.

Suparshvanatha, the seventh Tirthankara, made a significant contribution to the field of Indian philosophy by elucidating the doctrine of anekantavada, which pertains to non-absolutism. He provided a comprehensive explanation of the complex and diverse aspects of reality, as well as the constraints of human vision in comprehending the ultimate truth. The teachings of Suparshvanatha espoused the principles of intellectual humility and tolerance, thereby cultivating an environment conducive to open communication and mutual regard among diverse philosophical traditions.

Chandraprabha, the eighth Tirthankara, left a lasting impact on Indian knowledge by imparting valuable lessons on the virtues of compassion and charity. He stressed the significance of altruistic service (seva) and compassion towards all sentient creatures, cultivating a culture of benevolence and magnanimity. The teachings of Chandraprabha served as a source of inspiration for acts of humanitarianism and social welfare, encapsulating the essence of universal brotherhood.

Pushpadanta, the ninth Tirthankara, made significant contributions to the Indian knowledge system by placing great importance on spiritual discipline and self-transformation. The individual provided a comprehensive explanation of the concept of inner purification (anuvrata) as a method to surmount ignorance and achieve spiritual liberation. Pushpadanta's teachings emphasised the profound impact of moral behaviour and self-reflection beyond the cycle of birth and death.

Shitalanatha, the tenth Tirthankara, made significant contributions to the field of Indian philosophy through his elucidation of the essence of suffering and the means to attain freedom. He stressed the significance of equanimity (samata) in effectively dealing with the difficulties and hardships of life. Shitalanatha's teachings provide comfort to individuals struggling with existential distress, providing valuable understanding of the transient quality of worldly occurrences.

Shreyanasanatha, the eleventh Tirthankara, made significant contributions to the Indian knowledge system by imparting lessons on the acquisition of virtues and the elimination of vices. The speaker expounded upon the significance of ethical behaviour, known as Dharma, in promoting the welfare of both individuals and communities. Shreyanasanatha's focus on ethical uprightness and self-control motivated individuals to pursue greatness in their thinking, speech, and actions.

According to Vasupujya, the twelfth Tirthankara, his teachings on the nature of awareness and the pursuit of self-realisation have made noteworthy contributions to Indian philosophy. He elaborated on the concept of mindfulness (sati) as a method to surpass the constraints of the ego and gain an understanding of the interdependence of all existence. The teachings of Vasupujya served as a source of inspiration for individuals in their quest for self-exploration and spiritual enlightenment.

Vimalanatha, the thirteenth Tirthankara, enhanced the Indian knowledge system by highlighting the significance of mental and emotional purity. He elaborated on the concept of inner cleansing via detachment (vairagya) and introspection (anupreksha), directing individuals towards spiritual clarity and equanimity. Vimalanatha's teachings emphasised the profound impact of moral behaviour and self-consciousness in achieving freedom from worldly entanglements.

Anantnatha, the fourteenth Tirthankara, enhanced the Indian knowledge system by imparting teachings on the interdependence of all living beings and the idea of universal empathy. The individual underscored the intrinsic value and respect for all conscious entities, establishing an environment characterised by compassion and veneration for existence. The teachings of Anantnatha served as a source of inspiration for acts of kindness and altruism, fostering a profound sense of connectivity and solidarity among all sentient beings.

Dharmanatha, the fifteenth Tirthankara, made noteworthy contributions to the field of Indian philosophy by providing guidance on the journey towards spiritual freedom. The author elaborated on the concept of proper behaviour (samyak charitra) as a method for cleansing the mind and fostering virtuous attributes. Dharmanatha's teachings offered pragmatic counsel for the cultivation of ethical conduct and spiritual development, enabling individuals to surmount ignorance and achieve enlightenment.

Shantinatha, the sixteenth Tirthankara, enhanced the Indian knowledge system by highlighting the need for inner tranquillity and calmness in effectively dealing with life's difficulties. He explained the concept of mental quietude (shanti) as a method to surpass suffering and achieve spiritual freedom. Shantinatha's teachings provided comfort to individuals struggling with intense emotions and restlessness, directing them towards a state of internal balance and tranquillity.

Kunthunatha, the seventeenth Tirthankara, made significant contributions to the Indian knowledge system by imparting teachings on the transient nature of earthly existence and the pursuit of higher wisdom. The individual provided a detailed explanation of the concept of detachment (vairagya) as a method to free the mind from the constraints of desire and attachment. Kunthunatha's teachings motivated individuals to detach themselves from transient gratifications and embark on the journey of attaining spiritual enlightenment.

Aranatha, the eighteenth Tirthankara, brought about substantial advancements in Indian philosophy by prioritising the development of virtues and the elimination of vices. The speaker expounded upon the significance of ethical behaviour, known as Dharma, in promoting the welfare of both individuals and communities. The teachings of Aranatha served as a source of inspiration for individuals who aspired to achieve excellence in their thoughts, words, and actions, so facilitating their spiritual growth and ethical uprightness.

Mallinatha, the nineteenth Tirthankara, enhanced the Indian knowledge system by highlighting the significance of self-awareness and introspection in the quest for spiritual development. He provided a detailed explanation of the concept of self-reflection (svadhyaya) as a method for fostering wisdom and self-actualisation. The teachings of Mallinatha urged individuals to explore the depths of their own awareness, revealing the inherent divinity that exists within.

Munisuvrata, the twentieth Tirthankara, made significant contributions to the Indian knowledge system by imparting lessons on the journey towards liberation and the elimination of ignorance. The individual elaborated on the concept of discernment (Viveka) as a method to surpass the constraints of the ego and attain the realisation of the ultimate truth. Munisuvrata's teachings motivated individuals to develop cognitive lucidity and spiritual perception, leading them towards enlightenment.

Naminatha, the twenty-first Tirthankara, made substantial contributions to Indian philosophy by clarifying the concept of karma and its consequences for spiritual development. The individual elaborated on the complexities of karmic bondage and the significance of intention (bhava) in influencing subsequent experiences. The teachings of Naminatha enhanced comprehension of karma theory, offering valuable insights into the principles of causality that control the cosmic order.

In the Indian knowledge system, Neminatha, the twenty-second Tirthankara, made significant contributions by placing great emphasis on the significance of non-attachment and renunciation in the quest for spiritual emancipation. He provided a detailed explanation of the concept of detachment (vairagya) as a method to surpass worldly cravings and achieve inner tranquillity. Neminatha's teachings served as a source of inspiration for individuals seeking to free themselves from attachment to material possessions and egoic identifications, so directing them towards the journey of self-realisation.

Parshvanatha, the twenty-third Tirthankara, made significant contributions to the Indian knowledge system by imparting the principles of non-violence and ethical behaviour. The individual provided a comprehensive analysis of the concept of ahimsa as a fundamental virtue that fosters both spiritual development and social cohesion. The teachings of Parshvanatha had a profound impact on promoting acts of compassion and charity, cultivating a culture characterised by non-violence and mutual respect among all living beings.

Mahavira, the twenty-fourth and most recent Tirthankara, made significant contributions to the Indian knowledge system by providing a thorough exposition of Jain philosophy and ethics. He explained the principles of non-violence (ahimsa), honesty (satya), non-stealing (asteya), chastity (brahmacharya), and non-possessiveness (aparigraha) as the five-fold route to spiritual emancipation. Mahavira's teachings serve as a source of inspiration for millions of followers globally, encapsulating the enduring wisdom and empathy of the Jain tradition.

Conclusion:

Jain Tirthankaras have made significant and diverse contributions to the Indian knowledge system, including several aspects such as ethics, philosophy, spirituality, and psychology. The teachings and exemplary lives of the Tirthankaras have served as a source of illumination for successive generations, motivating individuals to foster wisdom, compassion, and inner tranquillity. The enduring wisdom of these individuals continues to reverberate within the collective consciousness of humanity, providing guidance towards a more profound comprehension of both the individual and the cosmos.

References

Books:

Jain, J. P. (1998). Religion and Culture of the Jains. New Delhi: Bharatiya Jnanpith.

Shastri, K. (1995). Jainism and Indian Civilisation. Delhi: Motilal Banarsidass Publishers.

Articles:

Balbir, N. (2006). "Jain Contributions to Philosophy and logic." Philosophy East and West, 56(3), 391-405.

Jain, S. (2010). "Tirthankaras and the Development of Jain Thought." Journal of Indian Philosophy, 38(2), 105-125.

Wiley, K. (2009). "Jain Education and Its Role in the Preservation of Knowledge." Education and Culture, 25(2), 65-82.

Conference Papers:

Shah, N. (2014). "Jain Tirthankaras and Their Influence on Indian Ethical Systems." Paper presented at the International Conference on Jain Studies, Mumbai, India.

Web Resources:

Jain, V. (2021). "The Role of Tirthankaras in Shaping Jain Literature." Jainpedia. Retrieved from https://www.jainpedia.org/themes/people/tirthankaras.html

"Jain Tirthankaras and Their Contributions to Indian Knowledge System." Jain World. Retrieved from http://www.jainworld.com/education/jain-tirthankaras-contributions/

Chapter 10

Vasudhaiv Kutumbkam: Imaging Bharat on the International Front

U. P. Vibhute,
Assistant Professor, Department of Economics,
Peoples College, Nanded, M.S.

P.E. Vibhute,
Former Principal, Shri Havagiswami Mahavidyalaya, Udgir, M.S.

Growth is quantitative, whereas development is qualitative. Growth requires physical investment, whereas development requires human investment. Development begins with people and not with goods and or physical assets. Though economic growth is only one aspect of it, the farmer has invariably been equated with the latter as development. Various scholars have questioned the utility of this limited concept of development and argued that economic growth alone cannot promote the social, political, emotional, intellectual, and spiritual dimensions of development.

Bharat is a nation quite right in making constant endeavours to raise the standard of living. But the standard of life is more important than the standard of living. In Homoeopathy, Dr. Samuel Hanemann said in 1833 AD that life = Body + Mind + Vital Principles.

But according to my opinion, at least in Maharashtra's state, only Life = Body + Mind + Vitthal Principles. Because Maharashtra's vital is Vitthal, according to the father of homoeopathy, Dr. Hanemann, man's body is important, but mind is crucially very important. Therefore, for mind and body, we have to use Vitthal principles where

V = vegetarian in all respects, such as consumption, production, exchange, distribution, and international trade. This is the primary condition of Vitthal principles. The secondary condition is man should be intelligent. The third condition is TH: first, H is humility; second, H is humanity; and third, H is hard work; the fourth condition is TH, again means T = 3, and first, H is Harmony in body and mind. Second H = Honesty in mind. Third H Human Unity. A = All together and L = Love.

Someone has said, when ethics fails economics fails when economics fails everything including love fails because Maharashtra land is "Naad Bramha" therefore in Maharashtra's Varkari Sampraday is very important because of Vitthal Bhakt.

Vitthal is a God who is purely vegetarian and Varkari Sampraday is also purely vegetarian. In Bharata's holy land Vasudhaiv Kutumbkam is vital therefore Vasudhaiv Kutumbkam belongs to Vitthal principles in holy land like Rama, Krishna's, sages, and saints etc. Therefore according Vitthal principles must belongs to Vasudhaiv Kutumbkam. Therefore Vasudhaiv Kutumbkam is very crucial to become Bharat as a nation and also in international front.

भारत मे हिंदी मे ऐसा कहा है कि

आदमी साधनों से नही साधना से श्रेष्ठ बनता है |

आदमी भवनो से नही भावना से श्रेष्ठ बनता है |

आदमी उदाहरणसे नही आदमी उदार आचरण से श्रेष्ठ बनता है |

Therefore, according to our opinion, life has many facets, like life = line of intelligence to find excellence on one side and the other and, most importantly, the sideline of intelligence to find errors. One side of life belongs to excellence and excellence accrues when the soul awakens as a human being. The excellence side has been proved by Swami Vivekananda and others, and the most important side of errors has been proved by Mahatma Gautama Buddha and Mahatma Gandhi. This is possible only in Vasudhaiv Kutumbkam.

Confucius has said education breeds confidence, confidence breeds hope, and hope breeds peace. This is possible in individuals' lives, but there is a society in which Vasudhaiv Kutumbkam argues that it depends on Saptapadi of development and Saptapadi of development depends on the education system; therefore, the education system should be developed. It involves Saptapadi of development that can be argued as follows: education breeds character, character breeds confidence, confidence breeds capacity, and capacity breeds capital; all these 4 sides when maintaining equality should breed the square of credit then and only then credit breeds expectation of excellence among the society to create the best. Then and only then, expectation breeds peace; peace means zero defects and zero defects means quality. In terms of society, it depends on self-transformation. Scholars have said that when there is righteousness in the heart, There is beauty in the character. When there is beauty in the character, there is harmony in the home. When there is harmony in the home, there is order in the nation. There is order in the nation, and there is peace in the world. Therefore, the word heart is basically significant, and there are 5 qualities that have to be created that are humility, excellence, accountability, respect and trustworthiness an individual heart. But the character has been four-fold approaches

1. Non-violence
2. Truth
3. Not to theft
4. Brahmcharya

The first approach, non-violence, depends on consumption patterns. All 3 sides depend on non-violence; therefore, non-violence is a crucial approach to building character for non-violence, and the consumption pattern should be vegetarian. Therefore, non-violence is a crucial approach to building character. For non-violence, the consumption pattern should be vegetarian; therefore, all the families should come together and make the consumption pattern vegetarian. Vegetarian patterns should lead to agriculture-oriented and animal-oriented if the green revolution in the agriculture sector is the white revolution in milk production. Grey revolution and blue revolution may be expected in space and software technology, respectively. Then, it should create eradicate poverty, reduce unemployment, and it will lead to a clean environment. This is possible in Vasudhaiv Kutumbkam; therefore, Vasudhaiv Kutumbkam may lead to

1. Think Bharat
2. Team Bharat, and
3. Total innovation of Bharat is possible only when Vasudhaiv Kutumbkam holds well in the world.

Man is a social being. Amongst all human life is the most evolved creation in the universe. Excellence or superiority of human life as compared to other living beings can be easily identified. In the case of other creatures, their life is manipulated by man in his own interest. Man is the only unique creation in the universe; that is, under certain parameters, he is free to make his own destiny.

For every man, understanding becomes fruitful only when it is sustained by sympathetic feeling in joy and sorrow without ethical culture there is no solution for humanity.

Einstein says a man's ethical behaviour should be based effectively on sympathy, education and social ties and needs. Equilibrium is also known as development, but development depends on matter and spirit. Modern society, especially in the third world, including India, is worried about what is called value deterioration or value crisis, from which they are suffering. For value formation, views of great men with clear thinking are required. Science, culture, polity, economy, religion and philosophy, art, literature, in fact, or knowledge and skills have their certain base basic needs that man feels. In modern society, we will see more advanced industrialisation, a scientific and technological base, and vast vistas that have been opened up for the fulfilment of human desires for wealth and power. Indian culture and modernity are both complementary. We have to form an honourable social system that can produce a balanced personality and provide an honourable, fairly comfortable, and satisfying life to all, with freedom guided by discipline and more or less harmony in individual and social life. Structural transformation may lead to new society where freedom goes with discipline, justice goes with merit, right goes with duty, moral and spiritual values go with material welfare, and the whole or the collectively respect the part of the unit. Culture is a kind of hold all term to which nothing human is alien. What kind of houses people build and what kind of scientific research they engage in or what kind of technological advances, they are making are indicators of their culture. Spirit is preserved and embalmed in Bhartiya culture.

According to our opinion, Mahatma Basaveshwar and present econometrics are the following 4 properties for human beings for the purpose of development.

1. Propensity of the person.
2. Trials towards the propensity of the person.
3. Successful trials towards the best within the society.
4. Purusharth, i.e., Dasohav, economics, development, knowledge.

This is possible only when in Vasudhaiv Kutumbkam. It holds well within society; then, we will accrue the above 4 properties of human beings, and life will become fruitful; otherwise, it will not. According to Mahatma Basaveshwar, these are the 4 properties of a human being, but according to our opinion, a human being must hold the 8th dynamics of metaphysics of L. Ron Hubbard's. It will lead to automatically.

1. Think Bharat
2. Team Bharat
3. Total innovation of Bharat.

Think Bharat. This kind of thought will lead to the eradication of poverty. Team Bharat, this kind of thoughts will lead to reduced unemployment and total innovation in Bharat. This kind of thinking will lead to a clean environment. Means that zero poverty. Zero unemployment and zero carbon emissions are these 3 zero concepts of the world which Mohammad Yunus, Nobel laureate, has been holding good within the world, but in our opinion, Vasudhaiv Kutumbkam's approach will be accepted by the world for human being development. Then, it is possible to 3 zero concepts. I have, therefore, Vasudhaiv Kutumbkam as an image of Bharat and on the international front, too.

The following are the 12 parameters for human excellence.

1. Self-control 2. Compassion 3. Self-Reliance 4. Concentration 5. Knowledge 6. Devotion 7. Honesty 8. Discipline 9. Will power 10. Dedication 11. Confident 12. Strength.

All these 12 parameters of human excellence can be converted into 3 dimensions

1. Bliss
2. Peace
3. Freedom.

The following characters are necessary and are better suited to build a peaceful society that can be created within the society as such

1. We become natural creators
2. We become more compassionate and understand pain and suffering
3. We create more sacrifices

4. We become listener

5. We possess more tolerance.

6. We must be born teachers

7. We deserve freedom and equality to build our lives and carriers

8. We can build a peaceful neighbourhood and then we can contribute to world peace.

References

Dr. P.E. Vibhute, Unpublished Thesis, "District Development Plan, a Case Study of Nanded District." SRTMU Nanded, 2000.

Opcit pp137

Ghodke N.B. (Ed) The welfare economist, a monthly economic journal vol III Dec 1981. NO. 3 pp1

Mathur P.N., The Problems of values, edited in, Ruhela S.P., Human Values and Education, Sterling Publisher Pvt. Ltd., New Delhi, 1986 P 1.

Ibid pp 14.

Dr. Das A.K., A Treatise Organon of Medicine Part I Souvik Homeo Publications Calcatta 1995. P 53.

L. Ron Hubbbard, Scientology a new slant of life, Bridge Publication Inc. 5006 E Olmpic Boleyard Commerce California.

Muhammad Yunus, A world of Three Zero, Hachette Book Publishing Pvt. Ltd. and Hachette UK Company, 2017.

Dr. S.G. Dolegodar Patil, Dr. D.T. Angadi, (Ed) Sonorous Vibrations of Spiritualism and Mysticism in Indian Writing in English, Kalyan Literary Publishers. Kalburgi.

Chapter 11

Vishwa Guru Basaveshwara: A Universal Star

'Poorna Chandra' Annapurna C. Badihaveli,
Former Principal, Government College Chitguppa, Karnataka.

N.S. Hungund,
Associate Professor & Head, Dept. of Mathematics,
Shri Havagiswami College, Udgir, Maharashtra.

Sri Basaveshwara, the great Saint, Poet, and Philosopher of Karnataka, occupies a very prominent place among the mystics and religious reformers of Bharatam, the land of the descendants of Bharat. There was a time when the phrase 'Citizen of the world' lists the highest watermark of culture. Apparently, he is a person whose heart is as large as the universe and whose mind is as vast as a glance of the whole creation.

It is a matter of pride for Karnataka that it has produced the Universal Star in the twelfth century. His vision was unclouded and he sought to realise the life of individual as well as the collectivity i.e., the Supreme Universality of Vision. If Allam Prabhu was the God Man of his time, Lord Basaveshwara was the Universal Man - Vishwa Manava.

Lord Basaveshwara is one of the great saints who heralded social change in medieval India. Lord Basaveshwara lived his life divinely, fearing none and hating none. He came as a deliverer, preaching oneness and equality among the people in general. He thought of human society as a 'Democracy of Souls' with inherent respect and affection for all.

He was a great Saint and social reformer. We should try not merely to express our appreciation towards his valuable preaching, but we should put them into practice in our daily lives. Lord Basava was not an academic philosopher. He neither planned his views nor did he build a philosophical system. He preached the reality of existence, God, and human beings of the mortal world. This robust outlook enlivens Basava to be wakeful of material life. He eradicated untouchability by his advocacy of welcoming all devotees into Veerashavism, irrespective of their caste, creed, and birth. He insisted on devotion and intellect and advocated for equality for each and everyone in the eyes of the Maker.

Lord Basava was one of the greatest religious and social revolutionaries of all time who revolted against the tyranny of the varnashram system. He was an embodiment of all great human values and virtues. His far-sightedness, preaching, and inspiring leadership have had a tremendous impact on the lives of the people of south India for centuries. They mainly emphasised the importance of 'Kayak,' which means work, proclaiming "work is heaven." Himself being a firm believer in practising his own precepts, He tried to transform ordinary men and women into godly human beings through his Vachanas.

His Vachanas are couched in simple and elegant language; he explained his profound ideas in the common speech encouraged with power of simplicity and beauty of language. He rendered his lofty thoughts in the form of Vachanas in a language which is easily understood by the humble lay man. His religious and spiritual discipline, virtues, intense love, and inner peace are fully reflected in his Vachanas.

The 'Vachanas' is the oldest literary genre in Kannada literature. The term "Vachana" earlier covered a very wide range of writings, which included the preaching and experiences of Basava and other pioneers, like Madar Channayya, Dohar Kakkayya, Jedar Dasimayya and many others. Innumerable saints, both men and women, contributed to the Vachanas Sahitya in Kannada. These writers succeeded in eliminating the artificial distance between the language of old Kannada and the spoken language of the common people. Thus, they restored the language of the common man to its rightful place in the literary process. Their words were regarded as "Vachan Veda," and their way of living came to be known as the "Vachan Dharma" It must be acknowledged that Basava's works owed inspiration to his followers at large.

The 'Vachanas' literally mean spontaneous utterances that embody Basava's experiences and those of his followers. The perfect freedom of talk and thought was exhibited in the Vachanas. They are different from the scriptures. They are an expression and a means of connecting the human and the divine words. They are the verbal expressions of infinite experiences. They finely appeal to everyone and everywhere for their great mind of common sense and wisdom. They express, explore, explain, and comment on recurrent experiences of people in simple language.

The foundation of 'Anubhava Mantap' is an outstanding work by Lord Basava. It was a place where Vachanas were recited, and philosophical discourses were undertaken. However, it was Basavanna who made the substance of his personal experiences through his Vachanas available to the common man. Many Veerashaiva Saints created a whole literature, 'Vachana Sahitya,' the main quality of which was honesty and a deep exploration of experiences. Vachana is not simply a composition; there is a profound intensity of expression.

Basavanna's language is a vast subject itself. He harmonises the Sanskrit with Kannada so perfectly that they do not jar. Most Vachanas turn out to be independent artistic entities. They give us a sense of an epic poem. Thus, Basavanna's individuality finds profound fulfillment in his Vachanas. Undoubtedly, the Vachanas of Lord Basava and his followers stand unique in the history of Kannada literature.

Lord Basava lays down a code of conduct for his followers in the following Vachana, these commandments engrave in every one's heart.

Thou shall not steal nor kill

Let no falsehood foul thy tongue.

Nor anger burn thy brow

Bear with one another,

And suffer all men,

Stand not high in thy own esteem,

So shall thy ways.

Both of heart and demeanour

Proclaim thy purity.

And shall favour find.

Of Lord Kudal Sangama Deva.

He mainly emphasised the value of adherence to truth, good actions, faith in God i.e one's own self, respect for women, purity in both internal and external. His outlook and perception towards life seem to be simple; but practising the same is very difficult. Undoubtedly, he strictly practised what he preached.

He worked unceasingly for the emancipation of womanhood and for the socio-economic and religious equality of women folk. It is Basava who revolutionised primitive thought and brought about a synthesis of approaches to the matters of religious and spiritual freedom for each and every soul on this earth. He envisaged the message of universal love and brotherhood.

Basava was the main force behind the establishment of 'Anubhav Mantap, ' the forum of religious discussions and experiences. It was an ideal Parliament. He nurtured it mainly with the assistance of Allam Prabhu and Chennabasava. A profound study of the functioning of 'Anubhav Mantap' is bound to give more definitive ideas of Basava's attitudes towards womanhood. The Mantap had a good number of women as its members, viz, Akka Mahadevi, Satyavve, Aydakki Lakkamma, Sankavve, Lingamma and many more. The discourses with Allama and many other Sharanas, especially with Akka Mahadevi, are the most illustrious and noteworthy chapters. Women were regarded as in no way inferior to men, even in spiritual matters. Consequently, the contributions of women in religious experiences were not only heartily welcomed but also highly appreciated and encouraged. He called Akka Mahadevi 'Akka' though she was younger than him. He profoundly appreciated and respected her spiritual experiences.

The contemporary age is especially an Age of Secularism. The pursuit of spiritual path, leading towards of the realisation of the Supreme Being, is totally ignored. Lord Basava's preaching of twelfth century hold relevance in the present situation. He will always be remembered for his strenuous work for the upliftment of humanity at large.

It is a pity that all his preaching and philosophy are found in the Kannada language. It is almost necessary that this writing should be made known throughout the world.

It is no exaggeration to say that the message of Basaveshwara is like a reservoir into which all previous thoughts flowed out. Kind like Buddha, Simple like Mahaveera, Gentle like Jesus, Bold like Mohammad, Basava Strikes us almost as a Wonder of Creation. It is an account of his lofty ideas and great revolutionary change that he brought about restoring human dignity that Basava shines as a star in the minds of human beings even today and will continue to dazzle as a Universal Star.

References

Basavaraj K.R. *Basaveshwar, his life, Vision, and Works.* Dharwar.

Mudgal H.G. *Basavas Gift - One Society to India.* Basav Journal. Vol.28. Basav Samiti, Bangalore.

Virupakshappa. B. *Basav Path.* Vol. 12. Basav Samiti, Banglore.

Basavanal, S.S. & Iyangar, Srinivas K.R. *Musings of Basava*

Yaravintelimath, C. R. *Vachanas of Women Saints.* Basav Samiti, Bangalore.

Shahapur, Agni. *Basav Marga.* Vol. 2.

Chapter 12

Sikh Gurus and Their Contribution to Indian Knowledge System

Pratik P. Surana,
Chief Mentor and Founder,
Quantum Infotrainers & Consultants Pvt. Ltd. Pune, Maharashtra.

The lively and egalitarian religion of Sikhism, which was established in the 15th century by Guru Nanak Dev Ji, has had a profound impact on India's intellectual, cultural, and spiritual landscape. The teachings of the 10 Sikh Gurus, who personified the values of equality, service, and devotion to the divine, are fundamental to Sikhism. Philosophy, ethics, and spirituality have all been greatly enhanced by the deep contributions that each Guru has made to the Indian knowledge system through their enlightened insight and exemplary lives. Let us explore the unique contributions made by each Sikh Guru and their long-lasting influence on Indian philosophy.

1. **Guru Nanak Dev Ji:** The founder of Sikhism, Guru Nanak, transformed Indian spirituality by promoting the equality and oneness of all people (Ik Onkar). His emphasis was on the significance of compassion, selfless service (seva), and devotion to the almighty (Nam Simran). Sikh philosophy is based on the teachings of Guru Nanak, who emphasised the pursuit of morality and truth in all facets of life.

2. **Guru Angad Dev Ji:** By emphasising education and linguistic reform, Guru Angad Dev, the second Sikh Guru, made important contributions to the Indian knowledge system. In order to advance spiritual instruction and literacy, he founded pathshalas, or schools,

and standardised the Gurmukhi script. The propagation of Sikh teachings was aided by Guru Angad Dev's efforts in language and educational reform, which also enhanced India's rich cultural legacy.

3. **Guru Amar Das Ji:** By emphasising social equality and community welfare, Guru Amar Das, the third Sikh Guru, contributed to Indian spirituality. He ended traditions that were discriminatory, such as the caste system, and instituted the langar system of community kitchens, which serve free meals to anybody, regardless of social standing. A more equitable and inclusive society was made possible by the teachings of Guru Amar Das on compassion and equality.

4. **Guru Ram Das Ji:** By emphasising devotion (Bhakti) and spiritual discipline, Guru Ram Das, the fourth Sikh Guru, enhanced the Indian knowledge system. He founded the city of Amritsar and constructed the Golden Temple, or Harmandir Sahib, which is a revered site of devotion for Sikhs all over the world. Seekers were motivated to develop a close relationship with the divine and conduct lives of service and virtue by Guru Ram Das's teachings on humility and devotion.

5. **Guru Arjan Dev Ji:** The Guru Granth Sahib, the core text of Sikhism, was compiled by the fifth Sikh Guru, who made significant contributions to Indian spirituality. In addition, he placed the foundation stone for the Harmandir Sahib, highlighting the significance of group devotion and spiritual harmony. The literary and philosophical legacy of India was enhanced by the compilation of holy songs from Sikh and other spiritual traditions by Guru Arjan Dev.

6. **Guru Hargobind Ji:** By emphasising spiritual sovereignty and martial bravery, Guru Hargobind, the sixth Sikh Guru, added to the

Indian knowledge system. He formed the Khalsa martial tradition and taught Sikh soldiers how to fight injustice and oppression. The bravery and resiliency of Guru Hargobind motivated Sikhs to defend morality and the dignity of all living things.

7. **Guru Har Rai Ji:** By emphasising kindness and environmental care, Guru Har Rai, the seventh Sikh Guru, enhanced the Indian knowledge base. He created gardens and animal sanctuaries and was well known for his love of the outdoors and his attempts to conserve wildlife. The greater Indian concept of ecological harmony was reflected in Guru Har Rai's teachings on environmental sustainability and respect for all living forms.

8. **Guru Har Krishan Ji:** The eighth Sikh Guru, Guru Har Krishan, embodied compassion, and healing, and made a profound impact on Indian spirituality. Guru Har Krishan, in spite of his brief life, showed great compassion for the ill and suffering during Delhi's smallpox outbreak. His altruistic efforts and heavenly favour brought comfort to a great number of people, demonstrating the restorative influence of love and empathy.

9. **Guru Tegh Bahadur Ji:** By standing out for human rights and religious freedom, the ninth Sikh Guru contributed to the Indian knowledge system. In order to defend Hindus' freedom to follow their religion and stave off religious persecution at the hands of Mughal emperor Aurangzeb, he gave his life. The martyrdom of Guru Tegh Bahadur served as a reminder of the value of religious tolerance and the inherent right to conscience freedom.

10. **Guru Gobind Singh Ji:** By founding the Khalsa Panth and the Amrit, or Khalsa baptism process, Guru Gobind Singh, the tenth Sikh Guru, made significant contributions to Indian spirituality. He converted the Sikhs into a martial community committed to preserving equality, justice, and virtue. Sikhs are still motivated

to live brave and moral lives by the courage, selflessness, and spiritual sovereignty imparted by Guru Gobind Singh.

The foundational text of Sikhism, the Guru Granth Sahib, offers deep insights into many facets of life, spirituality, and Indian knowledge. Although its main focus is spirituality, it also discusses social, intellectual, and ethical issues that are relevant to the larger body of Indian knowledge. The Guru Granth Sahib makes the following allusions, which illustrate his viewpoint on the Indian knowledge system:

1. **Regarding the essence of existence and creation:** "ਏਕੋਅੰਕਾ ਰੁਸਤਿਗੁਰੁਪੂਰਾਜੋਨਦਰੀਕਰੇਸੁਹਓਾਇ॥." (Ang 611 in the Guru Granth Sahib) Meaning: "The One Reality is the True Guru, the Perfect Guru; whatever pleases Him comes to pass."

This stanza emphasises the central idea of Sikh philosophy, known as Ik Onkar, which is the conviction that there is only one Universal Creator. It embodies the Indian view that all things are interrelated and that the diversity of creation is rooted in divine unity.

1. **Righteous Living and Ethical Behaviour:** "ਸੋਕਿਉਮੰਦਾਆਖੀਐਜਿਤੁਜੰਮਹਿਰਾਜਾਨ॥" (Guru Granth Sahib, Ang 474) What does it mean to name someone bad? Kings are born of her."

2. This passage, which reflects the Indian values of respect for all living forms and the conviction that every person has the capacity for spiritual development and enlightenment, underlines the significance of appreciating the inherent worth and dignity of every human.

3. **On Seeking Wisdom and Knowledge:** "ਪੜਿਐਨਾਹੀਭੇਦੁਬੁਝਿਐਪਾਵਣਾ॥" Translation: "Reading and studying without understanding, the difference between right and wrong, is worthless" (Guru Granth Sahib, Ang 356).

This stanza emphasises how crucial it is to comprehend information's underlying meaning and significance in addition to merely absorbing it. It reflects the Indian emphasis on wisdom acquired by self-examination and discernment as opposed to information collection alone.

1. **Regarding Enlightenment and Spiritual Liberation:** "ਸੇਵਾਬੁਧਿਹੈਜੁਗਤਿਹੈਗੁਰਮੁਖਿਗਿਆਨੁਆਂਇ॥ ਇਥ. (Sahib of Guru Granth, Ang 1239) Meaning: "Serving God is wisdom; through the Guru's instructions, the Gurmukh obtains spiritual wisdom."

2. This passage highlights how achieving spiritual enlightenment can be transformed with commitment and service. It reflects the Indian idea that discovering one's true essence and breaking free from the cycle of birth and death can be accomplished via spiritual activities and direction from enlightened individuals or Gurus. These quotes from the Guru Granth Sahib shed light on Sikh beliefs regarding the nature of reality, moral behaviour, the quest for knowledge, and spiritual liberation, among other facets of the Indian knowledge system. They exhibit the syncretic character of Sikh philosophy, which emphasises the universal values of love, compassion, and devotion to the almighty while drawing inspiration from other Indian spiritual traditions.

3. **Regarding Unity and Universal Truth:** "ਆਪੇਜਾਨੈਆਪੇਦੇਇ॥ਨਾਨਕਹੁ ਕਮੀਆਵਣਜਾਇ॥." (Ang 1) Guru Granth Sahib Translation: "He is the one who gives and knows." We come and go by His command, O Nanak. The idea of divine sovereignty and the connection of all existence to the will of God are emphasised in this verse. It represents the conviction that the cosmos is governed by a cosmic order, or hukam, and the Indian notion of the fundamental unity of all creation.

4. **On Humanity and Compassion:** "ਸੇਵਾਕਰਤਹੋਇਨਹਿਕਾਮੀ॥ਤਸਿਕਉਹੋਤ ਪਰਾਪਤਸੁਆਮੀ॥." (Ang 286 in the Guru Granth Sahib) Translation:

"Desire is released via service. A servant like that receives the Lord as his recompense." This passage highlights the spiritual benefits and transformational power of selfless service, or seva. It embodies the compassion and charity of Indian culture, stressing the need to help others receive heavenly grace and spiritual fulfilment.

5. **Regarding the Delusion of Ego and Attachment:** "ਜਿਨ੍ਹਿਹਰਿਸੇ ਤੀਸਬਦੁਨਚੀਨ੍ਹਿਆਬਿਖਮੁਭਰਮੁਭੁਲਾਾ॥"

   Translation (Guru Granth Sahib, Ang 168): "Those who have not acknowledged the Shabad, the Word of the Lord, are misled by uncertainty and the dreadful global sea." This passage highlights the significance of realising the divine presence within oneself and cautions against the dangers of ignorance and spiritual blindness. It expresses the Indian view that in order to achieve spiritual realisation, one must rise above attachment and earthly delusions, as well as the ego's role in maintaining illusion (Maya).

6. **Regarding the Unification of Humanity and Divine Love:** "ਸਭਉਅ੍ਰਬਿੰਦਹੈਸਭੁਗੋਬਿੰਦਹੈਗੋਬਿੰਦਬਿਨੁਨਹਤੀਨਹੀਤਧ੦ਢਤਤ." (Ang 488 in the Guru Granth Sahib) Translation: "Everyone is the universe's ruler; everyone is the universe's ruler."

   There is none at all without the Lord." This passage emphasises how all beings are inherently divine and how divine love is global. It highlights the divine's presence within each person and the unity of all humanity under the protection of divine grace, reflecting the Indian concept of divine immanence.

7. Within the context of the Indian knowledge system, these quotes from the Guru Granth Sahib offer significant insights into Sikh beliefs on spirituality, ethics, and the interconnection of all existence. They are reflections of the ageless knowledge and universal truths that uplift truth-seekers and aspirants to a higher level of consciousness everywhere.

In conclusion, the Sikh Gurus made significant and varied contributions to spirituality, ethics, social justice, and cultural heritage within the Indian knowledge system. The Sikh Gurus have made a lasting impact on Indian society by modelling compassion, equality, and devotion to the holy through their enlightened wisdom and impeccable lives. Humanity's hearts and minds are still touched by their timeless teachings, which point the way toward a future that is more inclusive, equitable, and spiritually vibrant.

References

Books:

Singh, K. (2006). *A History of the Sikhs: Volume 1: 1469-1839*. 2nd ed. New Delhi: Oxford University Press.

McLeod, W. H. (1996). *The Sikh World: An Encyclopaedia Survey of Sikh Religion and Culture*. New York: Macmillan Publishing.

Singh, H. (1994). *The Encyclopaedia of Sikhism*. Patiala: Punjabi University.

Articles:

Grewal, J. S. (2009). "The Contribution of Guru Nanak to Indian Society." *Journal of Punjab Studies*, 16(2), 45-60.

Singh, P. (2013). "Sikh Gurus and the Evolution of Sikh Thought." *Studies in Humanities and Social Sciences*, 20(1), 27-38.

Mandair, A. S. (2010). "Sikhism and Its Philosophical Contributions to Indian Thought." *Philosophy East and West*, 60(4), 528-553.

Edited Volumes:

Singh, P., & Fenech, L. E. (eds.) (2014). *The Oxford Handbook of Sikh Studies*. Oxford: Oxford University Press.

Shackle, C., Singh, G., & Mandair, A. S. (eds.) (2001). *Sikh Religion, Culture and Ethnicity*. Richmond: Curzon Press.

Dissertation:

Kaur, G. (2007). *The Impact of Sikh Gurus on Indian Ethical and Social Systems*. Ph.D. dissertation, University of Toronto.

Conference Paper:

Dhillon, B. S. (2015). "Educational Contributions of Sikh Gurus." Paper presented at the International Conference on Sikh Studies, Vancouver, Canada.

Web Resources:

Singh, R. (2022). "The Role of Sikh Gurus in the Indian Knowledge Tradition." SikhNet. Retrieved from https://www.sikhnet.com/sikh-Gurus-role-indian-knowledge-tradition

"Contributions of Sikh Gurus to Indian Philosophy and Literature." Sikh Dharma International. Retrieved from https://www.sikhdharma.org/contributions-of-sikh-Gurus-to-indian-philosophy

Chapter 13

Understanding the Role of Yoga in Indian Education and Personal Well-Being

Divya Ramprasad Maheshwari,
Associate Professor & Head, Department of English,
Tolani Commerce College, Adipur, Kachchh, Gujarat.

"Yoga is the journey of the self, through the self, to the self."

–The Bhagavad Gita

"Close your eyes for a moment and imagine yourself standing at the threshold of a journey - one that promises not just knowledge but a profound transformation of mind, body, and spirit. As you step into the chapter pages of exploration, prepare to be transported into the heart of Indian education, where the ancient wisdom of yoga intertwines seamlessly with the modern pursuit of personal well-being, where tradition meets innovation and the quest for knowledge is instilled with the essence of inner harmony."

Introduction

The heart of Indian education represents a unique blend of ancient wisdom and modern aspirations. Here, the practice of yoga, rooted in centuries-old traditions, is flawlessly integrated with contemporary approaches to personal well-being. This fusion fosters an environment where tradition meets innovation, allowing the pursuit of knowledge to be infused with the essence of inner harmony. At its core, it embodies a holistic approach to education, nurturing not only intellectual growth but also emotional and spiritual development.

In the tapestry of Indian culture, the intertwining relationship among yoga, education, and personal well-being forms a cornerstone deeply rooted in spiritual, philosophical, and practical realms.

Yoga, Education, and Personal Well-being in India: A Holistic Perspective

Originating from ancient Indian traditions, yoga embodies a multi-faceted approach encompassing physical postures, breath control, meditation, and ethical principles. Within the educational landscape, yoga emerges as a holistic tool, nurturing not only physical health but also mental intelligibility, emotional balance, and ethical development among students.

Yoga's integration into education unveils a myriad of benefits, ranging from enhancing cognitive abilities and concentration to managing stress and fostering resilience. Beyond academic success, it cultivates values like compassion and self-discipline, shaping responsible and ethical individuals within society. Moreover, yoga transcends the physical realm, offering a spiritual and philosophical journey towards self-realisation and inner harmony.

In the Indian context, yoga is not merely a practice but a way of life, enriching educational curricula with profound insights into self-awareness, interconnectedness, and purpose. This holistic approach to education aligns with the ancient ethos of nurturing body, mind, and spirit in harmony with the universe, paving the way for holistic development and well-being. Thus, the integration of yoga into education stands as a vital endeavour, embodying the essence of Indian wisdom and its timeless quest for holistic living.

Yoga: Embracing Wisdom for Inner Harmony

The present chapter captures the essence of yoga's profound traditional roots and its timeless quest for inner harmony and enlightenment. Dating back millennia, the yoga is depicted as a path to self-realisation and union with the divine, offering liberation from the cycle of birth and death and finds its origins in ancient Indian scriptures like the Vedas and Upanishads, where its philosophical underpinnings emphasise its spiritual significance.

The yoga Sutras of Patanjali, composed around 400 CE, serve as a comprehensive guide, outlining yoga as a holistic system for attaining inner harmony and enlightenment. Patanjali's yoga Sutras provide a systematic framework for understanding and practising yoga, guiding individuals through ethical principles, physical postures, breath control, concentration, meditation, and, ultimately, enlightenment. This philosophical treatise serves as a beacon of wisdom for those seeking to delve deeper into yoga's transformative potential. The chapter also explores how yoga has dynamically evolved to cater to the changing demands of contemporary society while retaining its traditional essence.

Evolution of Yoga: Meeting Modern Society's Needs

The chapter talks about how yoga has changed over time to fit modern life while still keeping its original principles. It shows how yoga has adapted to meet the needs of today's world while staying true to its traditional roots.

1. **Diverse Practices**: Yoga has expanded beyond its traditional forms, adopting various styles and approaches to suit the preferences and lifestyles of modern practitioners. Whether it's vigorous flow or gentle restorative yoga, there's a practice tailored to meet the diverse needs of individuals today.

2. **Integration with Modern Science**: The convergence between traditional yoga practices and modern scientific principles has led to the development of therapeutic yoga programmes. These programmes are designed to address specific health conditions backed by scientific research, such as stress, anxiety, chronic pain, and PTSD (Post-Traumatic Stress Disorder).

3. **Accessible Platforms**: Technology has made yoga more accessible than ever before, with online platforms offering virtual classes and tutorials. This accessibility has democratised yoga, enabling individuals worldwide to practice from their convenient zones.

4. **Yoga in Education**: Recognising its holistic benefits, some educational institutions have integrated yoga into their curriculum to support students' physical and mental well-being. These yoga programmes emphasise mindfulness, stress reduction, and character development, creating a conducive learning environment.

5. **Corporate Wellness Programmes**: In response to the needs of modern workplaces, yoga has become a part of corporate wellness initiatives. Employers understand the importance of promoting employee health and productivity, offering yoga classes and mindfulness sessions as part of workplace wellness programmes.

Thus, yoga's evolution showcases its adaptability to meet the evolving needs of society while remaining rooted in its timeless principles of self-awareness, inner harmony, and holistic well-being.

Yoga in Education: Cultivating Holistic Development

The transformative role of yoga aims at fostering comprehensive growth among students. This integration extends beyond physical exercises to encompass mental, emotional, and spiritual well-being, utilising yoga as a powerful tool to cultivate mindfulness, concentration, and resilience.

In Schools:

Many schools in India have integrated yoga into their daily routines, incorporating yoga sessions into the curriculum. These sessions typically include physical postures, breathing exercises, and relaxation techniques, enabling students to improve physical health while learning stress management, focus enhancement, and self-discipline.

Yoga as a Subject:

Some educational institutions offer yoga as a formal subject, allowing students to study the philosophy, history, and principles of yoga alongside practical sessions. This comprehensive approach enables students to deepen their understanding of yoga's holistic benefits and cultural significance.

University Programmes:

Universities in India have recognised the importance of incorporating yoga into higher education, offering courses and programmes in yoga studies, teacher training, and research. These programmes promote not only physical fitness but also critical thinking, self-reflection, and personal growth.

Mindfulness and Emotional Well-being:

Yoga practices in educational settings emphasise mindfulness and emotional regulation through techniques like meditation and relaxation. By equipping students with these life skills, schools and universities aim to cultivate well-rounded individuals who are academically proficient and emotionally resilient.

Thus, the integration of yoga into education in India reflects a holistic approach to student development, acknowledging the interconnectedness of physical, mental, and emotional well-being. By embracing yoga practices, educational institutions strive to nurture individuals who are not only intellectually capable but also emotionally balanced and resilient, prepared to navigate life's challenges with grace and resilience.

Expanding Horizons: Yoga's Impact on Personal Well-being

The chapter explores the profound implications of yoga beyond the realm of education, reaching into various aspects of personal life.

Physical Health:

Regular yoga practice offers a multitude of physical health benefits, such as increased flexibility, strength, and balance. It also aids in alleviating chronic pain, improving cardiovascular health, and boosting the immune system. Through breath control techniques, yoga enhances respiratory function and induces relaxation, contributing to overall physical well-being.

Mental Health:

Yoga is renowned for its positive effects on mental health, providing tools to manage stress, anxiety, and depression. Mindfulness practices like meditation and deep breathing foster present-moment awareness and reduce rumination, promoting emotional resilience and psychological well-being. Moreover, yoga encourages self-reflection, facilitating a deeper understanding of one's thoughts and emotions.

Emotional Balance:

Yoga fosters emotional intelligence and inner peace, regulating the nervous system and balancing neurotransmitters to promote emotional stability and mood regulation. This emotional equilibrium translates into improved relationships, enhanced social interactions and a greater sense of fulfilment.

Spiritual Progress:

For many practitioners, yoga serves as a spiritual journey, facilitating inner transformation and spiritual awakening through practices like meditation and self-inquiry. It encourages the exploration of existential questions and the pursuit of meaning, leading to profound spiritual growth and self-realisation.

Lifestyle Changes:

Engaging in yoga often inspires individuals to adopt healthier lifestyle choices, including mindful eating, regular exercise, and self-care practices. The holistic nature of yoga promotes harmony between mind, body, and spirit, leading to sustained improvements in overall well-being and quality of life.

Here, one can understand that yoga offers a comprehensive framework for personal well-being that transcends physical fitness and extends into mental, emotional, and spiritual dimensions. By integrating yoga practices into daily life, individuals can experience profound transformations that enhance their health, happiness, and sense of fulfilment.

Yoga Across India: Promoting Health, Vision, and Growth

The chapter also delves into the pervasive influence of yoga within Indian society, serving as a catalyst for promoting physical health, mental clarity, and spiritual growth.

Individual Practitioners:

Yoga has permeated the daily routines of individuals across India, with many incorporating it into their lives to maintain physical fitness, enhance mental focus, and cultivate inner peace. Whether practising at home, in local parks, or at yoga studios, individuals harness yoga's transformative power to elevate their overall well-being.

Community Centres and Ashrams:

Community centres and ashrams serve as focal points for yoga practice and spiritual exploration in both urban and rural areas. Offering classes, workshops, and retreats led by experienced instructors and spiritual leaders, these centres foster a sense of unity and shared purpose among participants, providing immersive experiences for deepening one's yoga practice and spiritual journey.

Yoga Festivals and Events:

India hosts numerous yoga festivals and events that celebrate the rich heritage of yoga and facilitate opportunities for practitioners to deepen their practice, connect with others, and learn from renowned teachers and Gurus. These gatherings promote community engagement, cultural exchange, and the dissemination of yoga's teachings to a broader audience.

Government Initiatives:

Recognising yoga's significance for public health and well-being, the Indian government has implemented various initiatives to promote yoga nationwide. Observing International Day of Yoga on June 21st, government - sponsored programmes provide training and certification for yoga instructors, ensuring quality instruction and accessibility to yoga for all.

Integration into Healthcare:

Yoga has been integrated into mainstream healthcare systems in India as a complementary therapy for various health conditions. Hospitals and clinics offer yoga therapy programmes for patients, reflecting the growing recognition of yoga's therapeutic benefits and its potential to enhance conventional medical treatments.

Yoga's widespread adoption in India underscores its profound impact on physical health, mental well-being, and spiritual growth. Across diverse settings and communities, yoga serves as a unifying force, promoting holistic living and inner transformation among individuals and society as a whole.

Journey to Inner Peace: Embracing Yoga for Self-Discovery

The transformative path individuals undertake when embracing yoga leads to profound self-discovery and inner fulfilment.

Self-Exploration:

Through yoga practices like meditation, breathwork, and self-reflection, individuals embark on a journey of self-exploration, uncovering unconscious patterns, beliefs, and emotions. This process allows them to gain insight into their true nature beyond societal conditioning.

Connection to the Self:

Yoga fosters a deep connection to the inner self, heightening awareness of thoughts, feelings, and sensations. Through mindfulness and asana practices, individuals learn to listen to their intuition, fostering authenticity and alignment with their true essence.

Release of Limiting Beliefs:

As individuals progress in their yoga journey, they confront and release limiting beliefs and negative thought patterns. Practices like pranayama and meditation cultivate mental clarity and emotional resilience, enabling individuals to let go of fear and self-judgement.

Expansion of Consciousness:

Yoga facilitates expanded states of consciousness, transcending the individual self and experiencing interconnectedness with all existence. Through meditation and devotion, individuals tap into a deeper sense of unity, recognising the divinity within themselves and all beings.

Integration and Wholeness:

As individuals integrate insights gained from yoga, they embody a greater sense of wholeness. Mind, body, and spirit align, and inner conflicts dissolve, leading to inner peace and fulfilment beyond external circumstances.

In short, by embracing yoga, individuals embark on a sacred journey of self-discovery and self-realisation, uncovering their infinite potential and experiencing the joy of living in harmony with their true essence.

Yoga: Transformative Force in Indian Education and Well-being

Yoga's blend of tradition and innovation serves as a transformative force in Indian education and well-being, promoting holistic development, interconnectedness, and positive societal change. Through yoga, individuals and communities awaken to their highest potential and contribute to a more compassionate and harmonious world. It serves as a catalyst for holistic development and interconnectedness.

Integration into Education:

Yoga is integrated into Indian education as more than just physical exercise but as a comprehensive system for personal growth. Schools and universities offer classes blending traditional teachings with modern approaches, fostering inner harmony, emotional resilience, and ethical values alongside academic knowledge.

Holistic Development:

Yoga nurtures physical, mental, emotional, and spiritual dimensions through practices like asanas, pranayama, and meditation, promoting well-rounded development beyond academic achievements to encompass personal growth and fulfilment.

Interconnectedness of Knowledge and Inner Harmony:

Yoga emphasises the interconnectedness of knowledge and inner harmony, fostering a deeper understanding of self, relationships, and the world. This integrated approach cultivates compassion and reverence for all life, leading to a more compassionate and sustainable society.

Profound Impact on Individuals and Communities:

Yoga empowers individuals and communities to lead healthier, happier lives, fostering self-awareness, resilience, and social bonds. Collective yoga practice strengthens solidarity and promotes inclusivity, contributing to a more harmonious society.

Contribution to Society:

Yoga's transformative power extends to society, promoting holistic well-being and ethical values. As more people embrace yoga, they become agents of positive change, inspiring integrity, kindness, and mindfulness in others.

Conclusion

This way, yoga stands as a beacon of transformative power within Indian education and personal well-being, blending tradition with innovation to create a holistic approach to growth and fulfilment. Its integration into educational institutions underscores its ability to nurture not only academic knowledge but also inner harmony and resilience.

From schools to universities, yoga fosters holistic development and contributes to the well-being of individuals and communities alike. As individuals embark on the path of self-discovery through yoga, they unlock the gates to inner peace and fulfilment. By embracing yoga, they cultivate not only physical health and mental clarity but also tap into their spiritual potential, fostering a deeper sense of connection and purpose in life.

Yoga's timeless wisdom guides us towards a more compassionate, harmonious existence, inspiring us to embrace its transformative power for growth, healing, and self-discovery. As we continue to explore its role in Indian education and personal well-being, let us embark on this journey with openness and dedication, enriching our lives and the lives of those around us!!!

References

Deshpande, S., & Nagendra, H. R. (2015). Yoga: The Indian Heritage. Journal of Ayurveda and Integrative 2. Medicine, 6(3), 180–182. [Reference for historical significance of yoga]

Singh, S., Singh, K. P., Singh, A. P., & Singh, D. (2018). Yoga and Mental Health: Current Perspectives. Indian Journal of Psychiatry, 60(Suppl 3), S388–S392. [Reference for global popularity of yoga]

https://zoedolan.medium.com/a-iconoclast-9a6bb9cb7313

https://www.goodreads.com/quotes/316337

https://www.facebook.com/SureshKumaRainaOfficial/videos/-yoga-is-the-journey-of-the-self-through-the-self-to-the-self-the-bhagavad gita-/5279934868711117/

https://beyogi.com/live-yoga/self-discovery-yoga/

https://ijrpr.com/uploads/V5ISSUE1/IJRPR22194.pdf

Chapter 14

Indian Hermeneutics: Texts and Method of Interpretation

Ambika Datta Sharma,
Senior Professor & Head, Department of Philosophy,
Dr. Harisingh Gour Vishwavidyalaya Sagar, M.P.

Mohit Tandon,
Assistant Professor, Department of Philosophy,
Savitribai Phule Pune University, Pune, Maharashtra.

Indian textual tradition has originally been the tradition of scriptures known as *Āgama* and *Nigamaśāstra*. They have been treated by different philosophical schools, either as *pauruṣeya* (man-made) or *apauruṣeya* (divine). Whatever has been the debate about their being so, it is an incontrovertible belief that such scriptures were first preached by Brahmāand intuited by risis and munis and then such intuited wisdom aphoristic in nature transmitted to eligible pupils in the form of verbal instructions/discourse. This is how scriptural wisdom evolved and flourished in oral tradition. In Indian textual tradition (*Vāṅgmaya*), 'Brahmā' is popularly known as 'First God' (*Ādideva*) and is considered a primal teacher or *Śāsta*of all scriptures, knowledge, or sciences. *Śāsta*etymologically means the ruler. This is why primal texts of all knowledge or sciences are called śāstra or śāsana. The *śāstra*s preached by Brahmā are also called *tantra* because of their being extremely extensive or comprehensive. Subsequently, ṛisis and munis condensed *śāstra*spreachedby Brahmāinto aphoristic language (*sūtra*s) and made them useful as per their times. This is the reason that *śāstra*s were taken as 'said by' or rather 'revealed by' ṛiṣis (*prokta*). This feature of 'said' (*prokta*) is '*Yattenaproktamna* *ca tenakṛtam.*' That is, a special speech, discourse, or recitation of what has been 'preached' or 'created' by someone since scriptures revealed or preached by Brahmā known as *śāstra*, *śāsana* and *tantr a* (*Divyam Varṣasahastramprovācnacāntamjagām*) were 'said' or 'spoken' by ṛiṣi-munis they are called *Anuśāstra*, *Anuśāsana* and *Anutantra*.

I

Hence, in the light of the above-mentioned belief/supposition of Indian mythology, it can be maintained that presenting *śāstra*s (scriptures/texts) as the body of knowledge actualised in literal or text form (*Vāṅgmaya-vigraha*) is a later development. It's a different matter that its history has also been very miraculous. It is worth knowing that initial acts of writing texts, i.e., literalizing *anuśāstra*, *anuśāsana* and *anutantra* by ṛisis and munis were not considered as praiseworthy acts. This is why Niruktakāra Yāska considered those ṛiṣis belonging to the inferior category who had not 'realised' the truth (*Dharma*) in themselves but only grasped it as preached or 'said' knowledge.[2] Again, Yāska, commenting on such lower category ṛiṣis, says that only those who had not realised the truth (*Dharma*) in themselves used to inscribe (write) texts with the help of *mantras* and preached knowledge, i.e. *śāstras*.[3] Surprisingly, in Indian tradition, Buddha also has said something similar to Yāska's statement regarding the act of text-writing. Buddha says, "Those (brahmins) who used to live ini.e... ests building huts and meditate therein, started living civic life near village or city writing texts due to not being able to realise meditation. Earlier, such an act was considered inferior, but today, the same is considered a superior act."[4]

So, on the basis of the above-mentioned references, it can be maintained that the act of writing a text was not counted as a great act until a certain period in Indian *śāstra* tradition. In fact, such abuse of acts of writing texts was more an advocacy of 'oral tradition,' of the unwritten form of *śāstra*- tradition and its underlined intellectual sub-traditions. It seems as if presenting *śāstras* in codified and literalised (written) form was seen as actually to sully them. And adherents of non-authorship or divinity (apauruṣeyatva) of *śāstras* really believed to be so. In Pāṇinīya teachings, reading of written text has been said to be a mean reading (*ṣadetepāthakādhamā*). In Mahābhārata, inscribers and polluters of *Vedas* have been heavily criticised.[5] In such a situation, advocacy of heard and oral (*śruta* and *vācika*) tradition seems quite natural. In fact, the greatest characteristic of *śāstratraditions' being* an oral flow is that in this form only, these intellectual traditions remain connected with life experiences and thereby possess such a form of life which not only incorporates faithful adherence to ideals, rules, and customs but also their application in everyday life. Such a life form not only has the element of faith (*śraddhā*) but also corresponding conduct (*niṣthā*). So, this *naiṣthika* form of life is a matter of living the *śāstra*. Even today, one can find families in India which consider the lifelong practice/living of *śāstra* and its knowledge system as their prime duty (*sva-Dharma*). But its biggest demerit is that intellectual traditions in this form become conservative due to its sectarian faithfulness and secrecy and thus fall victim to narcissism in the absence of healthy inter-faith dialogue. Such effects, to a great extent, can be seen in the propagation, dissemination, and development of Indian *āgama-nigamaśāstra* tradition and its magnified (*upavṛaṅhit*) different intellectual sub-traditions.

On the other hand, we also notice that efforts of transforming prevalent oral *sastra*-traditions into textual/literal tradition have been given utmost importance in Indian tradition. Even in *Brāhmaṇa* tradition, the Sūtrakāra, who is given the status of 'First revealer' of *śāstras* (*ādya-vāgvigrah-kartā*), has been glorified as God (*bhagavān*).[6] In this regard, some others have been named as 'Oh Brahman.'[7] Similarly, in *Śramaṇa* (*Bauddha*) traditions, the significance of efforts done for the compilation (*sāngāyana*) of *Buddha-vacant through* organising ceremonial assemblies is well known since before compilation it all was part of heard and oral (*śruta* and *vācika*) tradition itself. The real intent of giving such importance to the one who first textualises orally-continued *śāstra*-tradition, i.e., sūtrakāra, is that he is the person who is full of the knowledge of preached or revealed *śāstras* and capable of grasping them at an intuitive level. In fact, the significance of *sūtras* is only that it is the seeded textualisation (*bījbhūta-vāgvigraha*) of a *śāstra*-tradition. In Yāska's terminology, only a highly capable/great ṛiṣi (or śrutarṣi) can form such textual *sūtras* in a higher cognitive state of '*bhāvanāprakarṣaparyanta.*' This is why there arises a dire need to unbind/untie the *sūtra* through interpretation. It is worth mentioning that a *sūtra* is a condensed and most synthesised form of words persisting at least for 3 moments (first moment of utterance, second of persistence and third of cessation, i.e., *trayadhvika*) and is analysed later. So, it can be maintained that it is *sūtra*, which is the first literalisation or textualisation (*ādya-vāgvigraha*) of any *anuśāstra* or *anutantra* in Indian tradition. By making '*sūtra*' foundational, the development of the textual tradition of *anuśāstra* took place in a later period through *Bhāṣya, Vārtika, Vṛitti* and *Tīka*.

Some believe also that the evolution of *Sūtra*-style was an enterprise of keeping *śāstras* and *vidyās* (scriptures and knowledge) alive in oral tradition. This is because it was comparatively easier to keep *vidyās* (knowledge/wisdom) free from memory loss and preserve them till infinity through their practice in *sūtra*-form. Once *sūtra* is learned, its impression (*saṃskāra*) remains lifelong. With regard to *Sāṃkhyaśāstra,* Yuktidīpikākāra, while revealing its sense, has rightly said that the right understanding of this Kapila-preached great (*Sāṃkhya*) *śāstra* (system) is not possible even in hundred years because it is too vast and comprehensive. Keeping this in mind, munis with sharp intelligence and pure wisdom (i.e., Sāṃkhyācāryas) have written the *śāstra* in summarised / short text form for the benefit of pupils.[8] Even if it is so, there is no harm in believing that *sutra* only is the First text (*ādya-vāgvigraha*) of any *anuśāstra* tradition in Indian heritage. Again, this possibility also cannot be denied that *sutras* of various knowledge systems were popular in oral tradition till a certain period of time, and later, they were systematised and inscribed. This is why most of the wisdom or knowledge of Indian tradition was intertwined with *sutra*-style. Within the permitted limit of known history, the first evolution of *sutra*-style seems to have taken place perhaps in *the Vyākaraṇa* tradition. *Sūtras* of *Pāṇinīya* tradition are considered to be the most ancient *Sūtras* of Indian *Sūtra*-tradition.[9]

II

Although the first textualisation of *anuśāstras* in Indian tradition has been done in *sūtra*-style, nevertheless, the number of numerous types of texts in the form of interpretative texts (*vyākhyātmakavāgvigraha*) found in Indian *śāstra*-literature (philosophical and religious both) and the way in which the *śāstra*-tradition has been flourished through such texts is exceptional and rare in any other tradition. In the 18th chapter of *Pārāśarpurāna*, the extension of *anuśāstras* from *sūtra* to *tīka* is beautifully explained, which is notable in this regard.[10] Hence, at first, it would be relevant to understand the intent of *sūtra*-styled textualisation. In *Viṣṇudharmottara Purāṇa*, defining *sūtra*, it has been said that essence-like (*sārvid*) and universally applicable knowledge-content (*viśwatonmukhajñān-rāśi*) containing least letters (*alpākshara*) and apodictic terms (*asandigdhapada*) is *sūtra* in which there is no possibility of repetition and break in order.

> *"Alpāksharamsandigdhamsārwadviśwatomukham,*
>
> *Astobhamanvadyam ca sūtramsūtravidoviduḥ."*

Although *sutra*-texts like *Gṛihyasūtra*, *śulvasutra,* etc., are found in Vedic literature also, definitionally, the discussion of *sūtra*-style and its types is firstly found in *Vyākaraṇa* tradition only. In the interpretation of *Mugdhābodha*, Durgādās has mentioned 6 types of *sutras* – *Sanjñā, Paribhāṣā, Vidhi, Niyam, Atideśa* and *adhikārasūtra*.

> *"Sanjñā, caParibhāṣā ca vidhirniyameva ca,*
> *Atideśoadhikāraścasadvidhamsūtralakṣnam."*

Here, it is notable that the use of such classification of *sutras* is mostly seen in *Vyākaranaśāstra*. In *sutras* of other *śāstras*, many types are not found. For example, in *Vyākaranaśāstrav riddhirādaicasanjñā-vidhāyakasūtras* are called *'sanjñā-sūtra.'* In the state of discordance *sutras* which bring order are called *'paribhāṣā-sūtra.'* (*Aniayameniyamkāriniparibhāṣā*). For example, *'tasminnitinirdiṣṭapūrvasya'* is *paribhāṣā-sūtra* due to which *yaṇa* of *ikāra* is intended in *suddhupāsya*-use, not of *ukāra*. Similarly, *sutras* proposing *'ikoyaṇacī'* are called *'vidhisūtra.' 'Kratadhitasamāsāśca'* is *'niyamasūtra.'* The use of *vidhi* and *niyama*, of both types of *sutra*, is seen in *Mīmāṁsā* tradition. According to *Mīmāṁsāśāstra*, vidhāyaka is *vidhi* and *pākṣikavidhāyaka* is *niyama*.[11] Similarly, if an utterance is contextually referred to/related elsewhere, it is called *atideśa*. So, *'sthānivadādeśoanalvidho'* is *atideśasūtra*. *'Adhikārasūtra'* is one on the basis of which only one type of activity goes on in a *prakaraṇa* (particular discourse based on a particular philosophical issue), e.g., the term *'samarthaḥ'* is *vidhisūtra*, and it is applied in the whole case of *samāsa*.

Again, in *the Āyurveda* tradition, the classification/division of *sutras* has been elaborated in another mode. Interpreting *Caraka Saṅhitā* Dalhana has mentioned 4 types of *sutra*. The first of these, *'Guru Sūtra,'* is a sermon/instruction given by the Guru/teacher. *Ekadeśīya*-thought is referred to by *'ekīyasūtra,'* and the thought added by pratisanskartā (redactor) of the text is called *'pratisanskṛatasūtra.'* In fact, the inclusion/addition of new thoughts in any growing (pravardhamān) *śāstra*-tradition happens through *pratisanskṛatasūtras* only. This is why it is said,[12]

"Vistāryatileśoktamsaṅkṣiptyativistaram,

Saṅskartākurutetantrampurāṇam ca punarnavam."

In the same way, we find tripartite classification/division of *sutras* in Nyāyadarśana. Since the elaboration of substances, in the Nyāya-thought-process, has been done through the method of *uddeśa, lakṣaṇa* and *parīkṣā,* the first *sūtra* of *Nyāyasūtra* is called *uddeśasūtra,* and the *sūtras* of the first and fifth chapter are *lakṣaṇasūtras.* *Parīkṣāsūtras* are intertwined (nibaddha) in the rest of the 3 chapters. Śrī Lakṣmīpuramśrīniwāsācārya, in his text called 'Mānameyarahasya Ślokavārtika,[13] has mentioned *sutras* of 3 types while referring to a text named *Śrutaprakāśikā.*

Sūtramtrividhamprāyaḥpūrvācāryeḥnirūpitam,

upadeśātmakamtvādyamvyākhyānamtadanantaram,

Upapādanaśāstramsyāttratīyamnyāyapūrvakam.

This means earlier ācāryas have told *sutras* of 3 types: *upadeśātmaka* (sermons/preaching), *vyākhyānātmaka* (explanative), and*upapādānātmaka* (elliptical, i.e., have another meaning besides what it expresses as primary meaning). In fact, such classification/ division of *sutras* seems to be the translation of *uddeśa, lakṣaṇa* and *parīkṣā* only, since the meaning of *upadeśātmaka* is *nāma-saṅkīrtana* and *vyākhyāna* means introduction of form, i.e., *lakshaṇa* and *upapādana* is obviously done through *parīkṣāṇa-vidhi* (testing) itself. In this way, it is noticed that the classifications/ divisions of *sutras* as introduced in *Vyākaraṇa* tradition, *Āyurveda* tradition and *Nyāya* tradition are actually divisions of sections (*vibhāgabheda*), not of form (*swarūpabheda*) and this sectional-division is helpful in synthetisation of meaning (*arthānvayana*) of concerned *śāstra.* The nomenclature of these, too, seems to be in accordance with the nature and procedure of concerned *śāstras.*

III

In this way, whatever manner in which the division of sections (*vibhāgabheda*) of *sūtras* as per thought process of different *śāstras* were done, it is clear that *sūtras* originally are synthesised word-content possessing the condensed form of knowledge. The synthesised form of *sūtras* cannot and should not be understood in the sense of mere linguistic abbreviations. Rather, the thought inherent in *sūtra* should be understood in the sense of conceptualising it into its fundamental concept. When a *śāstra*-tradition with its entire conceptual scheme is presented in *sūtra*-collections, it is really a highly condensed structure/form of the concerned thoughts. This is why they were later *stashed* to be interpreted to reveal their intended meaning. Patanjali has rightly said, '*Vyākhyāntoviśeṣapratipattirn ahisandehādlakṣaṇam*' which means a special intended meaning is known through interpretation. (or explanation). Doubt doesn't make subject matter impure or disproved. Therefore, in Indian philosophical tradition, generally, 6 rules have been proposed for the interpretation of *sūtras*. In *Parāśaropurāṇa* [14] these 6 rules and their order have been elaborated in this way-

Padacceda[15] *padārthoktivigrahovākyayojana,*

Ākṣepaścasamādhānamvyākhyānamṣadvidhamatam.

That is, if the interpretation of the text presented as sutra-collection / form of a *śāstra* is done applying these 6 methods viz *padacceda*, (breaking up terms) *pratipādya-abhikathana*, (ascertainment of subject matter) *vyutpatti-pradarśana*, (demonstration of term's origin, etymology) *vākya-yojna*, (sentential form) *ākṣepa* (*pūrva-pakṣa*) (objection, problem) and *samādhāna* (*uttarpakṣa*) (reply, solution), the intended / true meaning of the text is revealed in its proper/right form. The interpreter first breaks up terms of sentences of the case/issue to be interpreted. The same is called *padacceda* or *anvaya*. For instance, Vācaspti Miśra, in 'Nyāyasūci

Nibandha' while breaking up 528 *Nyāya-sūtras* has divided them into 1966 terms (*padas*). Then there are *prātipadikas* (root-words) and *vibhaktis* (partitions) in terms (*padas*). The identification of meaning expressed by both is *padārthokti* (assertion of meaning of terms). Again, there are distinct meanings of *samāsa-pada* (compound term), *taddhitapratyayānta-pada* (causal term) and *kṛadanta-pada* (so-generated term), and *nāma* (name) and *dhātu* (root) of their own. Their explanation is done on the basis of 'vigraha' (division /separation) or 'vyutpattī' (etymological origin). The interpreter is also supposed to form sentences according to her view. It is worth pointing out that where there is no subject term (*kartā*) and verb term (*kriyā*), the sentence formation is done by *adhyāhāra*, i.e., by supposing them (as a necessary element). The presence of doubt or *pūrvapakṣa* in the context or case-to-be-interpreted as *ākṣepa* (objection) and presentation of reply based on means/proof (*pramāṇa*) and logic (*tarka*) is *samādhāna* (solution).

The acceptance of these 6 rules of interpretation has been almost system-independent in Indian tradition. In *Viṣṇudharmottarpurāṇa*, another six-typed interpretation of *sūtras* has been repeated.

Ārambhoathāpisambandaḥsūtrārthastadaviśeṣaṇam,

Codakamparihārasyavyākhyāsūtrasyaṣadvidhā.

That is, in the interpretation of *sūtra*, the following things are expected: consistently related context (*avatarana*), subject's relation with the case/issue, ascertainment of subject matter (*prtipādya*), refinement of the intent of its adjective, highlighting/ producing the *pūrvapakṣa* and its resolution. The same thing has been said in different words, i.e., for interpretation *sūtrārtha* (meaning of *sūtra*), *padārtha* (meaning of term), *hetu* (reason/cause), *krama* (serial / order), *nirukti* (description/definition) and *sammyakaprastuti* (proper/ right presentation) are essential.

Sūtrārthaścapadārthaścahetuścakramaśastathā,
Niruktamayavinyāsovyākhyāyogasyaṣadvidhā.

In another widely-heard *śloka* too, while mentioning the six-fold mechanism of interpretation, it is said that what is required for interpretation is an introduction (*avataraṇa*), demonstration of the etymological origin of the term (*vyutpatti-pradarśana*), ascertainment of subject matter or theme (*pratipādya-kathana*), highlighting/ producing the doubt (*sandeha-utthāpana*), its resolution (*nirākaraṇa* of doubt) and then establishing the own thesis. (*siddhānta-upsthāpana*). Here, the sentential scheme has not been mentioned, but it can be seen as inherent in the mechanism.

Upodghātaḥ[16] *prathamtaḥpadārthaḥpadvigraḥ,*
Avimarśaḥpratyavasthāvyākhyatantrasyaṣadvidhā.

A five-fold method of interpretation similar to the above-mentioned six-fold method is also there, which is known as '*Pūrva-Mīmāṁsāvyākhyāpaddhati.*' According to it, while thinking over a particular subject, the force of thesis and anti-thesis is assessed, and accordingly, judgement is drawn. This is how this method is applied in *Mīmāṁsāśāstra*. The mere mention of the subject is not sufficient for the judgement. Rather than performing thorough cogitation or reflection, the conceptualisation of 'it is what it is' (*idmittham*) is done. Here, the five-fold procedure of reflection has been referred to. First, the subject of contention is introduced, and then a possible question/ problem about it is raised. The arguments of the former (opponent's) position (*pūrva-pakṣa*) are demonstrated, showing incriminating / obstructive evidence / proof the former position is denied or rejected and then means / proofs affirming the defended position (*Uttara-pakṣa* or *siddhānta*) are demonstrated. In this way, proving the absence of incriminating/obstructive evidence/proof in one's own position and showing consistent proof of one's own position, i.e., doctrine, is established.

Viṣayoviśayaścaivapūrvapakṣastathottaraḥ,
saṅgatiścetipañcāṅgamśāstreadhikaraṇamsmratam.

It is noticeable that this five-*sūtrīya* thought system is termed '*adhikaraṇa*' (locative case/reference/head) in Mīmāṃsaśāstra. The application of *adhikaraṇa*-based interpretive method is seen in Vedānta and Mīmāṃsaśāstra only. The author of '*Jaimininyāyamala*' has divided Mīmāṃsaśāstra into 2 thousand *adhikaraṇas*. Again, as auxiliary elements of these *adhikaraṇas*, 11 sub-divisions are given such as *pramāṇa, bheda, śeṣatva, prayukti, krama, adhikāra, atideśa, uha, bādha,* tantra and *prasanga-rūpa*. In fact, these sub-components can be understood in both forms, auxiliary elements, as well as determining factors of *adhikaraṇa*.

Dharmodvādaślakṣaṇyovyutpādyastatralakṣanaiḥ,
pramāṇabhedaśeṣatvaprayuktikramasaṅjñakaḥ.
adhikaroatideśaścasāmānyenaviśeṣataḥ,
uhobādhaścatantram ca prasangaścoditakramāt.[17]

For the determination of '*vidhi*' in the above-mentioned *adhikaraṇa*-based interpretive method and for showing consistency of the action-oriented (*kriyārthaka*) Vedas through hermeneutics of invocation and condemnation, and thus for determination of meanings, these six-fold *pramāṇas* have been explained in *Mīmāṃsaśāstra*. Although these 6 means (*pramāṇas*) are used for determining meaning extensively in *Mīmāṃsaśāstra* only in a summarised way, these are also accepted as a general principle of hermeneutics (meaning-determination). The six-fold factors of meaning-determination are, *śruti, liṅga, vākya, prakaraṇa, sthāna* and *samākhya*.[18] In this regard, in *Mīmāṃsaśāstra*, this method also allowed that *prāmāṇya* (authenticity**)** of *pūrva-purva* happens to be strong and in the same degree the *prāmāṇya* (authenticity) of *uttara-uttara* happens to be weaker in the context of meaning-determination. That means the prior source of wisdom/ knowledge, i.e., *sūtra*, is considered the most authentic one and later sources like *bhāṣya, vārtika, tīkā* etc are considered comparatively as having weaker authentication. In other words, prior is more authentic than posterior. In this method, *the nirpekṣa* (independent/ unconditional) word is called *śruti.* (*nirpakṣhokhaḥśruti*). *Liṅga* refers to a sentence which does not express meaning directly but rather expresses its meaning in another context. (*liṅganāmāny aparamsad anyārthadyotkamvākyam*). In the context of meaning-determination, *samabhivyavahāra* (proximity of words to ascertain the meaning) is called 'vākya,' and its function is the simultaneous utterance of descriptive (*vācaka*) terms of part and whole (*aṅga* and *aṅgī*). Similarly, where 2 sentences have an expectancy of each other for a fuller expression of meaning, it is called *prakaraṇa* (subject/topic) (*ubhayākāṅkṣaprakarṇam*). A particular *sannidhi* (proximity) is called 'sthāna' (place). It's another (*apara*) name (*saṅjñā*) is krama (order) too. In the case of meaning determination, the determination of *śruti- krama, pātha-krama* and *pravṛitti-krama* is actually *sthāna. Samākhya* means 'name' since sometimes names too are helpful in meaning-determination. For example, by the name 'Ram Kumar, ' it becomes clear that the name-holder must be a Hindu. However, such type of meaning-determination is not publicly done because it is possible that someone holds the name 'Shivadās' yet he might not be a follower of Shaivism. This is why *sthāna* and *samākhya* are placed in the last among the factors of meaning-determinations.

In the act of interpretation, not only compliance with appropriate six-fold or five-fold methods and six-fold auxiliary means of meaning-determination is necessary, but also some other kind of elocutionary alertness is required for making interpretation complete and indicative (*parikara*). Ācārya Abhinavagupta, in the very beginning of his *Abhinava Bhārti*, has instructed such kinds of scholarly alertness. According to him, firstly, where many types of readings are available, the original reading must be decided according to meaning, order and context. The rest of the readings must be referred to as *pātha-bheda* (difference of readings) without neglecting any of them. Similarly, if, while interpreting, the mutual difference among contexts is noticed, then it is the duty of the interpreter to resolve it. With this, intended meanings become complete. Along with this, rendering of intended meaning must be in accordance with *uddeśya* (objective/purpose). Initiating the act of interpretation by making the case or context consistent and resolving repetitions as per their being general and particular sense makes interpretation sound and errorless. At the end, the interpreter must also collect the main intents (gist) while concluding the subject matter. Abhinavgupta has performed all these duties in the interpretation of *Nātyaśāstra*.

Upādeyasyasampāthastadanasyapratīknam,

sfutavyākhyāvirodhānāmparihāraḥsupūrṇatā,

lakṣyānusarṇamśliṣṭamvaktavyosavivecanam,

saṅgatipaunaruktyānāmsamādhānamnākulam.

Sangrahaścaityayamvyākhyāprakāroatrasamāśritā.

IV

Now, it is also relevant to discuss those various types of *anuśāstrīya* interpretive texts composed in different *śāstra* traditions, more or less applying the above-mentioned constitutive elements of interpretation. Consideration of the nature of these texts throws some specific light on the Indian method of interpretation. Although any text can be seen as interpretive in one way or another, those texts, which are definitionally considered as purposely interpretive texts and have been composed in almost all *śāstra* traditions, disclose the stylistic characteristic of types of interpretation. The main types and classification of such texts are as follows:

Vṛitti: - *Vṛitti* is the text which presents the intended meaning of *sūtra* as it is in a very concise manner. Characterising it, it is said in the *prakaraṇa* (chapter/head) named 'Nirdeśa' of *Kāvya Mīmāṁsaśāstra* that – 'Sakalasūtrāṇāmvivaraṇamvṛittiḥ.' It means only those things are included in *vritti* which are inherent in *sūtra*. In a *vritti*, leaving extension and abbreviation aside, only that much is said as much is required for a clear grasp of the subject matter. The inclusion of unwanted, repeated and rationale-less subjects is absolutely prohibited in *vritti*. The name *vritti* itself informs the same, since very first only 'as it is and unmixed *vritti* is formed in the *citta* (consciousness). In *Viṣṇudharmottarapurāna*, throwing light on stylistic characteristics of *vritti* it, it is said that –

> *Sūtraṣveva hi tatsarvamyadvrattosamudāhṛtam,*
>
> *vistāroktammatimsantisamāsoktamnagṛhyate.*
>
> *Samāsavistarohatvavaktavyamyadvivakṣitam,*
>
> *apārthvyāhatamcaivapunaruktamtathaiva ca.*
>
> *Tathāvibhinnasaṅsthānamyuktihīnamviverjayet,*
>
> *Abhidhānamcānyatvamnaitānisyurkārṇāt.*

Again, *vritti* have been mentioned as having 6 attributes in *the Chāya* interpretation of *Mahābhāsya*. That is, *vritti* should be decorated at some place with **nipātana (use of exceptional words),** at some place with separation of unity of *sūtra* (*yogavibhāga*), at a difficult place with teaching of Guru, at some place with withdrawal of intent instructed in *Vārtika* etc, at some place with refinement of subject by the principle of change in *śāstra* and at some place with an independent disclosure of intended meaning.

> *Nipātnātyogavibhāgadarśnāt,*
>
> *gurupdeśānuvartikādapi.*
>
> *svātantryasiddhehpartantradarśnāt*
>
> *Prasādyellakṣaṇtoathṣadvidheḥ.*[19]

In fact, due to the above-mentioned attributes, *vritti*-based interpretation becomes pure or clear. The knowledge of the doctrine is easily received, and the spirit/nature of the concerned *śāstra* is also grasped. Hence, *vritti* in Indian interpretive methodology has a specific style. That is why *vrittis* on *sūtras* of most of the *śāstras* are certainly found. The tradition of writing *vrittis* on *sūtras* has been an age-old tradition, and writing *vrittis* on *kārikā* texts seems to be a tradition of a later period. *Vritti* on some *kārikā* texts have been written by authors of *kārikā* itself. For example, Dignāga has himself written a *vritti* on *Pramānsamuccaya*. Dharmakīrti has written *Svopagyavritti* on the *svārthānumāna* chapter of *Pramānvārtika*. When *vritti*-text again commented upon, it is termed as the text named '*paddhatī*' (*sūtravrit tivivecanampaddhatiḥ*).

Bhāṣya, Vārtika: - The second category of interpretive texts in Indian tradition is that of *Bhāṣyas*, *vārtikas* and commentary texts written on them. Indian *śāstra* tradition comparatively got enriched more through this type of text. The richest form of Indian *śāstra* tradition is seen in these texts. The continuity, dynamism, and development of knowledge full of repudiation and vindication which is seen in *bhāṣya-vārtika* texts of *Vyākaraṇa*, *Nyāya*, *Mīmāṁsa*, *Vedānta* and *Bauddha* tradition, such a committed-ness and readiness is unavailable anywhere else. This is the reason different *śāstra* traditions confronted each other, and consequently, mutual understanding evolved among them, and in this way, gradually, they happened to be critical in nature.

Introducing *bhāṣya*-text, śāstrakāras have unanimously admitted that where sentential meaning expressing the intent of *sūtras* is stated by *sūtra*-fitted sentences is called *bhāṣya*.

> *Sūtrārthovarṇyateyatravākyaisūtrānusāribhiḥ,*
> *svapadāni ca varṇyantebhāṣyambhāṣya vidoviduḥ.*[20]

The importance of bhāṣyakāra lies in his really being a śāstrakāra. Here, in this regard, the meaning of śāstrakāra is that the bhāṣyakāra systematises *sutras* into *addhyāya* (chapter), *āhnika* (appeal/ introduction), *prakaraṇa* (subject/topic), *adhikaraṇa* (reference/ locative case) etc according to the conceptual scheme of concerned *śāstra*. In this way, after preparing a coherent collection, he prepares a *sutra*-fitted sentential structure and reveals the intended meaning of *sutras* interpreting terms consisting in sentential structure. Hence, it can be maintained that all terms used in *bhāṣya* manifest (*vyākrata*) intended meaning of *sutras* being applied with meaningfulness and precision.

In the rich tradition of writing, *bhāṣya* on *sutras sutrakāra* and bhāṣyakāra are 2 different persons. However, the exception is also found in some places. Certain ācāryas having been written *sutra-* texts wrote *bhāṣyas* on them too. Kautilya (Viṣṇugupta)[21] has stated that many times, mutual discrepancy (*vipratipatti*) is seen among bhāṣyakāras of *śāstras*. Therefore, I, myself, have composed *sutras* of *Arthaśāstra* as well as written *bhāṣya* on it. Similarly, Jaina Ācārya Umāswāti has composed *Tattvārthādhigamasutra* and presented its *bhāṣya*-interpretation also. But Kautilya's above-mentioned statement forcefully echoes that there must be maximum consistency of thought between *sutra* and *bhāṣya*. There should not be any room for deviation between the 2. In fact, authentication of *bhāṣya* lies in it only. Notwithstanding, there manifests a kind of deviation in this criterion of *bhāṣya*-text in the Buddhist tradition. The *sutras* of Abhidharmakośa are of Vasubandhu, but his own *bhāṣya* on has been written with a different point of view. That is why Saṅghabhadra has written *punarbhāṣya* on Abhidharmakośa in opposition to Vasubandhu.

In this way, *bhāṣya*-texts of different *śāstras* have their own characteristics too. These characteristics can be taken as inherent or already expressed (*gatartha*) in the talent of bhāṣyakāra. However, bhāṣyakāra's minimal obligation is limited to the 'as it is' disclosure of intent of *sūtras*. It's being critical is not necessary. Although natural criticality inserted/involved (akṣipta) in interpretation remains more or less present in *sūtras* and *bhāṣyas*, too, the actual critical form of *sūtra-bhāṣya*-created-*śāstras* comes to the fore through *vārtika* texts itself. That is why vārtikakāra, interpreting all 3 aspects, *ukta* (said), *anukta* (not said) and *durukta* (difficult to say) in the *bhāṣya* formulates the intent of *śāstra* with high order criticality. –

> *uktānuktaduruktānāmcintāyatrapravartate,*
>
> *tam granthamvārtikamprāhuḥvārtikajñāmanīsiṇaḥ.*

Often, *vārtikas* or *vārtika*-localised texts are surely available in all *śāstra* traditions. Generally, it is interpretive text on *bhāṣya*, but in *Vyākaraṇa* tradition, *vārtika* texts have been written first and later *bhāṣyas*. Perhaps due to this exception, *bhāṣya*, written by Patanjali, has been given the status of *Mahābhāṣya*. In *Bauddha-nyāya* tradition, too, Prajñākaragupta has written *Alaṅkārabhāṣya* after Dharmakīrti's Pramāṇavārtika. It is unanimously admitted, considering the characteristics of *vārtika* texts, that there must be eight-fold features in the *vārtika* text. These are- a statement of purpose or objective, demonstration of problem or doubt, presentation of doctrine with resolving doubt, clarification of particular meaning through lecture/discourse, demonstration of quality, i.e., to justify one's claim or statement by means of proof and logic, maintenance of economy while not saying anything useless and avoiding redundant extension and giving only required statement without any repetition.

> *Prayojanamsansśayanirṇayo ca,*
>
> *vyākhyāviśeṣoguṇalāghavam ca.*
>
> *kṛatavyudāsoakratasśāsnam ca,*
>
> *savārtiko Dharma guṇoavaśca.*[22]

Saṅgraha and Prakaraṇa Texts: -

'*Saṅgraha*' texts (collection) have characteristics of their own in the tradition of interpretive texts. The oldest reference of such type of text is found in Vyādi-composed '*Vyākaraṇa Saṅgraha*' in *Mahābhāṣya*. In Vaiśeṣika tradition, the work of Praśastapāda is considered as *bhāṣya*-localised, but the author has called his work a *saṅgraha*, i.e., *Padārthadharmasaṅgraha*. Defining *saṅgraha*-text in *Pārāśaropurāna* and *Kāvyamīmāṁsa*, it has been maintained that the text in which things that were said in detail in *sūtra-bhāṣya* are presented in brief is called *saṅgraha* (*vistāreṇopadiṣṭanāmarthānāmsūtrabhāṣyayoḥ, sa ṅgrahoyaḥsamāsensaṅgrahaṅtaṅvidurbudhāḥ.*)[23] In Indian tradition, on the one hand, the word '*saṅgraha*' has been used in naming texts like *Tarkasaṅgraha* and *Arthasaṅgraha*, on the other hand, matured (developed) interpretive texts like *Nyāyabhūṣaṇa, Nyāyamanjarī, Vākyapadīya, Tatvasaṅgraha* and *Siddhāntaleśsaṅgraha* also are counted in the category of *saṅgraha*-texts. Hence, it is not clear that above-mentioned definition of *saṅgraha* text has been given focusing on which type of texts. In fact, the appropriateness of *saṅgraha*-texts comes to focus only when it was either written in that period of shastra tradition in which it was descended in an inscription from its oral form or it was written after the multi-dimensional development of *śāstra* tradition. For example, there are many schools of oral tradition in classical vocal music. There are different modes/ways/ qualities of singing the same particular raga. Similarly, there can be differences of opinion about (saṅgīt) *śāstras* in different Guru traditions. Therefore, if a *saṅgraha* text presents a summary of all of them, then its appropriateness is understandable. Again, if a text collects the differences of opinions and sectarian disagreements and even ekdeśīya (institutional) opinion and school differences which arise in the course of *sūtra*-based *bhāṣya, vārtika, tīka* and *anutīka*, even then it can meaningfully be called a *saṅgraha*. Such a *saṅgraha* text can be written in the later period of the development of a *śāstra* tradition. In such a *saṅgraha* text, the author's interpretive role lies in the analysis of the intent of differences in viewpoints and in the right presentation of doctrines. Texts like *Nyāyabhūṣaṇa, Nyāyamañjarī, Tatvasaṅgraha* and *Siddhāntaleśsaṅgraha* can be seen as belonging to this category.

In Indian tradition, another type of interpretive text is that of 'Prakaraṇa' texts. In *Pārāśaropurāna*, defining its characteristic, it is said that "The text in which a part of *śāstra* is clearly and extensively explained is called *Prakaraṇa* text. (*Śāstraikadeśasambaddhaṁśāstr akāryāntaresthitam, āhuḥprakaraṇamnāmgranthabhedamvipaścitaḥ.*)

[24] Śāliknātha's Prakaraṇapañcika, Gaṅgeśopāddhyāy's Tatvacintāmaṇi[25] can be called its standardised form. Similarly, many short or long *Prakaraṇa*-texts have been written in different traditions in which particular doctrine-centric different viewpoints have been collected, discussed, and criticised, and subsequently, their own thesis/position has been established.

The structure of *Prakaraṇa*-texts can also be understood from another point of view. That is, it can be seen in the multi-polar and system-centric dynamicity of the development of Indian *darśanas* that after a phase, some fundamental type of metaphysical and epistemological doctrines/theories establish their own autonomy beyond the sectarian or school-centric commitment of different *darśanas*. The identification of such variedly developed doctrines can be made in the form of those *prakaraṇas* which are concerned with all sects/schools of Indian *darśanas*, and it is expected from all those philosophical systems that they render/propose their own position/ thesis in the concerned subject/area/topic. In this way, when one initiates text-writing keeping a *prakaraṇa*-doctrine at the centre and collects alternative interpretations of that doctrine, reviews them, and establishes one's own position/thesis, then the author's effort takes the form of *prakaraṇa* text in a specific sense. Such *prakaraṇa*-texts have been actually written discussing *prakaraṇa*-wise (subject / topic-wise) problems like *Prāmāṇyavāda, Viṣayatāvāda, Khyātivāda, Apohavāda, Bhāvanāvāda, Vidhivāda, Kṣaṇikavāda, Vyāptivāda* etc. However, there are still many metaphysical or epistemological *prakaraṇas* (subjects/topics) in the Indian tradition of *darśanas* which either *prakaraṇa*-texts have not been written on, or such *prakaraṇas* have not been adequately identified. For example, *Pramāṇavyavasthāvāda, Pramāṇasamplavavāda, Indriya-prāpyakāritvavāda* etc. are very significant *prakaraṇas* in themselves, which no *prakaraṇa*-text is available on. **26** Hence, today, the creative space for writing *prakaraṇa*-texts in Indian philosophical tradition is still available. Such types of texts can be written in more than one way, e.g., within the limits of the school/sect/system, from an inter-sect / school/system point of view, and even include western philosophical determinables.[27]

In this way, we find that there are 2 fundamental types of interpretational texts making *sūtras* their basic reference point – *vritti* and *bhāṣya*. Both manifest the intent of *sūtra*-text in their own way. Again, 'paddhatī' on *vritti* and 'vārtika' on *bhāṣya* also intimately related to *sūtras*. Therefore, these can also be taken as texts related to *sūtra*-interpretation. The vārtikakāras of Nyāya tradition at first, in the text, actually address the *sūtrakāra, Akṣapāda* Gautama itself (*Ya dakṣapādopravaromunīnāmśamāyaśāstramjagatojagād*).[28] Moreover, all other types of *tīka* (commentary) texts which are known with multiple names are sub-interpretations.[29] In these sub-interpretations, too, the *sūtra*-oriented rootedness is not sacrificed. Rather, skills used in discourse (*vyākhyāngata Kauśal*) and all their determinations are sparks of universally applicable (*viśwatomukha*) *sūtra* itself.

V

Now here, it is also worth noting that the instructions that our earlier ācāryas have given about types, classifications, divisions (*Bhedas*) and methods of interpretation here and there are applied more or less in the act of interpretation. However, this does not mean that all these are mechanical methods of interpretation and anyone can interpret these methods. Hence, some qualifications are required for being an interpreter, too, and only then will he/she be the right user of methods of interpretation. Notably, it is essential for an interpreter to be the knower/expert of concerned *śastra* as well, as he must be '*padavākyapramāṇajña*' (authority on language and logic). There has been a custom of calling an expert/scholar padavākyapramāṇajña.' Here '*pada*' means *Vyākaraṇaśāstra*, '*vākya*' means *Mīmāṁsāśāstra* and '*pramāṇa*' means *Nyāyaśāstra*. The knower of all these 3 *śāstras* is called a '*padavākyapramāṇajña*.' Only such a person can be a lecturer/scholar of *śāstras* of both kinds, i.e., *svayūthya* (*śāstra* belonging to own tradition) and *paryūthya* (*śāstra* belonging to other tradition). The methods as constituents of interpretation which have been mentioned earlier, nobody can employ them without being '*padavākyapramāṇajña*[30] Although all 3 *śāstras* indicated by these 3 terms also effectuate the *puruṣārtha-catuṣṭaya* (accomplish 4 *puruṣārthas*), but their ultimate or superior (*anyatam*) nature is to think with polemic method (*vāda-vidhānapaddhatī*) and incessantly furthering the process of interpretation. From this point of view, calling these 3 *śāstras* as '*vādavārta*' and '*mānvārta*' *prakriyā-śāstra* seems more appropriate. This is why these 3 *śāstras*, even being independent of each other, are supportive of other *śāstras*. *Vyākaraṇa* and *Nyāyaśāstra* are often called lamp-like supporters of all *śāstras*.[31] *Mīmāṁsa* too, in a way, is a *parīkṣāśāstra* (text of examination) for determination of *Vedavākyas*. The *sūtra*, '*Tasyanimittapariṣṭiḥ*,' implies the same. *Mīmāṁsāśāstra*, in *Pāraskaragṛihyasūtra*, has been straightforwardly termed as '*tarka*' (*Vidhivirdheyastarkaścavedaḥ*). In this statement of Pāraskara, the term *vidhi* indicates the *brāhmaṇa*-section of Veda, *Vidhya* indicates *Mantra*-section, and *Tarka* indicates *Mīmāṁsāśāstra*. Vācaspati Miśra has also called *Mīmāṁsāśāstra* as *Yuktiśāstra* or *Tarkaśāstra* referring to *Pāraskaragṛihyasūtra* (*Mīm āṁsāsañjñakastarkaḥsarvovedasamudbhavaḥ*). Hence, it can be said that *vyākaraṇa* (*padaśāstra*) constitutes the body of literature of interpretation, and *Mīmāṁsāśāstra* (*vākyaśāstra*) and *Nyāya* (*pramāṇaśāstra*) perform analysis and justification/authentication of them. For interpreters, in Indian tradition, the knowledge of all these 3 *śāstras* is even more expected.

Moreover, among the qualifications of a skilled/expert interpreter, the knowledge of *tantra-yuktis* (systemic arguments) is also included in Indian tradition. There has been an age-old tradition of *śāstra-svoboda* (understating the *śāstra*), *śāstra-nirmāṇa* (creating the *śāstra*) and the application of *tantra-yuktis* (arguments) as qualitative elements (*guṇasūtra*) of its interpretation. Its references are found here and there in the texts of *Āyurveda*, Kautilya's Arthaśāstra and *Viṣṇudharmottarapurāṇa*. Even some scholars claim that *tantra-yuks* have been skillfully used in Pāṇini's Aṣṭādhyāyī. A work of Ācārya Nīlmegha named *Tantrayukti* has also been found in the 13th century. The glory of *tantra-yuktis* for *śāstra-nirmāṇa* and *śāstra-avabodha* have been praised very ceremonially in *Caraka Saṁhitā* and *Śuśruta Saṁhitā*.[32] Again, 2 purposes of *tantra-yuktis* have been mentioned- *vākyaprayojana* (sentence-making) and *arthaprayojana* (meaning-making).[33] Connecting the unconnected sentences is *vākyaprayojana* and making shrunken, unclear and inconsistency meaning consistent is *arthaprayojana*.

Here in the word *Tantrayukti*, the meaning of the term 'tantra' *refers* to the body of literature of purposefully and considerably well-connected sentences.[34] The method or means through which such body of literature is composed is called *yukti* (*yuktisabdaḥkhalūpāyavāchi, yujyojanetasminyuktiritirupambhavati*). In this sense, *tantra-yuktis* are useful in both ways, for creating a body of literature (discourse) and again for understanding it. In modern terminology, *tantra* means to the body of 'text' and *yukti* means 'texture.' Hence, the way in which the knowledge of texture can be utilised for creating the text as well as understanding the text, in the same way, the utilisation of *tantra-yuktis* is possible for creating an interpretable system and for understanding the structure/formation of the interpreted system. Now, since the interpreter creates/constitutes a body of literature through his / her act of interpretation, therefore it is essential for him/ her to be aware / expert of *tantra-yuktis*. There might be disagreement about the actual number of *tantra-yuktis* available as means of *tantra* (system/body), but the popular figure of *tantra-yuktis* is 32 in the Indian tradition of interpretation. The name and their features are as follows:[35]

Yamarthamdhikratyochyatetadadhikaranam;   Yen vākyārthoyujyatesayogah; Sūtrapadeyoarthoadhikratahsapadārthah; Yadnyatyuktimadarthasyasādhanamsahetvarthah; Samāsvacanamudd eśahvistāravacanamnirdeśahevamevaityupdeśah; Anenakārnenetyap deśahprakratasyānāgatenasādhanampradeśahati-krāntenanātideśah; Abhiprāyānukaranamapavargah;   Yenārthahpari-samāpyatepadenāh āryenasavākyaśeṣah; Yadkīrtitamartha-māpādyatesārthāpatih; Pra kārenāmihitoarthahkenacidupodghātenapunarūcyamānahprasaṅg ah; Sarvatrayastathāsaekāntah; Kvacittathākvacidanyathāsoanekā ntah; Pratiṣedhavacanampūrva-pakṣah; Tasyottaravacanamnirnayah; Prakaranānupūrvyavidhānam;   Tasyapratilomyaviparyayah; Ityuktāmitiatikrāntavīkṣanam;   Pratravakṣyāmiityanāgatavīkṣana m; Ubhayatohetudarśansanśayah; Tatrātiśayavarnāvyākhyānam; Paramatāpratisandhonumatih;   Parerasanmatahsvasanjñālokep ratītamudāharanamnirvacanam;   Tadyuktinidarśanamdrṣṭāntah; Idamvāidamvetivikalpah; Idamcedamcetisamuccyah; Anyathāyadjñāt amyuktitaścedgamyatetadūhyamiti; Itidvātrinśattantrayuktyāh.

Considering the antiquity of the above-mentioned 32 *tantra-yuktis* and the conceptual scheme operative in its background, it seems that it would have been devised as a general law of aggregating *sūtras* of a particular *śāstra* popular in oral tradition. This is why its application in the creation of *sūtra*-texts is clearly visible. The interpretational method and the discourse style which are applied in interpretive texts like *sūtra*-based *bhāṣya-vārtikas* of later period, the more or less withdrawal and effect of *tantra-yuks* can be seen in them. The shadow-interpreter (Chaya) of *VyākaranaMahābhāṣya* has evaluated these exact 32 *tantra-yuktis* as qualities of interpretation. (*Dvātriṅsat aprakārāṇāmsamāveśaḥvyākhyāṁkartavyaḥ*).

VI

In this way, we find that the method of interpretation of Indian tradition begins with the conception of the *tantra* (system). For the construction of the body of literature of such *tantra*, its means, i.e., *tantra-yuks*, were devised. Subsequently, six-fold and five-*fold* interpretive methods have been evolved subsequently for this purpose. Some attributes or predicates have also been indicated for the enrichment of interpretation and conceptual illumination. The manner in which interpreters have incorporated these interpretive techniques and attributes in their interpretations is based on their skills/temperament; the consequence is that different types of texts were produced or created. As a result of such an accomplishment, we witness the thought-building process and its institutionalisation, which reflects the coordination and inconsonance with *sutras* on the one hand and innovative critical creativity on the other. The manner in which the Indian *śāstra*-tradition flourished for thousands of years through this coordination can be a matter of pride for any intellectual tradition. Really speaking, the Indian *śāstra* tradition has not been a rare item of the distant past lying in a museum but an alive tradition of contemplative thought discipline. But we have no hesitation in saying that although the rich tradition of Indian hermeneutics (*śrutyārtha-paryālocana*) and continuously evolving critical commentarial tradition hasn't gone extinct like river *Saraswati* but certainly has gone contaminated, impure like *Ganges*. Hence, today, there is a dire need to imbibe Vācaspati Miśra's like commitment, which envisages - "*Icchāmikimapipuṇyamdustarakuniba ndhapaṅkmagnānām, Udyotkaragavīnāmatijartīnāmsamuddharaṇāt.*" So that the modernity of Indian intellectual tradition can be saved from oblivion and, at the same time, regained. At this juncture, it is pertinent to note that Indian commentarial tradition has exhibited a unique art of texturing, i.e., in the paradigm of *Sūtra-Bhāṣya-Tīkā* and through this paradigm, it exhibits its intellectual wisdom, making such texts' philosophical treatises. This tradition introduces newer ways of thinking, rationalising, theorising, or philosophising, which can enable a universal reader/interpreter/philosopher to have the right kind of philosophical dialogue with texts. In other words, it can enable the reader/interpreter/philosopher to grasp the true philosophical spirit of the text. Hence, this great intellectual tradition needs to be restored, maintained, re-lived, and further explored for the sake of philosophy itself since the Indian way of thinking provides newer ways (different from the west) of pursuing philosophical inquiry into the nature of reality and self, language, and meanings. The hermeneutic insights and the unique rationality inherent in Indian commentarial tradition can be helpful if applied universally within the undergoing process of modernity in developing a more coherent, reasonable, and better framework for understanding a civilisation and having dialogue among civilisations.

Notes and References:

1. Mahabhasya – 4-3-101

2. Nirukta 1/20, *Sākṣātkratadharmāṇariṣayobabhūvusteavarebhyoas ākṣātkratadharmabhyaupadeśenmantrānasamprāduḥ.*

3. Ibid, *Upadeśāyaglāyantoavarebilmgrahaṇāyemamgranthamsamā mnāsiṣurvedam ca vedāṅgāni ca.*

4. See, *Dīghanikāya, Aggañjayasutta*

5. Mahābhārata, Ch.63/28, *Vedavikrayiṇaścaivavedānāñcaivadūṣak āḥ; vedānāṅlekhakāścaivatevainirayagāminaḥ.*

6. Many references are found terming sūtrakāras as *Bhagawān.* For example, the term 'BhagawānSūtrakāra' has been used in '*Utthanikā*'

of '*Śārīraka Sūtra.*' Again, the address 'BhagawānBādarāyaṇa' has been used in '*Utthanikā*' of 4-4-22 also. Similarly, while commenting on '*siddheśabdārthasambandhe*' in *Mahābhāṣya*, it has been said, '*Kathampunarindambhagwataḥ Pāṇinerācāryasyalakṣaṇampravṛat tam.*' Similarly, Medhātithi says while commenting on *Manusmṛiti* (1-1) that '*tathā hi Bhagawān Pāṇinirnuktaivaprayojanam..........*' In the same way, many references are found addressing Bhāṣyakaras too as *Bhagawān*. For example, ĀcāryaŚaṅkara has said '*Varṇā evaśabdāitibhagawānupavarśaḥ*' for Upavarśa. (Brahmasūtra ŚaṅkaraBhāṣya, 1,3,28) Similarly, Śabara Swāmi has remembered Upavarśa with the term *Bhagawān*. (*Vṛttikāravacanātpratijñāms aṅśayamcāvagacchāmaḥ; AtraBhagwānācāryaidamudāhṛtya –* Śābara Bhāṣya - 12,1,16).

7. Niruktakāra has said, Oh Brahma, i.e., whose Brahma is Uha (13,1,13). Again, it has been said in a mantra of Ṛgveda that *Oh Brahma-ṛtwijas* should be chosen leaving *ṛtwijas* who are incapable of doing uha (telling /uttering / knowing?) of/the meaning of mantra. (*OhBrahmāṇoṅvicarantiutatve* - Ṛgveda, 8,2,24)

8. See, *Yuktidīpikā* on *Sāṁkhyakārikā - 4,5-*

    Na tasyādhigamaḥśakyaḥkartumvarṣaśatairapi,

    Bhūyastvāditisañcintyamunibhiḥsukṣmbuddhibhiḥ.

    Granthenālpenasaṅkṣipyatadārśamanuśāsnam,

    Nibaddhammalaprajñaiḥśiṣyāṇāmhitkāmyayā.

9. *Śāstras* written in *sutra*-style were present even before Pāṇini's*sutras*. Pāṇini himself has mentioned it- (*Pārāśaryaśilāl ibhyāmbhikṣunaṭsūtrayaḥ*, Aṣṭādhyāyī-4-3-110). Again, before Pāṇini there were previous śabdikaācāryas (of oral tradition?) like Āpiśali, Kāśakṛtsna and Bhāgurietc whose *sutras* were full-fledged grammar with *dhātus* and *gaṇas*. (Vaidika Siddhānta Mīmāṁsā - Yudhiṣṭhira Mīmāṁsaka, page-242).

10. See, JICPR, Vol.1-96, Notes and Queries, English translation of significant parts of 18th chapter of Pārāśaropurāṇa, AmbikāduttaŚarmā.

11. Tantravārtika, 1-2-3-4, *Vidhiratyantam prāptauoniyamaḥpākṣike sati, tatracānyatra ca prāptauoparisaṅkhyetigīyate.*

12. Caraka Saṁhitā, Siddhi Sthāna, 12/65-66, It is noticeable that in every new discourse (*pravacana*) where there is inclusion of new element due to discourse or *saṁskāras*, the older or ancient element remains secure. The restoration or redaction of tantra of Agniveśa's Āyurveda was done by Caraka (Vaiśampāyana). The following *pada* has occurred in *Kāśikā* interpretation of *Mahābhāṣya* (4-3-104): 'Carakaiti Vaiśampāyanasyākhyā.' This is why it was named as *Caraka Saṁhitā*. (*Agniveśakratetantre Carakapratisaṅskrate*). Again, in later period, there have been redactor/restorer/editor of *Caraka Saṁhitā* named Dṛdhbala and redactor of *Pātañjala Mahābhāṣya* named Candrācārya.

13. Śāstravāda Prakaraṇa – p. 453,

14. Pārāśaropurāṇa – Ch. 18, śloka-17

15. Procedures like Padaccheda (breaking up terms) is essential for interpretation. This is why, the followers of Bhavadāsa, in Sucarita Miśra'stīkā (commentary) of Ślokavārtika, Pratijñāsūtra, have mocked/ridiculed that this new commentator does not perform the procedure of breaking up the terms, so he does not know the true meaning of *sūtras*. (Yataḥ *padacchedādinakaroti, tasmānnāy abhinevābhāṣyakāraḥsūtrārthavijānīta*)

16. Ācārya Māthara, in his *Vṛtti* of *Sāṅkhyakārikā*, has mentioned the feature of *upodghāta* as – *Sthānamnimittamvaktā ca, śrotāśrotraprayojanam, Sambandhādyabhidhānam ca, upodghātaḥsauccyate.*

17. Jaimini Nyāyamālā Vistara- 1/12-13

18. *śruti-liṅga-vākya-prakaraṇa-sthāna-samākhyānamsamvāyepārada urbalyamarthavaprakarṣāt-* Mīmāṅsā Sūtra, 3-3-14

19. Chāyā interpretation of Vyākaraṇa Mahābhāṣya – p. 2

20. Apart from this definition of *Bhāṣya* given in *Viṣṇudharmottara Purāṇa* it has been said in Śiśupāla Vadha (2-24), "The statement extending the condensed meaning of short sentences (*sutras*) is called Bhāṣya. *"Saṅkṣiptasyāpyatoasyaivavākyastārthagarīyasaḥ; Suvistaratarāvācobhāṣyabhūtābhavantu me."*

21. Arthaśāstra - *Dṛṣṭvāvipratipattimbahudhāśāstreṣubhāṣyakārānaṇ ām; Svyameva Viṣṇuguptaścakārasūtrambhāṣyam ca.*

22. I have grasped this *śloka* on eight-fold attributes of *Vārtika*-texts listening to my Gurus, Swāmī Yogīndrānanda and later Ācārya Kiśornāth Jhā.

23. Rājaśekhara, Kāvyamīmāṁsā, Ch. 2, 23. Rājaśekhara has defined *Cūrṇi* and *Pañjikā* texts as well as *Kārikā* texts.

24. Pārāśaropurāṇa, Ch. 18, śloka 21-22

25. The '*Tatvacintāmaṇi*' of Gaṅgeśopādhyaya is a prakaraṇa-text from the perspective of entire Nyāya tradition, but in the context of Navya-Nyāya tradition it is Ākara-text? TheNyāya-Vaiśeṣika tradition was continued to be seen as the same stream of philosophical thought in its later phase too, this is why many *prakaraṇa*-texts have been written giving importance to different viewpoints, such as *Nyāyasāra* by Bhāsarvajña, *Tārkikarakṣā* by Varadarāja, *Tarkabhāṣā* by Keśavamiśra, *Nyāyalīlāvati* by Vallabhācārya, *Bhāṣāpariccheda* by Viśwanātha and *Nyāyasiddhāntadīpa* by Śaśadhara.

26. ŚrīLakṣmīpuramŚrīnivāsācārya has formulated Indian Darśanas into 156 *prakaraṇas* in his text *Mānameyarahasyaślokavārtika*. Perhaps this is the only text in which Indian philosophy has been elaborated by dividing it intoprakaraṇas and not into schools or systems. However, this great effort of his is not critical but more like descriptive *prakaraṇasaṅgraha*.

27. Currently, B.K. Matilal's work '*Perception*' can be considered as top-grade *prakaraṇa*-text. Similarly, among *prakaraṇa*-texts written in Hindi Prof. ViśwambharaPāhī's '*VaiśeṣikaPadārthavyavasthākāPadd hatimūlakaVimarśa*' and Prof. ĀnandaMiśra's '*SaṁvitprakāśaVāda*' are worth mentioning.

28. In another context Udyotkara Bhāradwāj has given importance to Sūtrakāra and Bhāṣyakāra both - *Yadakṣapādapratibhobhāṣyam Vātsyāyanojagau; Akārimahatastasya Bhāradwājenvārtikam.*

29. The famous titles of *Upavyākhyā*-texts in Indian tradition are as follows: *Tātparya Tīkā, Gūdhārtha, Subodhinī, Parīkṣa, Samīkṣa, Pradīpa, Prakāśa, Prakāśikā, Udyotana, Dīpa, Āloka, Taraṅgiṇī, Darpan, Paribhāṣā, Vivaraṇa, Amṛta, Sphuṭārtha, Maṅjūṣā, Tīkā, Tippaṇī, Kaumudi, Muktāvali Tarkabhāṣā, Manoramā, Praudhamanoramā, Kucamardinī, Dīpikā Pariśuddhi, Maṅjari, Sajjīvanī, Ghaṇṭāpatha, Locana, Rasamaṅjari, Surabhi, Prapūrṇi, Yuktisneha, Kalpataru, Parimala, Jayamaṅgalā, Tattvavivecanam, Tattvayāthārthyadīpanam, Tattvabindu, Tattvasamīkṣā, Caṅdrikā, Taruvasanta, Akutobhayā, Ratnākara, Kāśikā, Sudhā, Sarvopahāriṇī, Mitākṣarā, Ujjīvanī, Ajitā, Pārāyaṇa, Ābharaṇa, Mandana, Vimalā, Śikhā, Kaṇikā, Viveka, Ratnamālikā, Avali, Mandala, Dīdhīti, Cchāyā, Bhāskara, Mitabhāṣiṇī, Paṅjikā, Bodhinī, Makaranda, Alaṅkāra, Mārtanda, Siddhi, Kalāpa, Rahasya, Kaustubha, Prabhāvalī, Nirṇaya, Prabhā, Mukhamardana, Saurabha, Saugandhya, Uddhāra, Vardhana, Mallikā, Upanyāsa, etc.*

30. Interpretershave also humbly expressed their knowledge of Nyāyaśāstra and Mīmāṁsāśāstra in order to show / prove the authenticity / truth of their interpretations. For example, '*Kaṇādam Pāṇanīyam ca sarvaśāstropakārāt*' is famous independently of any system or school. Similarly, Gaṅgeśa introducing himself in the very beginning of *Tattvacintāmaṇi*, states,

Anvīkṣānayamākalayyagurubhirjñārtvāguruṇāmmatam,

cintādivyavilocanena ca tayohsāramvilokārivalam.

tantredoṣagaṇenadurgamtaresiddhāntadīkṣāguruḥ,

Gangeśastanutemitenavacasāśrītattvacintāmaṇim.

Similarly, VācaspatiMiśra (second) has also stated in the very beginning of his work *'Kṛtyadīpa'* that – *'Vaṅśejātaḥkaluṣarahiteka rmamīmāṁsakānāmanvīkṣāyāmgurukaruṇayālabdhatattvāvabodh aḥ;'* Dharmarājādhvarīndra has also expressed his knowledgeability about *Nyāyaśāstra* in the beginning of his *Vedāntaparibhāṣā* saying that – 'I have written a commentary on *Tattvacintāmaṇi* titled as *Tarkacūḍāmaṇi* which is capable of refuting 10 commentaries.' (*"Yen cintāmaṇautīkādaśatīkāvibhaṅjinī, Tarkacūḍāmaṇināmakrat āvidvanmanoramā"*)

31. This is a famous statement for Nyāyaśāstra – *"Pradīpaḥsarvavid yānāmupāyaḥsarvakarmaṇām, Āśrayaḥsarvadharmāṇāmśāśvadān vīkṣikīmatā."* Similarly, in praise of Vyākaraṇa Śāstra it has been said in *'Padamañjarī'*- *'Upāsanīyamyatnenaśāstramvyākaraṇamma hat; Pradīpabhūtasarvāsāvidyānāmyadavasthitam."*

32. It has been said in *Śuśruta Saṅhitā* –

    Sāmānyadarśanenāsāṅvyavasthāsampradarśitā,

    viśeṣastuyathāyogamupadhāryovipaścitā.

    dvātrinśadayuktayohyotāstantrasāragaveṣaṇe,

    yohyotadvidhivadvettidīpībhūtāstubuddhimāna.

33. ŚuśrutaSaṅhitā – *Asadvādiprayuktānāmvākyānāmpratiṣedhanam,*

    svavākyasiddhirapi ca kriyatetantrayuktitaḥ.

    vaktānoktāstu ye hyarthālīnāyecāpyanirmalā,

    leśoktā ye ca kecitsyurateśāmcāpiprasādhanam.

34. Vātsyāyana interpreting the term 'tantra' has said – *'Tantram-itaretarābhisambaddha-syārthasamūhasyopdeśaḥ-śāstram.'* *Vātsyāyana Bhāṣya – 1-1-26*

35. The collection of 32 '*tantra-yuktis*' and their names as mentioned in the 'Chāyā' (shadow) interpretation of *Mahābhāṣya* are as follows: *Adhikaraṇa, Vidhāna, yoga, Padārtha, Hetvartha, Uddeśa, Nirdeśa, Upadeśa, Atideśa, Apadeśa, Pradeśa, Upamāna, Arthāpatti, Saṁśaya, Prasaṅga, Viparyaya, Vākyaśeṣa, Anumata, Vyākhyāna, Nirvacana, Nidarśana, Apavarga, Svasaṅjñā, Pūrvapakṣa, Uttarapakṣa, Ekānta, Anāgatāpekṣaṇa, Atikrāntāvekṣaṇa, Niyoga, Vikalpa, Samuccaya and uhya.*

Chapter 15

Implementation of Linguistic Diversity in Education System: Is it simplicity within Complexity?

Anita Mudkanna,
Former Principal
Jawahar Arts, Science & Commerce College, Anadur, Tamilnadu.

The current education system supports the supremacy of English, which hinders the development of the personality of the child and slows down the pace of learning. According to psychological studies of children, they can able to learn effortlessly and speedily in their mother tongue or regional language. The new education policy discusses encouraging and supporting linguistic diversity for the betterment of the teaching and learning process. The education system has 4 major pillars - learners, tutors, curricula, and infrastructure facilities. Keeping these 4 in mind, the new education system lays emphasis on the use of the mother tongue for the medium of primary education, which aims to advance children in the field of education by keeping them connected to their mother tongue and culture. The main problem in a bilingual country where we find cultural diversity, like India, is that deciding which language to use as a medium of coaching is really complicated.

The linguistic approach connects us with our language and speech, which helps us to preserve this multi-lingual society. It is necessary that children have the chance to learn different languages from school to college level as we observe that children are not able to attain the basic language skills at school level and they are lacking the skill of reading, writing and knowledge of letter etc. Experience is that when these children are admitted to colleges and universities, they not only take any interest in language and literature studies but also avoid attending classes. Considering the terms of language in a policy of the NEP, questions may arise in the minds of many learners and teachers about whether multilingualism and multiculturalism are able to prove the power of language. None of us is quite sure to give appropriate answers, but the time will.

Now, this is the time that it takes to learn English can be expected in the expansion of knowledge. Therefore, changing the medium of education in government and private schools in the initial phase will produce very positive results. While giving priority to the local language in each state, English Language is not denied, and students are not imposed to choose any language. There is a freedom to them that they have to select 3 languages as per their understanding. The use of local language/ mother language/ regional language in teaching science, social sciences, and mathematics is applicable in primary education patterns. By using this methodology, the basic concepts will be clear, and they will learn them easily. During this age group, the medium of instruction that has been set in the mother tongue or regional language will have comprehensive consequences, and our national spirit will also be strengthened. Now, it is obligatory for both government and private schools, which is the biggest achievement of the new education policy.

Many world-famous language scientists and academicians like Steven Pinker, Noam Chomsky, Peter Trudgill, etc., have clearly mentioned that the language closest to the student's social language or their mother language is the most useful language for education. As we see the statement of the sociologist Peter Trudgill, we understand that he believes that the socialisation of language in the education system makes education easy and knowledgeable.

"Language as a social phenomenon is closely engaged with the social organisation and value systems of society (p. 8)."

In this way, if a language represents a region or a particular society, then it will be easy for any child from the background of that society to understand the basic education in their language. The language through which the child first communicates with his mother, family, and environment, if he gets an education in the same language for the first few years, will improve his conceptual development. As Rutherford mentioned in his statement quite significant, he says, *"There is a minimum of one characteristic that's common to each successful language-learning experience we've ever known, which is that the learner is exposed a method or another to an adequate amount of the info of the language to be learned"* (p.18).

Early childhood care and education have been included in the education policy, keeping in mind the versatile development of children. Considering that it is a significant initiative that has been taken to use the mother tongue or regional language for primary and secondary education, it is the best way to involve students in a stream of education. Removing the overbearing of English as a medium of primary-level education and wide-ranging use of Indian languages will see far-reaching results in basic education. This will cover the way for the advancement of native languages, as well as help in the development of the spirit of Indianness and national unity. As we study the objectives of NEP 2020 and the place of multilingualism in the policy, we have found the following opportunities that will be helpful for learners, society, and the nation.

Significance of Mother Tongue:

Mother tongue is a natural language of each and every child, which he learns without any linguistics study. The language of any region represents its social status rather than linguistics. In this way, the mother tongue or regional language can express its social values and knowledge to the entire occultation of the new generation through elementary education. So, it will be easy for any child coming from any background in that society to grasp basic education in their language. Govindraj Ethiraj rightly said,

"The closer the school language is to the language that the child is familiar with, what is going to build a robust."

Translation Methodology:

The concept of the Indian Institute of Translation and Interpretation in new education policy under which the work of translating and new interpretation from various fields of knowledge. It strengthens local languages, and it can be done easily. Not only the translation methodology but also the new education policy highlights that the teaching of all languages will be supplemented through advanced and practical methods. Importance is given to teaching the students by mingling cultural aspects of languages such as local songs, movies, drama, storytelling, verse, etc.

As suggested in 'The National Knowledge Commission,' the 'National Translation Mission translation of tribal language is initial responsibility and these commission will work as institute where there is a comprehensive translation initiative in all Indian languages including English. These tribal languages should be placed at the national front which is going to die.'

Hindi as the language of nationality:

Making it the official language and enshrining it as a symbol of nationality should be the priority of the new education policy. The aim of the new education policy is to make the people aware that they can develop when they fully use all Indian languages, including Hindi, because it's a national language. The root of Indian nationality is its merged culture, which connects with the languages of India. Therefore, policy focused on teaching the languages of the Union and the States is important to keep unity and national pride.

Sanskrit as Mainstream of Curriculum:

Sanskrit will be included in the mainstream curriculum. It will not be limited to single-stream Sanskrit schools and universities but will be kept in wider perception as we know that Sanskrit is known as the Mother of Indian languages. Indian epics, medicine, linguistics theories, mathematics, astronomy, philosophy, linguistics, dramaturgy, yoga, and more were originally written in Sanskrit, so teaching in Sanskrit t will be made interesting, innovative, and more informative therefore in NEP 2020 Sanskrit is placed as an important modern language.

Three-language Formula:

The New Education policy is rightly ready to implement a three-language formula to support multilingualism at the school level. Its emphasis on the pattern of the three-language formula will be applied to the need to promote statutory requirements, people, regions, union goals, multilingualism, and national unity. It emphasises the utilisation of a national language as a teaching medium up to Class 5 of the kids, and if the students up to the fifth class are interested in learning the language more than 3, they can do so. Language diversity in new education policy helps to preserve this multi-lingual society, and it is necessary that children have the opportunity to learn multi-lingual proficiency from school education to college and university education. We all are very familiar that the expressive capacity of a person living in a multi-lingual society can be seen and heard in every sphere of his life.

Challenges:

1. But to make these languages educative, there is an urgent need to strengthen them at the structural and conceptual level, i.e., without maintaining its standard, technical terms and manufacturing text, books there will be a lot of difficulty in making these languages as a medium of teaching.

2. Higher quality textbooks in all subjects including science will be made available in-home languages / mother tongue. In NEP 2020 the explanation is given regarding the translation is that all efforts will be made to prepare multi-lingual textbooks and excellent teaching material regarding science and mathematics. It becomes very helpful for students to think and speak on both subjects in both languages that is in mother tongue and English.

3. There will be a major effort from both the Central and State Governments to recruit a large number of language teachers in all the regional languages across the country.

4. Translation is an extremely difficult task. In literature like drama, poetry, and fiction, where the emotional aspect is dominant, translating this is most difficult for rendering in a new language, which is the aesthetic experience of the original author, who has communicated to his readers in his own language. The expression of this experience is inextricably connected with idioms, images, and nuances of the source language, so it becomes a challenge to find exact equivalents in the receptor language to convey the same experience.

Conclusion

Language is an important pillar in our education system, strengthening the societal fabric in general and imparting education to children in particular. But, due to the existing centralised structure and diversity in language, no local or regional languages have been given importance or supremacy over other languages in India. The three-language formula in the policy document will certainly give enhancement to our education system and eradicate social inequality. No doubt, most of the reforms in the NEP 2020 are very appreciative and helpful for society to develop, but as we studied the challenges while implementing the policy, we find that this is a huge burden on administrators, parents, teachers, and students. The availability of a lot of opportunities, choices, freedom to leave the course, online courses, etc., may be seen as good as a rainbow, but the question is, is it admirable in the future? Is it possible to collect data on local language culture and translate it properly? India is a multi-lingual country where many languages are spoken, and there is a variation in the mother language, so it is a big task for a translator to translate cultural oral literature properly. Of course, the importance of multilingualism is good conceptually, but practically, it's too complicated because people leave villages for a better life; they even know their cultural hegemony. It's new hope for a new world with a new theory of education; just wait and watch and go ahead with a positive mindset.

References

MHRD "National Education Policy 2020," Ministry of Human Resource Development, Government of India, New Delhi.

Trudgill, P. "Sociolinguistics: An introduction to language and society." Fourth edition Penguin, UK, 2000.

Rutherford, William E. "Second Language Grammar: Learning and Teaching." London; New York: Longman.1987

Govindraj Ethiraj (August 5, 2020) "National Education Policy 2020: Instruction Should Be In The Language Of The Playground" https://www.indiaspend.com/national-education-policy-2020-instruction-should-be-in-the-language-of-the-playground/ Retrieved on 30.11.2020

Anthrogogic English Language Classroom and Samvad as a Base for Questioning Technique

Shree Deepa,
Associate Professor, Centre for English Language Studies,
University of Hyderabad, Hyderabad, Telangana.

A. Amartheja,
Research Scholar, Centre for English Language Studies,
University of Hyderabad, Hyderabad, Telangana.

In India, questioning skills are typically not taught in many English language (EL) classrooms at the UG (undergraduate) level. The main emphasis in these classes is on question structures and formulation, including lexical items, question tags, and potentially interrogative question forms. Specifically, these classes focus more on teaching question construction and question syntax. There is a growing necessity to implement Samvad questioning techniques in English language classrooms in light of the current NEP2020, particularly for adult students studying in mainstream higher education classrooms. There is an even more necessity to root and route such teaching in the Indian Knowledge systems (IKS). One such branch is the Samvad perspective, which is the theoretical structure that uses questioning techniques through IKS. Students can build real-world knowledge and improve their questioning skills with the support of the Samvad teaching system. It is believed that asking questions through discussion can assist pupils in integrating new concepts or information with what they already know. By allowing students to express their ideas and perspectives, dialogic teaching enables them to "think, interpret, and generate new understandings." (Nystrand, 1997). During dialogic engagement, speakers actively listen to one another, share information, and collaborate to create new meanings through reciprocal understanding. Samvad teaching entails teachers' questioning strategies, which must be understood outside of the classroom surroundings (textbooks and printed materials) and through the learners' real-life experiences. Samvad questioning encourages pupils to approach the idea in a 'logic-based' manner, producing their own evidence and arguments. Samvad teaching is a strategy that facilitates the teaching and learning process through interactive conversations, question posing, and response, resulting in the formation of new questions, comprehensions, and ideas. Samvad teaching employs open and divergent questions that encourage students and teachers to think, exchange, and develop diverse ideas in order to construct knowledge collaboratively.

Samvad and IKS relevance:

According to the Cologne Digital Sanskrit Dictionary (Wisdom Library), the word Samvad has been used in several ancient writings, which give different meanings. Those contextual meanings are briefly discussed hereafter: Samvad means

- To speak together or at the same time (Aitereya-Brahmana, Chandogya Upanishad)
- To converse with or about (Rig-Veda; Atharvaveda; Taittriya Samhita; Brahmana)
- To sound together or in concord (Atharvaveda)
- To agree, accord, consent (Harivamsa; Mrcchakatika; Kathasaritsagara)
- To coincide, fit together (Ratnavali)

- To speak, to address (Bhagavathapurana)
- To designate, to call, name (Srutabodha)
- To cause to converse with or about (Sathapatha-Brahmana)
- To invite or call upon to speak (Hitopadesa)
- To cause to sound, play (Mahabharatha, Kathasarithsagara)

Samvada is a Sanskrit term that means "wording together" or "discoursing together" and can also be used to denote discourse. Sam stands for together and Vada for word. Patton, L. (2003) states the different meanings of Samvada in her literary essay, "Samvada: A Literary Resource for Conflict Negotiation in Classical India." Patton claims that Samvada used to mean 'bargain' in Brahmanas; conversation discussion, or dialogue in the Dharma Sutras; an account, incident story in the yuddhakaanda of the Ramayana; dispute in the Mahabharata; agreement and concord in the Mimamsa Sutras, Tantravartika (1.2.22;1.2.47) and in the Jain text Prabandhacintamani (52.4). Patton has included the Gita text as Samvada between Arjuna and Krishna. She points out that these examples, which 'are named as samvada of ancient classical Indian text,' are indeed 'indigenous genre.' The Indian *Vada*-tradition explores contending different philosophical perspectives and concepts, to be precise, through long public debates; in any debate, there was a winner or a loser, but the long-run debates sharpened the boundaries of philosophical thoughts (Clayton, J. 2006: 36).

Prince, B. Claims that "The Samvada model accepts the freedom to be different and respects the difference of communities and traditions and equality of different traditions however without subscribing to a liberal neutral point." Prince further states," In a dialogue between traditions, the strength of one community compensates the weaknesses of others." He asserts that there are 3 steps in Samvada, i.e., first, *to know oneself* in a manner to know the traditions that build the enquiring self, its logicism, its authoritative texts, and the narrative of these texts; secondly, *understand the other-* other in their in tradition and its rationality like learning a new language; and finally, *the act of dialogue between oneself and the other* to the fulfil the purpose of dialogically living together. For the purpose of this task, the teacher selected to introduce Vikrama-Bethal stories and Yaksha Prashnas.

India was the birthplace of the stories about Vikram and the vampire. A king named Vikram and a ghost named Betal are the subjects of these tales. Sanskrit was the original language used to write the stories. Stories meant to teach moral lessons to listeners or readers make up the collection of tales.

King Vikram initially pledged to send Betal on a journey to fulfil his prayers. Throughout their journey, Betal was adamant about telling a narrative and asking Vikram a question at the conclusion. But he modified it with a few requirements. First, Betal would take off and return to their starting point if Vikram provided the correct response. Secondly, Vikram's time will run out if he doesn't respond. Finally, Betal will tell a fresh narrative, and Vikram will continue on the path if he doesn't know the solution.

The Yaksha Prashna, also referred to as the Akshardhama, the Dharma Baka Upakhyana, or Yudhishthira's questions and answers exchange in the Hindu epic Mahabharata, tells the tale of this exchange. The story takes place when the Pandavas are coming to the end of their twelve-year exile in the forest, and it first occurs in the Vana Parva. The Madhya Parva of the Mahabharata has this conversation between Yudhishthira and the Yaksha, also referred to as the Dharma Baka Upakhyan, or the Legend of the Virtuous Crane.

Anthrogogy:

While andragogy (Knowles, 1984) is intended for the teaching-learning process of adult learners, pedagogy is intended for the teaching-learning process of children. The term "anthrogogy" (Trott, 1991) is appropriate for this purpose because the word "androgogy" or "andragogy" is sexist in its orientation and has to be replaced with a gender-neutral yet compassionate phrase. Under "teaching all adults (all genders) who are and has its own set of principles of teaching and testing where the emphasis is on living a life of a cohabitant alongside other beings peacefully on planet earth," the word "anthrogogy" (Deepa, 2022; Trott, 1991) is used. This setting pertains to classes in mainstream higher education, such as undergraduate programmes in India, where students are required to be at least 18 years of age and have registered for an undergraduate course in a regular mode (Deepa, 2022). Adult learners are expected to act, behave, and assume responsibility like adults in anthrogogic classrooms; in pedagogic classrooms, on the other hand, the teacher assists students in becoming capable of learning. According to Deepa and Durairajan (2023), the term "anthrogogy" suggests that adult learners in traditional higher education programmes and offline and online classrooms should be accountable for their academic goals and adhere to deadlines for completing tasks and assessments. Because students in anthrogogical classrooms are autonomous adult learners capable of independent thought, interpretation, and understanding generation, Samvad inquiry is welcomed in these settings.

Methodology:

This paper adopts a qualitative approach to carry out the study and assess the impact of Samvad questioning techniques in English Language classrooms at the undergraduate level in a central university in India.

Sample: 40 undergraduate students registered for Integrated M.Sc. Physics programme. The primary author of this paper is the course instructor, and the secondary author is the classroom observer (the researcher).

Research Tools: The teacher's diary, the researcher's diary, the reflective essays submitted by students, and focused group interviews were used to answer and fill up the research gap encountered in the literature.

Procedure: This study involved the interventions of the teacher and the researcher. For this task, the teacher was the instructor, and the researcher was kept as an observer in the classroom. The teacher conducted a task for almost 2 week-duration (4 hours a week). The teacher introduced ancient Indian tales from the Indian epics related to the questioning techniques, i.e., Vikram-Bethal stories, Yaksha Prashnas, and Nachiketha stories, as a pre-task. Further, the teacher explained the importance of the art of questioning in real-world contexts and its relevance to the above tales, namely the connection between Samvad's questioning and the tales. After the pre-task, the students were aware of the importance of the art of questioning.

The entire classroom was divided into 7 groups, depending on their comfort level, to reach optimum learning among adult learners. The teacher introduced the major task for the classroom by bringing the newspaper inlet advertisement as task material. The teacher created a fictitious situation to shop on behalf of the teacher and instructed them to make a shopping list for the budget of 2600/-. Each group had a chance to ask the teacher a maximum of 3 questions to make the shopping list. The condition for this task by the teacher was they could utilise the total amount of 2600/- and buy only those items that were useful to the teacher. The students were expected to ask questions and make a shopping list based on the reasons and assumptions why they chose them.

The students worked on the budget list from the newspaper inlet. Some groups utilised the 3 questions, some groups 2, and some did not use their chance to ask questions. Based on the replies given by the teacher, they made the final shopping list. For some questions, the teacher, instead of answering the questions, posed questions back to make them realise some things on their own. After the students had created the primary shopping list, the teacher gave them points based on the useful items in their list and their reasons and assumptions for arriving at the final list.

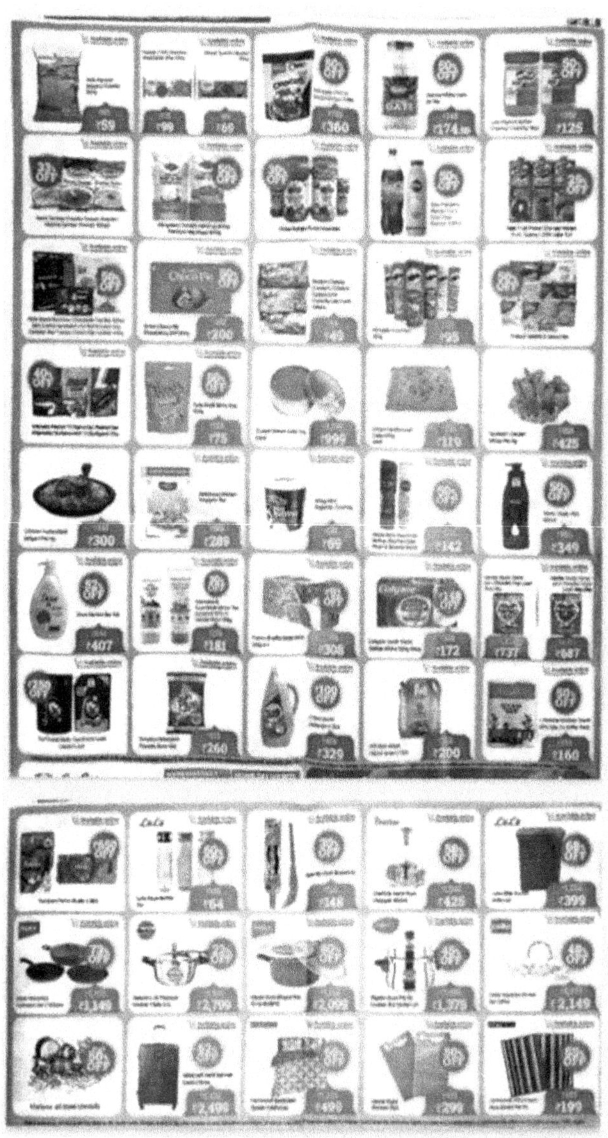

After the primary round of questions, the teacher gave them a chance to improve their list, and those who did not use their questions properly got a chance to ask a few more questions and utilise the chance this time. After utilising the chance, the students submitted their shopping lists. From this, the students could find the importance of the art of questioning in real-life contexts through dialogic questioning. Thus, the teacher drew students' attention through an engaging task by using questioning techniques from their daily life experiences. This technique was gleaned from the Samvad framework. The students were guided towards realising that it is not just important to ask questions but also utilise the opportunities that present themselves in front of adults, which in a pedagogic sense go either unnoticed or silenced or are disallowed. This, when carried into the undergraduate classrooms, remains the same. But in anthrogogic classrooms, the contrast has to be initially pointed out, as this study did, and the findings concur.

Results and Conclusions:

Throughout the task, the students were engaged and enthusiastic. The questions asked by the students mainly dealt with themes like the teacher's daily routine, health issues, food habits, family food choices, etc. For instance, the following questions were encountered by students.

> *"What are the Fruits and Vegetables that you don't prefer to buy in the pamphlet?"*
>
> *"Do you wish to buy dry fruits?"*
>
> *"What do you prefer, home needs or food items?"*
>
> *"Do you have any medical prescription while taking food?*
>
> *"Are you planning to go somewhere for a vacation?"*

The students made their final lists and mentioned their reasons and assumptions for selecting items in the lists. For instance, they chose oats because oats are high in antioxidants called avenanthramides, which are not found in any other cereal grains, and they might improve heart health. Likely, in this instance, they came up with such many instances. Some of the shopping lists made by students are shown below.

Grocery list

GROUP-MATTER AND METAPHORS

S.No	Item	Quantity	Price distribution Rs	Total Rs
1	Chefline Hand Push Chopper 900ml	1	425	425
2	Almonds Californian	500 g	349	349
3	Cashew Nuts White 320	500 g	349	349
4	Apple Red Gold	1 kg	199	199
5	Fortune Chakki Fresh Atta	(1*2) Kg	37*2	74
6	Nivea Body Milk	600 ml	349	349
7	Milkymist Probiotic Curd	1 Kg	69	69
8	Manna White Oats	1Kg	174.5	174.5
9	Surf Excel Matic Top/FrontLoad Liquid	3.2 L	247	247
10	Potato Premium	(1*0.5) Kg	14.5	14.5
11	Tata Sampann Toor Dal	1 Kg	67%*225	151
12	Sona Masoori Rice	(1*2) Kg	50*2	100
13	Musambi	(1*0.75) Kg	52*0.75	39
14	Lady's Finger	1 Kg	28	28
15	Musk Melon	1 Kg	32	32
	Total			2600

SAVINGS- **Rs.1794**

SIGMA SHOPPING CENTRE

NO. 209, COLLEGE FOR INTEGRATED STUDIES,
UNIVERSITY OF HYDERABAD,
GACHIBOWLI, HYDERABAD - 500046

CUSTOMER NAME : Dr. Shree Deepa

CUSTOMER ID : 23IPMP0X

CUSTOMER CONTACT : 9685130176

DATE OF PURCHASE : 16-10-2023

TIME : 11:33 AM (IST)

MODE OF PAYMENT : PAYTM

I.No.	Item Name	Rate	Quantity	Amount
1.	Muskmelon	₹32 /kg	1 kg	32.00
2.	Lady's Finger	₹28 / kg	1.5 kg	42.00
3.	Watermelon Kiran	₹19 / kg	1 kg	19.00
4.	Musambi	₹52/ kg	1 kg	52.00
5.	Almonds Californian	₹349/.5 kg	.5 kg	349.00
6.	Cashew Nuts White 320	₹349/.5 kg	.5 kg	349.00
7.	Walnut Chile	₹649/.5kg	.5 kg	649.00
8.	Ajwa Dates	₹525/.5 kg	.5 kg	525.00
9.	Dry Fig Ropeless	₹1099 /kg	.4 kg	440.00
10.	Peanut Plain (Brown)	₹143 /kg	1 kg	143.00

TOTAL AMOUNT : ₹2600.00

CGST = 5% Inclusive

GGST = 5% Inclusive

₹2600.00

PAID

Address for Door Delivery:
XXX, Faculty Quarters,
University of Hyderabad,
Gachibowli, Hyderabad-500046.

You saved ₹843.00

AIM: To prepare a Budget worth ₹2600.00/- from the given pamphlet.

SUBMITTED: A Bill worth ₹2600.00/- : Entirely Handwritten

ASSUMPTIONS: The necessities listed by ma'am in answer to our question last week are still the needful.

The appropriate requirements were listed.

REASON: Bill seemed quite a nice idea for a creative budget.

COPYRIGHTS PERMISSION: Customer's Name, Contact and Address for Door Delivery.

From the reflective essays submitted by students, the task was engaging and made them aware of the art of questioning techniques. The students said that the framing questions in real-life contexts made them realise the importance of daily life experiences.

Thus, this chapter deals with how Samvad questioning techniques were used in English Language classrooms. Anthrogogic classrooms always encourage or maximise the scope for self-efficient learning among adult learners. The groups responded to the session actively through WhatsApp for questions, answers, and feedback. In anthrogogic learning spaces, when students need more straightforward answers, they could arrive at answers by further questioning, moving far away from teaching the syntax of the interrogative, which usually does not happen in many language classrooms in India. The Samvaad questioning system suggests that this method might be applied in English classes where knowledge is valued. On the other hand, people value their cultural heritage and worldview, which helps them make sense of their words, ideas, and behaviours.

References

Alexander, R.J. (2008). *Towards Dialogic Teaching: Rethinking Classroom Talk* (4th edition). York: Dialogos.

Deepa, Shree. (2022). *Pedagogic scaffolding and anthrogogic learning contexts: Issues in metaphor mismathch.* Journal of English language teachers' interaction forum vol XIII.2:3-7

Deepa, Shree. (2022, August). *Thought seeds in anthrogogic learning contexts.* Journal of Indian education, 48(22).

Deepa, Shree. (2022, July). *Options in multiple choice questions: Oh Really! Yours sincerely Adult learners!* Language and Language Teaching: A peer reviewed journal (UGC CARE LISTED). Vol 11.2.22: 81-86e

Doukmak, R. (2014). *Are you sure You don't have any Questions? Dialogic Teaching as a way to promote Students' Questions.* Elited. Vol 16.

Mercer, N. (2000). *Words and Minds: How We Use Language to Think Together.* Abingdon: Routledge.

Mercer, N., Wegerif, R. & Dawes, L. (1999). *Children's talk and the development of reasoning in the classroom.* British Educational Research Journal.25/1, 95-111.

Nystrand, M. (1997). *Opening dialogue: Understanding the dynamics of language and learning in the English classroom.* New York, NY: Teachers College Press.

Paul, R. & Elder, L. (2006). *The Thinker's Guide to the Art of Socratic Questioning.* Foundations for Critical Thinking. Dillion Beach: CA.

Trott, D. C. (1991, October). *Anthrogogy.* Paper presented at the meeting of the American Association for Adult and Continuing Education, Montreal, Quebec.

Walsh, J.A. & Sattes, B.D. (2011). *Thinking Through Quality Questioning: Deepening Student Engagement.* Crowin/Sage : California.

Yang, Z. & Brindley, S. (2023). *Engaging students in dialogic interactions through questioning.* ELT Journal. Volume77/2.

Yildrim, S. & Uzun, S. (2021). *An Overview of Dialogic Teaching and Its Implications on Learning.* International Journal of Education, Technology and Science. 1(2) (2021) 135–153.

Chapter 17

From Tradition to Innovation: The Natya Shastra's Role in the Evolution of the Indian Knowledge System and Contemporary Performing Arts

Rajesh Mahesh Kale,
Assistant Professor, Department of English,
Santosh Bhimrao Patil Arts, Commerce and Science College,
Mandrup, Dist. Solapur, M.S.

The intersection of the Indian Knowledge System (IKS) and the Natya Shastra underscores a paradigmatic example of the synthesis between rigorous intellectual inquiry and the profound spirituality characteristic of Indian epistemological traditions. The Natya Shastra, as an integral component of the IKS, embodies an interdisciplinary approach, amalgamating elements of aesthetics, dramaturgy, musicology, and psychology, thereby serving as a conduit for the transmission of cultural and philosophical tenets across generations. This seminal text not only elucidates the technical disciplines involved in the performing arts but also, perhaps more crucially, delineates the underlying philosophical frameworks that inform these practices. In doing so, it exemplifies the quintessential ethos of the IKS, where the pursuit of knowledge is intrinsically linked to the quest for spiritual and moral development. Through the lens of research-oriented analysis, the Natya Shastra emerges not merely as a historical artefact but as a living testament to the dynamic and integrative nature of Indian scholarship, offering rich avenues for contemporary exploration and interpretation.

The Natya Shastra, an ancient encyclopaedic treatise on the performing arts authored by the sage Bharata Muni, is a monumental work that has profoundly influenced the cultural and artistic landscape of India. Situated at the intersection of art, culture, and spirituality, this seminal text presents a comprehensive overview of theatre arts, encompassing drama, dance, music, and aesthetic theory. Its composition, believed to date back to between 200 BCE and 200 CE, marks a pivotal epoch in the annals of Indian classical arts, setting the foundation for a rich tradition of performance that intertwines the artistic with the divine. This introduction aims to unfold the multi-faceted significance of the Natya Shastra within the Indian knowledge system, examining its historical context, philosophical underpinnings, and its overarching influence on the realms of dance, theatre, and music.

The genesis of the Natya Shastra is steeped in mythology and philosophy, reflective of its intrinsic link to the spiritual fabric of Indian society. According to legend, it was divinely inspired, conceived as a fifth Veda accessible to all varnas, transcending the limitations imposed on the original 4 Vedas. This ethos underscores the democratising vision of the Natya Shastra, positioning the performing arts as a universal medium for spiritual and emotional expression. The text itself is a vast compendium structured into 36 chapters, each delving into different aspects of performance art, from the intricacies of theatrical production and stagecraft to the nuances of gestural communication and the theoretical frameworks governing dance and music.

At the heart of the Natya Shastra lies its philosophical core, articulated through the concept of rasa, or aesthetic emotion, which Bharata Muni identifies as the ultimate purpose of performing arts. This notion of rasa as an experiential state to be evoked in the audience encapsulates the transformative potential of art, aiming to elevate individuals beyond the mundane to a realm of heightened emotional and spiritual awareness. The text's detailed exploration of the means to cultivate such experiences through performance techniques and aesthetic appreciation marks a significant contribution to the field of art theory, predating and influencing subsequent artistic traditions and philosophies both within and beyond the Indian context. Furthermore, Natya Shastra's impact extends well beyond the theoretical, deeply ingraining itself in the practical domain of art education and performance. Its systematic classification of dance movements, theatrical gestures, and musical scales has served as a foundational curriculum for generations of artists, shaping the evolution of numerous classical dance forms and regional theatre traditions across India. This enduring legacy is a testament to Natya Shastra's pivotal role in the perpetuation and revitalisation of Indian performing arts, ensuring their continuity and relevance in the face of changing times.

In dissecting the contributions of the Natya Shastra to the Indian knowledge system, it becomes evident that its significance is not merely historical or artistic but profoundly philosophical and cultural. It exemplifies the holistic approach to knowledge that characterises Indian intellectual and spiritual traditions, wherein art is not an isolated domain but an integral part of the broader quest for understanding human existence and the cosmos. As we delve deeper into the layers of meaning and insight enshrined in the Natya Shastra, we uncover not only the foundations of Indian classical arts but also the enduring principles of beauty, emotion, and transcendence that define the human experience.

Historical Context & structure:

The Natya Shastra, attributed to the sage Bharata Muni, is a foundational text of Indian classical arts, encapsulating the principles of drama, dance, and music and standing as a testament to the rich cultural and intellectual heritage of ancient India. This treatise, estimated to have been composed between 200 BCE and 200

CE, offers not only a deep dive into the performing arts but also a reflection of the society and philosophical thought of the time. Understanding its historical context and structure is essential for appreciating its comprehensive scope and enduring significance in the Indian Knowledge System (IKS).

Historical Context

The period during which the Natya Shastra was composed was marked by significant socio-political and cultural transformations in India. This era saw the rise and fall of several major dynasties and the spread of Buddhism and Jainism, which challenged the existing Vedic order and introduced new philosophical and ethical perspectives. It was a time of great intellectual ferment and artistic flourish, with patronage extending from Royal courts to the emerging merchant classes. Against this backdrop, the Natya Shastra emerged as a unifying cultural force, synthesising elements from various traditions and regions into a coherent system of performing arts. The text itself is said to have been inspired by a divine command to Bharata Muni, aimed at creating a fifth Veda that was accessible to all, regardless of caste or social standing. This narrative underscores the inclusive vision behind the Natya Shastra, positioning it as a means of moral and spiritual education for the broader society. It reflects the democratising impulse of the time, seeking to transcend the exclusivity of sacred knowledge and make it available through the universal medium of performance.

Structure and Content:

The Natya Shastra is an extensive work comprising 36 chapters that systematically cover every aspect of the performing arts, from theoretical foundations to practical applications. Its structure can be broadly categorised into 4 main areas: dramaturgy, dance, music, and aesthetic theory.

Dramaturgy:

The text lays down detailed guidelines for drama, including the construction of plots, characterisation, dialogues, and the use of literary devices. It outlines different genres of plays and the appropriate themes, moods, and costumes for each, providing a comprehensive framework for theatrical production.

Dance:

Bharata Muni describes various dance forms, movements (karanas), gestures (mudras), and expressions (bhavas), establishing a taxonomy that forms the basis of classical Indian dance. The emphasis on the communicative potential of dance, through the language of gesture and expression, highlights its role in storytelling and emotional evocation.

Music:

The treatise details the principles of music, including scales (ragas), rhythms (talas), and the integration of vocal and instrumental music. It recognises music as an essential element of drama and dance, contributing to the overall aesthetic experience.

Aesthetic Theory:

Perhaps the most profound contribution of the Natya Shastra is its exploration of rasa, or aesthetic emotion, which Bharata Muni identifies as the ultimate goal of performing arts. The theory of rasa articulates how art evokes specific emotional states in the audience, facilitating a shared experience of beauty and transcendence.

The comprehensive nature of the Natya Shastra, spanning theory and practice across multiple forms of art, reflects an integrated approach to knowledge characteristic of the IKS. It underscores the interconnectivity of various domains of human endeavour, weaving together the strands of philosophy, ethics, aesthetics, and spirituality into a coherent whole. Through its structured exposition, the Natya Shastra serves as a mirror to the complex social fabric and intellectual currents of ancient India, offering insights into the values, aspirations, and cosmological understandings of the time. Its enduring legacy lies in its ability to transcend its historical context, continuing to inspire and inform the practice and appreciation of the performing arts in contemporary society.

Philosophical Foundation:

The Natya Shastra, revered as the ancient bedrock of Indian performing arts, extends beyond its role as a mere instructional manual for dance, drama, and music. It encapsulates a profound philosophical framework, grounding the arts in the broader contours of Indian metaphysics and epistemology. This treatise, attributed to Bharata Muni, not only delineates the technical aspects of performing arts but also engages deeply with the aesthetic and spiritual dimensions of human experience, thus offering a rich tapestry of insights into the nature of reality, perception, and the transcendent potential of art.

The Concept of Rasa

At the heart of the Natya Shastra's philosophical foundations lies the concept of rasa, a term that, while literally translating to "juice" or "essence," signifies the aesthetic flavour or emotional sentiment experienced by the audience in the context of artistic performance. Bharata Muni identifies 8 primary Rasas - love, humour, sorrow, anger, heroism, fear, disgust, and wonder - each corresponding to a specific bhava (emotion) that the performance seeks to evoke in the spectator. This correlation between the performer's expression (bhava) and the audience's experience (rasa) encapsulates a sophisticated theory of aesthetic appreciation, positing that the goal of any artistic endeavour is to engender a shared emotional and spiritual experience that transcends the mundane.

The Interplay of the Material and the Spiritual

The philosophical edifice of the Natya Shastra is built upon the dual principles of materiality and spirituality, mirroring the broader Indian philosophical tradition that navigates the interplay between the empirical world (Prakriti) and the eternal spirit (Purusha). In this framework, performing arts serve as a medium through which the material aspects of existence - characterised by form, movement, rhythm, and sound - become vehicles for conveying deeper spiritual truths. This duality reflects the holistic understanding of human experience in Indian thought, where art becomes a bridge between the sensory and the supra-sensory, the temporal and the eternal.

The Educative and Liberative Function of Art

Further extending its philosophical scope, Natya Shastra posits that performing arts have an educative and liberating function. Through the dramatisation of mythological and historical narratives, art serves as a means of imparting moral and ethical lessons, shaping the character and consciousness of both the performer and the audience. This didactic aspect is intertwined with the notion of art as a pathway to liberation (moksha), offering a means to transcend the ego and attain a state of unity with the ultimate reality. By evoking rasa, art facilitates the dissolution of individual boundaries, enabling a collective experience of beauty and truth that leads to spiritual awakening.

Integration with Other Philosophical Systems

The philosophical underpinnings of the Natya Shastra also resonate with other Indian philosophical systems, such as Vedanta, which emphasises the non-duality of Brahman (ultimate reality) and the world, and Samkhya, with its analysis of Prakriti and Purusha. By embedding the performing arts within this rich philosophical context, the Natya Shastra not only elevates art to the status of spiritual practice but also reinforces the interconnectedness of all domains of knowledge within the Indian Knowledge System (IKS).

Foundational Framework for Classical Dance:

The impact of the Natya Shastra on Indian classical dance is unparalleled. It systematically categorises and details the movements, gestures, and expressions that form the basis of classical dance forms. The text delineates the concept of 'Nritta' (pure dance), 'Nritya' (expressive dance), and 'Natya' (dramatic storytelling), offering dancers a structured framework within which to explore and express a wide range of emotions and narratives. Classical dance forms like Bharatanatyam, Kathak, Odissi, and Kuchipudi draw heavily from the Natya Shastra's classifications of mudras (hand gestures) and bhavas (emotional states), using them to convey stories and emotions with precision and depth. The treatise's influence extends to the training methodologies employed in these dance forms, emphasising a holistic development that integrates physical technique with emotional expressivity and spiritual awareness.

Revitalisation of Dramatic Arts:

Drama, in the context of the Natya Shastra, is seen as a mimicry of the actions and behaviours of the world, intended to evoke a deeper understanding and appreciation of life's complexities. The text provides exhaustive guidance on various aspects of theatrical production, including scriptwriting, stage design, music, and acting, thereby laying the foundation for Sanskrit theatre. The treatise's principles have been instrumental in the development of traditional Indian theatre forms such as Kutiyattam (recognised by UNESCO as a Masterpiece of the Oral and Intangible Heritage of Humanity) and Yakshagana. By emphasising the interplay between dramatic narrative and aesthetic experience, the Natya Shastra has fostered a rich tradition of storytelling that remains vibrant in regional theatre practices across India.

Harmonising Musical Traditions:

Natya Shastra's treatment of music as an integral component of the performing arts has had a lasting impact on the evolution of Indian classical music. The text's classification of musical instruments, scales, and rhythms has informed both the Hindustani and Carnatic music traditions, providing a shared foundational vocabulary despite their regional variations. The treatise underscores the role of music in enhancing the emotional and aesthetic impact of dance and drama, advocating for a harmonious integration that elevates the overall performance. The principles outlined in the Natya Shastra continue to guide contemporary musicians and composers, serving as a reference point for both traditional and innovative musical explorations.

Continued Relevance and Global Influence:

The enduring legacy of the Natya Shastra lies in its ability to adapt and thrive amidst changing cultural and societal landscapes. Its comprehensive approach to the performing arts, rooted in a deep philosophical foundation, has enabled a continuity of tradition while also encouraging creative expression and adaptation. The treatise's influence extends beyond the Indian sub-continent, engaging with global discourses on performance theory, aesthetics, and the role of art in human society. As scholars, practitioners, and enthusiasts delve into the Natya Shastra's rich teachings, its insights continue to inspire a deeper appreciation of the performing arts as a medium of cultural expression, education, and spiritual exploration.

Conclusion:

The Natya Shastra stands as a monumental pillar within the Indian Knowledge System (IKS), embodying the synthesis of artistic expression, cultural wisdom, and spiritual insight. Its comprehensive exploration of dance, drama, and music not only enriches the Indian performing arts but also offers universal principles that resonate with global artistic practices. For educators and students alike, engaging with the Natya Shastra presents an unparalleled opportunity to delve into an ancient tradition that emphasises the holistic development of the individual—integrating physical discipline, emotional depth, and intellectual rigour. By incorporating its teachings into academic curricula and practical training, educators can provide students with a unique lens to view not only the performing arts but also the interconnectedness of human experience across cultures and time periods. The Natya Shastra, therefore, is not just a relic of the past but a living tradition that continues to inspire innovation, foster cultural dialogue, and contribute to the enrichment of the global arts landscape. Its place within the IKS is a testament to the enduring power of art to transcend boundaries, connect hearts, and elevate the human spirit, making it an invaluable resource for both the preservation of tradition and the exploration of new artistic frontiers.

References

Bharata Muni. "Natya Shastra." Translated by Manomohan Ghosh, Chowkhamba Sanskrit Series Office, 1951.

Ghosh, Manmohan. "Dramatic Concepts Greek and Indian: A Study of the Poetics and the Natyasastra." D.K. Printworld, 1995.

Appa Rao, P.S.R. "The Natya Shastra and the Indian Classical Dance." Journal of the Royal Asiatic Society of Great Britain and Ireland, no. 2, 1971, pp. 123-137.

Richmond, Farley. "Indian Theatre: Traditions of Performance." Asian Theatre Journal, vol. 9, no. 1, 1992, pp. 52-69.

"Natya Shastra: The Science of Indian Dramaturgy." Sangeet Natak Akademi, [no publication date], [URL]. Accessed 24 March 2024.

Kapoor, Sukriti. "Exploring the Influence of Natya Shastra on Modern Performing Arts." The Heritage Lab, 15 June 2020, [URL].

Chapter 18

Relevance of Indian Knowledge Systems in Morals and Ethics

Kasturi Sydaiah,
Assistant Professor of English,
BVRIT College of Engineering for Women, Hyderabad, Telangana.

Every human being wants to lead a happy life, which can be achieved once we realise the essence of human life, that is, we all came from same source- Supreme soul, all of our souls return to the source in the end.

Our human body consists of 37.2 trillion cells; if one cell gets affected, it will influence other cells, which leads to health issues. In other words, a person will not deliberately cut his hand, or his foot, or his face because all these are parts of his own body, and though an injury on his hand does not directly make his organs, such as a foot ache, he feels the pain from any part of his body. The foot, being ignorant and limited, is not conscious at once of the wound made in the hand, but the person is conscious of it and will not let the foot carry his body into a place where the hand will be injured. Of course, the foot ultimately suffers from the general fever of the whole body caused by a severe injury to any part of it, as ignorance of the unity of the body does not alter the fact of unity. And so the person who believes that the self is one, in him and in all others, also necessarily believes that in hurting any part, he is hurting himself. The one who uses that one body and lives and moves in all. If we could realise this and feel it always, we should always act for the highest good of all.

In life, every person wants to achieve 3 things: firstly, success in their career, secondly in life, and thirdly, to realise his own self, that is moksha or khaivalya.

In order to achieve them, we should follow the code of conduct, which consists of morals and ethics. The conduct of man is related to his surroundings as well as to himself/herself. We have to ascertain what is good in relation to those who form our surroundings, as well as in relation to the time and place of the actor, and we may take a wider and wider view of our surroundings according to the knowledge we possess. We have also to ascertain what is good for ourselves and in relation to ourselves. What is good for one man may not be so for others.

Morals are to bring about happiness by establishing harmonious relations between the members of a family, community, humanity, and harmonious relations between the inhabitants of the earth and those of other worlds of the system.

Career: If we were to succeed in our career, we should be honest in our efforts and give our best to get good results. How we behave with our colleagues is also very important. As Shirdi Sai Baba says, **"If you look at me I will look at you" in the same manner we should treat our colleagues in the way we want them to treat.** If we do so, we could cultivate good relations.

How we conduct our lives is imperative; when we don't care for others' praise and criticism, we could become Sthitapragna, who is well mature enough to lead in any situation in the face of life. Sthitapragna becomes indifferent to pleasure and pain; honesty is his armour, and simple truth is his utmost skill, according to Wotton.

Each religion has a different path to go on to reach God. The first thing we learn from religion is the unity of all selves. All human relations exist because of this unity, as Yajnavalkya explained to his wife Maitreyi when she prayed for him the secret of immortality. All-wife, sons, property, friends, worlds and even the Devas themselves are dear because the One-Self is in all.

"Vyasa has said 2 things in the whole of the 18 Puranas: Doing good to another is Punya (right); causing injury to another is Papa (wrong)."

As a general rule, when one helps another, makes him happy, then, whether he wishes it consciously or not, that happiness comes back to him by the law of action and reaction; this is expressed by the rule that Punya brings happiness. Exactly similar is the case regarding misery and Papa.

Happiness in any relationship depends on the parties to the relation fulfilling their duties to each other; that is, on their practising the virtues which are the fulfilment of the duties of the relation. Unhappiness in any relationship results if one or both parties do not fulfil their duties to each other; that is, if they practice vices, which are the absence of fulfilment of the duties of the relationship. A father and son are unhappy if the father shows the vices of harshness, oppression, and neglect, and the son shows the vices of disobedience, disrespect, and careless disregard. If father and son love each other, the virtues of that relation will be practised; if they hate each other, the vices of that relation will appear.

Self-realisation, which is the real goal of humanity, every one of us should realise; to achieve this, one should conduct oneself such as purity of speech, purity of thought, and purity of intention; always think of others' welfare, practice meditations, and see, feel oneness of Supreme self in everything and practice in day-to-day life.

The great Rishis knew that the Supreme soul and self of all souls is one. The authoritative declarations of the Shruti on general morality are final because they are based on this fact, and they can be defended by reason and shown to be of binding and universal obligation.

In the 10th Adhyaya of the Bhagavad Gita, Shri Krishna declares: "I am the Self, O Gudakesha, seated in the heart of all beings; I am the beginning, the middle, and also the end of beings." He then names Himself as many objects, such as sun and moon, mountain and tree, horse and cow, bird and serpent, and many others, and sums up in one all-embracing declaration.

India's way of life and culture are evaluated over 5000 years from the India Knowledge System, which consists of Vedas, Vedangas, Itihasa, Darmastras, Darshas, Nyayas, Upanishads, Ayurdeda, Puranas, Sribhagvadgita and Bhagavatham. All these teach you how to lead a happy life and attain moksha. The bottom line to achieve them is one should follow morals and ethics, why which one becomes a humble human being, who is very sensitive to the needs of others that is paropakarardam idam shariram (soul takes human form to help others).

To sum up, as long as human beings are yet to realise self and to run smoothly the day-to-day activities without attachment, we need to follow morals and ethics.

PEACE TO ALL BEINGS

References

Hindu Dharma by Pujyasri Chandrasekharendra Saraswati Swami

Sanatan Dharma by Central Hindu College, Benares, 1904.

https://egyankosh.ac.in/bitstream/123456789/34870/1/Unit-3.pdf

https://www.youtube.com/watch?v=1HIZHxpGaTg&list=PL-f2HTGDpinNlxEM6YvuACb3KM-qlbol1

Chapter 19

Glimpse of Indian Culture in Education

A. G. Joshi,
Associate Professor, Dept. of English,
Sambhajirao Kendre Mahavidylaya, Jalkot, Maharashtra.

The culture is a word that refers to the ways of life of the members of a society. Every society has its own identity, which is reflected in its norms, values, and modes of beliefs. Cultural heritage is a term broadly applied to reflections and expressions of ways of life living in a society. Culture is a matter that is passed from one generation to another generation. Cultural traditions are part of an education system. It allows students to connect with their history, values, ethics and so on. It also provides a sense of identity, community feeling, belonging, and understanding. Material and non-material cultures are significant as both tell us our journey from where it started and where it is now.

The culture of India is a matter of sub-cultures and traditions spread all over the Indian continent. Several elements of diverse Indian culture are Indian religions, yoga, Ayurveda, Literature, Languages, Cuisine, etc. Indian culture is one of the most ancient cultures, having unity in diversity. With more than 10 percent of people in India follow different religions, traditions, and customs. It gives birth to thousands of beliefs and sets of values. It is a nation that celebrates more than 50 festivals a year. India has a diversified culture, which contributes to its unity.

Diversified culture of India

Indian culture is an old culture in the world. It is a diverse culture in itself. India is a country where we have the presence of various religions. All these religions have their own belief system, tradition, and life style. But all these diverse factors contribute to the formation of a unique culture of India. All communities in India live in harmony while preserving their own distinct feature. The country has historical monuments which are the matters of pride of India.

Diversity in Architecture

India as a country and its architecture is highly diversified. It spans from ancient caves and monuments to modern sky scrapers. In the course of time, Indian architecture has risen with its application and mixture with new trends. In India, Dravidian style is famous. Dravidian style originated in south India whereas Nagra style was originated in north India.

Clothing and Food

India has a permanent name in the world because of its beautiful clothing. India has its own attire, like a dhoti-kurta, and every state has its own speciality. The sari is a favourite choice of Indian women. Another favourite choice among Indian women is the salwar kurta. In the case of food habits, Indians are fond of a variety of foods. North Indian, South Indian, and North-East Indian food is famous across the country. It is also known as Indian cuisine. This diversity is found in different regions that have diverse eating habits.

Religion

By the 42nd Constitutional Amendment of 1976, India is called a secular country. Hinduism, Jainism, Buddhism, Sikhism, etc., are significant religions in India. Indian religion has influenced and shaped the Indian culture. This amendment has ensured the people of India that the state will never have a religion of its own. All religions are equal to the state.

Indian Customs and Traditions

India has different traditions and customs. In south and north India, the festivals, art forms, dressing and even the way of wearing cloths is different in different communities and states.

Language

In India, it is said that language is changing at every 12 kilometres. Although, Hindi is the official language of the country and it is commonly spoken all over the country, yet many regional languages exist along with it. Each state of India has its own language but, in some states, more than 3 languages are used by the citizens.

Joint Family System

Family is an integral part of Indian society. Joint families with one member as the head of the family are generally found in all parts of the country. In India, arranged marriages are preferred and prevalent mostly. Whereas love marriages are looked down upon, and people prefer to marry among their own relatives and people of their respective castes.

Art

In Indian culture art forms have a distinct place. Each state is blessed with its unique art form which differs from others; Mohininatyan, Katthak, Ghoomer are some of the examples.

Festivals

The festivals of India are so worthful. Each state has its own festival. Oonam is the festival of Karla, which is characterised by, making of the social carpet to the pohela boishakh. Diwali and Eid celebrated all over the country. The festivals are both colourful and equally create social harmony.

Indian Music

Music plays a significant role in human life. Carnatic music, Hindustani music, Kirana music are most popular music forms in India. These are usually accompanied by the tune of the traditional musical instruments such as the tabla and veena. Indian music is quite soothing and pleasing to the ears compared to European music.

Literature

Literature is the wealth of any nation. India has been blessed with many classical writers and poets who reckoned India's name to the world. Rabindranath Tagore, Sarojini Naidu, and Toru Dutta made poetry their means of expression. Arbindo Ghose R K Narayan are prominent writers of India.

Celebrations

Numerous festivals and celebrations are in the Indian calendar. These festivals have grandeur and environment friendly. The country is home to many heritage sites and monuments like Ajanta and Ellora, Hampi, Meenakshi Temple, Ramappa Temple, Warangal Temple, etc. All these facts combined together make Indian culture unique and magnificent.

The Indian education system is the most well known system in the world. In ancient times, there were many universities like Vallabhi, Takshashila, Nalanda, etc. Those abodes of knowledge focused on the development of the pupils all around. In ancient times, i.e., the Vedic and Buddhist periods, education was provided in ashrams, temples, and forests. It is designed to nourish self-discipline, value education, and inner development, and these Gurukuls made pupils ready to face the challenges of the future. In the ancient period, the curriculum was dynamic. It consisted of Vedas, Upanishads, and Darshan Puranas, as well as Algebra, Geometry, yoga, Grammar, Aurveda and so on. It also focused on subjects like Economics, Military, Politics and Religion. The advantages of the ancient education system are:

- Focus on the all-round development
- Emphasis on practical education
- Acquisition of knowledge
- Classrooms provided a pleasant atmosphere
- No interference with the curriculum

Education and culture are interrelated. Culture guides the educational system. Culture plays an important role in shaping ideals, values, and ways of life in society. The cultural situation in society determines how education is to be given. In ancient times, when education was teacher-oriented, students were forced to impart knowledge. Now, it is asked to complete various tasks by giving importance to the child's interests, mental abilities, possibilities, needs, etc. School is a microcosm of society. So, it is natural that society's culture influences the school. Indian culture so far has given -

Secularism

By introducing a secular culture in schools, students can learn about the importance of heritage, people, and community. It raises awareness about citizenship and responsibility. Culture should be the core content of education, and it is the responsibility of the school administration to pass on the same to the new generations.

Tools of communication

Culture provides language codes for communication used for spoken and written purposes in the country. Language plays an important role in socialisation. Education offers students the opportunity to select their language and have a deeper understanding of their culture.

Stories

Stories of customs and traditions play an important role in culturing education. Indian stories are entertaining people for a long time. It also enables learners to learn about the values that can guide them in their future life. It prepares younger generations to face the challenges of life.

Indian History, Literature and Art

Indian history, literature, and art are important parts of Indian culture. It allows students to learn about India's rich cultural heritage and its contributions to the world. It helps students to understand what the world is like today. A well-planned curriculum must reflect the culture of the people for which it is planned for it to be a functional curriculum.

Indian Languages

Indian Languages are an important aspect of the country's cultural heritage and are included in the curriculum to promote linguistic diversity and cultural understanding. It plays a crucial role in preserving the rich cultural heritage and diverse identities of various regions. It also enables effective communication.

Ayurveda and Yoga

Ayurveda and Yoga are ancient gifts that India has in legacy. Ayurveda and Yoga both help to develop physically and mentally. Yoga helps in movement, breathing and meditation and Ayurveda is an herbal and environmental remedy for various diseases.

Philosophy and Religion

Philosophy and religion are ideal of spiritualism and humanism in India. The study of philosophy enhances a person's problem-solving capacities. It helps the individual to analyse concepts, definitions, arguments, and problems. Religious awareness of any country can contribute to the feeling of nationalism. So, curriculum has religious content as well.

- Culture also emphasises Indian values and cultural diversity. It is designed in such a way that all cultures should be respected.
- Culture guides individual patterns.
- Culture helps in the preparation of curriculum and text.
- It helps an individual to reflect on himself or herself.
- It helps in the adaptation or modification of existing culture
- It helps in creating a modern learning environment.

The presence of Indian culture is important in education because it is based on the ideals of truthfulness, connectivity, and humanity. It imparts a sense of awareness that helps to co-exist in society. Teaching children our culture means connecting them to our roots and nourishing them as responsible citizens.

References

Altekar, A.S. (1965) *Education in Ancient India*. Nand Kishore and Brothers, Varanasi.

Amala, P. Annie., P. Annapurna and D. Bhaskara Rao. (2004). *History of Education*. D.P.H. Publishing House, New Delhi.

Apte, D.G. (1961). *Our Educational Heritage*. Acharya Book Depot, Baroda.

Gardner, H. (1983). *Frames of Mind. The Theory of Multiple Intelligences*. New York: Basic Books.

Harp, B. and Brewer, J. (1996). *Reading and Writing: Teaching for the connections.* Harcourt Brace, Fort Worth, TX.

Mitra, V. (1964). *Education in Ancient India.* Arya Book Depot, New Delhi.

Mukerji, R.K. (1947). *Education in Ancient India.* Prentice-Hall Publishers, London.

Rai, B.C. (1966). *History of Indian Education.* Prakashan Kendra, Lucknow.

The concise Oxford Dictionary (1981). Oxford University Press, Delhi.

Prasad, Deepesh Chandra, (2007). *Philosophical Foundation of Education*, KSK Publishers, New Delhi.

Rawat, P.L. (1963). *History of Indian Education* (3rd Ed.). Ram Prasad and Sons, Agra.

Shah, A.B. and Rao, C.R.M. (Eds) (1965). *Tradition and Modernity in India*, Manaktalas, Bombay.

Chapter 20

Indian Education System: A Historical Perspective

J. G. More,
Assistant Professor, Department of English,
Kai. Bapusaheb Patil Ekambekar Mahavidyalaya, Udgir, Maharashtra.

There is a lot of cultural and legendary history in India, and the school system shows that it has strong roots in old traditions and philosophies and has changed a lot over thousands of years, shaping the intellectual, social, and moral fabric of Indian society. This system includes many ways of teaching, from the old Gurukul system to official schools and colleges today.

Understanding how the Indian education system has changed over time is important for figuring out all its subtleties and difficulties. By following its history from ancient times to the present day, including the Colonial Era, we can see the forces and factors that have shaped its path. Understanding this evolution helps us see how educational ideas, teaching methods, and social goals are both stable and changing over a period of time. The aim of this study is to examine the multi-faceted Indian education system, which encompasses its historical heritage, cultural context, and contemporary issues. By considering India's history, the study expects to appreciate how schooling functions at present and identify ways to make it better in the future.

Indian Education System from the time of the Vedas to the sixth century AD

India's education system during the Vedic period from 1500 BCE to 600 BCE had a strong societal basis and mirrored the values and objectives of that time. This was primarily achieved through talking with each other, and much knowledge was passed from one generation to another by an oral tradition, which included literature recitation. The Vedas, which are holy books, were the main source of education. They covered many topics, like philosophy, religion, rituals, grammar, and astronomy.

The Gurukul system, which was a personal and all-around way of learning that took place in the home of a Guru (teacher), was at the centre of education in ancient India. Gurukuls were usually built in remote places or hermitages in the woods, where it was quiet and good for learning. Gurukuls were structured in a way that was both casual and strict. Students lived with their teachers and learned by interacting with and watching them closely. The syllabus contained not only intellectual subjects but also moral character building, life skills, and physical fitness, among other things.

Gurus or teachers were very important in the Gurukul system and were looked up to. In addition to being teachers, they acted as religious leaders and mentors who moulded their students' characters and views about life. The methods used by teachers in training students included individual lessons, class discussions, debates, and practical activities for the students. This enabled teachers and students to establish strong bonds of confidence among themselves. Students, called shishyas, were involved in their own learning and showed their teacher respect by being humble, obedient, and devoted to them. As a result of doing things like helping with housework, gathering firewood, and serving their Guru, they learned the ideals of humility, service, and discipline.

6th century AD to the 12th century AD

During the classical time in India, which lasted from the 6th century AD to the 12th century AD, formal educational institutions like universities and monastic centres were built, which led to big improvements in education. These places were learning hubs that drew students and experts from all over the world. In this period, universities like Nalanda, Takshashila, and Vikramshila did very well. These were the centres of learning that taught a whole range of subjects like philosophy, mathematics, science, medicine, and languages. Monasteries like those in Buddhist and Jain traditions were crucial for the transmission of knowledge and the promotion of intellectualism.

This period saw important scholars who made their contributions to various fields of education that remain to date. Some important people in Indian history included Aryabhata, Varahamihira and Brahmagupta. Mathematics and science took science a leap forward in their development when Charaka and Sushruta became the first Ayurveda practitioners and surgeons. Sanatan Dharma philosophy was given impetus by Shankaracharya and Ramanuja, followed by Kalidasa and others who praised literature and arts. These were not only advanced thinkers, but they also nurtured the present generation's yearning for knowledge.

These schools covered a wide range of subjects from different directions each with its own way of teaching. Some subjects were taught through talks and conversations, while others were taught through experiments and real-time use. A culture of intellectual curiosity and new ideas grew because of the focus on debate, critical thinking, and independent research.

During this time, kings and families who supported education were very important to the growth of schools and the progress and development of learning. Kings like Chandragupta Maurya, Ashoka, and Harshavardhana were known for helping students and universities by providing funds and other resources for the smooth conduct of educational activities. Their support not only helped education grow but also raised the status of intellectuals in society.

The Middle Ages (12th century AD to 18th century AD)

When India was under Islamic dominion (12th to 18th centuries AD), its education system underwent transformations due to Persian culture as well as Islamic rule. During the time of Islamic rule, different educational practices came together, which is known as syncretism. Persian culture had an impact on the growth of literature, art, and building, which made the intellectual landscape of the sub-continent better.

One of the most important things that happened during this time was the growth of Islamic schools like Madrasas and Maktab. In the beginning, madrasas were places where people could learn, mostly about Islamic law, religion, and the Arabic language. Maktab, on the other hand, was like grade school, where kids learned basic reading, writing, and math skills along with religion. The Madrasas and Maktab system made it possible for Islamic education to spread across the Indian sub-continent. It also nurtured a new generation of scholars and intellectuals who were strongly rooted in Islamic principles.

Even though Islamic education was becoming more popular, there was still a lot of movement and contact between different types of education. This mixing of ideas led to the weaving together of Persian, Arabic, and Indian ways of knowing, creating a rich weave of learning that went beyond religious and cultural lines. Scholars from different fields had conversations, translated texts, and shared their thoughts, which made it intellectually lively and productive.

Traditional Indian education systems also got worse at the same time as these changes, especially after political and social unrest.

A smaller number of people went to traditional schools, which hurt scholarship and the protection of indigenous knowledge.

Time of the Colonies (18th century AD to 1947)

Indian education went through a lot of changes when the British ruled from the 18th century AD to 1947, which was known as the Colonial Era. As part of its colonial plan, the British East India Company brought western Education to India. Its goal was to train a class of Indians who could help the government and look out for British interests. Because of this, English-medium schools and colleges sprung up all over the country, and these were used to spread western ideas and knowledge.

Thomas Babington Macaulay's Minutes of 1835, which called for the Englishification of Indian schooling, was a major event at that time. Macaulay said that the English language and writings were better than the native languages and cultures. He also said that education should focus on teaching English to make a group of 'Anglicised Indians' who would be loyal to British rule. As a result of this strategy, indigenous languages, literature, and knowledge systems were pushed to the edges, which made Indians feel culturally inferior.

But, there were people who did not agree with the colonial schooling system. There were reform movements and resistance led by Indian nationalists, social reformers, and scholars who wanted to protect and support native education. Some of their activities were establishing schools at the village level, reviving traditional Gurukul systems, and advocating for an Indianized education system that incorporated local languages, cultures, and wisdom in teaching. Others who led the movement against western learning included Raja Ram Mohan Roy, Ishwar Chandra Vidyasagar, and Swami Vivekananda.

All these efforts however could not change India's colonial education system until its independence in 1947. But its legacy changed the way

Indians thought about schooling, language, and their own identity for a long time.

The period after independence (1947 and later)

Various changes would be realised in the educational sector after India had gained its independence. These resulted from several policies and reforms aimed at modernising education to make it more accessible. Several other initiatives have been launched by different governments targeting educational improvement since the Sargent Plan (1944), which led to the formation of the University Grant Commission (UGC) in 1956. It was emphasised in the Sargent Plan that schools should be made bigger and that science and technology should be emphasised. This set the stage for later changes.

One of the most important things that happened during this time was the growth of formal education, which was caused by efforts to make it easier for everyone to get an education and support fairness. Building a huge network of schools, colleges and universities across the country has made it much easier for people to register, especially in rural and underserved areas. But despite these efforts, problems with the quality of education still exist. Concerns have been made about old curricula, bad infrastructure, and a lack of teachers.

Since independence, there have been ongoing discussions and criticisms of different aspects of the school system. There are still a lot of problems with inequality, both in terms of access and results. These problems are caused by deep-seated socio-economic differences. Making education more like a business has also become a controversial topic, since many private schools make money ahead of quality.

Even with these problems, there have been important attempts to look into different educational models and ways of teaching. A wide range of students has been met by trying new ways of teaching, such as Montessori, hands-on learning, and digital tools, which have encouraged them to think critically. There is a growing number of people who are changing their mindset on education to a more holistic and learner-centred approach, innovation, problem-solving and lifelong learning. As India moves forward with its plans to change its schools, looking into and using these new models could help it meet the needs of a society that is changing quickly.

The Modern Indian School System

Presently, there are various types of educational institutions in India, such as schools, colleges, universities, and professional training centres. All these contribute significantly towards the building up of human capital in the country. However, the system continues to face problems that are caused by differences in social and economic status. Poverty, caste, gender, and the gap between urban and country areas all make it harder for some people to get a good education, which keeps inequality going. Even though people are trying to be more open and accepting, it is still difficult for people from marginalised groups to get quality education. In addition, the digital revolution has led to a move towards learning settings that are based on technology. More and more people think that digitalisation and using technology in schools are important ways to improve access, speed, and quality of learning. The digital divide is still a problem, though, especially in poor and remote places. Indian education has also become more internationalised because of globalisation, with more foreign colleges, partnerships, and exchange programmes. This can help people from different cultures learn from each other and share their knowledge, but it also brings up questions about how to protect traditional educational values and keep local issues relevant in the face of global impacts.

Conclusion

In conclusion, this journey has shed light on many aspects of the Indian education system, from its early days to how it has changed in recent years. Recapitulating the most important results makes it clear that even though the system has changed a lot over the years, some basic ideas have remained the same. When you think about the changes that have happened and the ones that have not happened in the Indian education system, you can see how well it has handled changes in society and politics and also see where it could be better. Looking ahead, the effects on future studies and directions show how important it is to promote fair, inclusive, and new ways of teaching. In this age of globalisation and change, it is also important to remember how important it is to protect and value India's rich educational history. India can continue to move towards excellence and the well-being of its people by embracing diversity, promoting indigenous knowledge systems, and pushing a whole-person approach to education.

References

Suresh Chandra Ghosh, "History of Education in India under the Rule of the East India Company," Oxford University Press, London, 1920.

Dharampal, "The Beautiful Tree: Indigenous Indian Education in the Eighteenth Century," Other India Press, Goa, 2000.

A.L. Basham, "The Wonder That Was India: A Survey of the Culture of the Indian Sub-Continent Before the Coming of the Muslims," Grove Press, New York, 1954.

B.R. Ambedkar, "Thoughts on Linguistic States," Government of Maharashtra, Mumbai, 1955.

Nalini Thakur, "Educational Thoughts and Ideals of Mahatma Gandhi," Concept Publishing Company, New Delhi, 1986.

R.S. Sharma, "Material Culture and Social Formations in Ancient India," Macmillan, New Delhi, 1983.

Yogendra Singh, "Modernisation of Indian Tradition: A Systemic Study of Social Change," Thomson Press, New Delhi, 1973.

K.N. Panikkar, "Culture and Consciousness in Modern India," Oxford University Press, New Delhi, 2011.

Krishna Kumar, "Political Agenda of Education: A Study of Colonialist and Nationalist Ideas," Sage Publications, New Delhi, 2005.

Ram Nath Sharma and Rajendra K. Sharma, "History of Education in India," Atlantic Publishers & Distributors, New Delhi, 2003.

Chapter 21

Implications of Indian Knowledge System

Shinde Prashant R.,
Associate Professor and Head,
Department of English, Shivneri Mahavidyalaya, Shirur Anantpal,
Maharashtra.

Theoretical and comprehensive Indian Knowledge System (IKS) is for effective and ethical communication, as well as the ancient wisdom of India. Keep in mind that it tries to respect Indian culture in the best way possible. This is done by invoking Natyashastra in daily communication. Natyashastra, commonly known as the fifth Veda, is a treatment of Indian arts. This proves the infinite importance and great value of ancient Indian knowledge. This article aims to make the country stronger by setting an example and also encouraging people to embrace and apply true knowledge to revitalise India. The knowledge is created around the impact of non-verbal communication, communication on the subconscious and how India has lost its originality as a result. This condition can also be reversed in IKS. Skills like hypnotising our wrong or destructive ideas (knowing the 7 principles according to Ayurveda and Yoga) should be taught to all generations for the benefit of all as independent people and strong countries.

Indian Knowledge System (IKS)

According to the official website of IKS https://iksindia.org, the Indian Information System (IKS) is an innovation centre under the Ministry of Education (MOE) located at AICTE, New Delhi. It was created to promote social research on all aspects of IKS and to preserve and publish IKS for further research and social applications. This education system in India is highly suitable to our cultural values. It has enough potential to compete with contemporary technical and global information systems. Essentially, it represents a clash between Westernisation and the conservation of indigenous cultures. Depending on the research framework, the argument favouring the preservation of indigenous culture or ICS is that the traits of a nation or an individual are closely linked to the cultural and social norms of that society, just like the unity among a community fosters a strong national identity in times of adversity.

Also, Indian values and traditional knowledge have a clear meaning regarding human beings - there will be a purpose or meaning of life through the concept called "Purushartha." Although there are other theories in the Four Vedas with a clear understanding of the good way of life, there is still a gap between knowledge and people. Art serves as a platform for exchanging creativity. It is a captivating and innovative way of acquiring knowledge that is accessible to all.

Thus, Natyashastra, popularly known as the fifth Veda, was born with the aim of dividing knowledge through ethics and reverence for the statue of Purushartha.

Natyashastra

The Natyashastra consists of 2 Sanskrit words: "Natya," meaning "action or representation;" and Shastra, meaning treatise or book of the law. It is an initiative that encourages all members of society to achieve Dharma (morality), artha (food prosperity) and kama (happiness) through arts. It is like a book about what is in the Vedas.

Performance

Since Natyashastra is a healing form of Indian art, drama is a unique medium of transferring knowledge and information throughout.

Types of Drama

Abhinaya (Natyshastra's term for drama) is the art of presenting a story through gestures, facial expressions, body movements and thoughts. It leads to personal change by following the principle of consciousness and how it relates to learning (integration of knowledge and identity). All aspects of Abhinayas are as follows:

1. Angika Abhinaya (Emotions of Body and Limbs)
2. Vachika abhinaya {Song and Speech}
3. Satvika abhinaya {Moods and Emotions}

For more information, the styles of these performances include Graceful, Lively, Flashy and Oral.

Philosophy or Laws of Natyashastra

Natyashastra covers many philosophies and laws that form the basis of the best art to be considered. These laws or principles emphasise the importance of orderliness, beauty, and adherence to tradition. There are 2 main concepts: "Rasa" and "Bhava," which are important to understand and experience the beauty and emotion of the performance. Art.

Rasa refers to the content or flavour of a performance that evokes a feeling or excitement in the audience (Bharata Muni, 2008). The Natyashastra describes 9 major Rasas namely joy (happiness), sadness, anger, fear, hatred, courage, miracles, peace, love and affection and teaches them through various arts such as music and dance, gestures, facial expressions, and speech.

Bhava refers to the emotional state of the actor (Bharata Muni, 2008). The definition of 'Bhavas' in theatre is to evoke emotions and feelings by creating a deep bond between the actor and the audience. Natyashastra also provides detailed instructions on all aspects of performing arts, including drama, music, dance, make up, clothing, and storytelling (Bharata Muni, 2008).

Aims and Limitations of the Study Purpose:

To develop an effective theoretical model of communication and ethics based on the principles of Natyashastra, aiming at the expansion of the Indian Knowledge System (IKS) and preservation of knowledge of Indian culture, promoting personal development, developing, and promoting the nation, Especially exploring the impact of non-verbal communication on the mind in the context of advertising remember to understand the impact of social media on personal perception and behaviour highlights. The potential loss of information authenticity and identity that India faces in the digital age. Explore the ideas and techniques provided by Natyashastra and other disciplines, such as Ayurveda and Yoga, to help people release false or hypnotic mental states.

Limitations

The model proposed in this research paper/article is theoretical in nature, and more research and practical applications are needed to evaluate its effectiveness.

The scope of this study mainly focuses on the use of "Natyashastra" in communication and the impact of media on the subconscious mind, leaving room for future research to include other Indian studies of Information System (IKS) and its wider implications.

The validity of the model depends indirectly on the user, just like the Natyashastra model is based on Sanathan (eternal) or personal morality and has only the ideal (since the goal of nation-building is an ideal).

Application

Impact of Media on the Subconscious

In this interconnected world, media plays an important role in shaping public opinion, thinking, influencing thoughts and influencing one's subconscious. It is important to remember that advertising (commercial, educational or entertainment) affects all positive emotions. This chapter explores the profound effects of various forms of media on people's thoughts, beliefs, and behaviours. It examines how certain images, descriptions, and words, especially subconscious cues and cues, influence images and subconscious mind patterns, influencing behaviour, values, and decision-making.

Performance Ethics and Sanathan Ethics

Performance ethics refers to the moral standards and standards that guide the conduct and behaviour of performers in performance, drama, and entertainment.

These ethical values include:

- Performers have a responsibility to maintain integrity, truth, and cultural awareness.
- Cultural appropriation, stereotypes, and the effects of theatre acting on marginalised communities must be known and recognised:
- Performers have a responsibility to promote inclusion Responsibility. Expressing sex, honesty, and justice through art.

With more knowledge, you get more power and feel more responsible. Therefore, the wisdom and knowledge that IkS gives us require us to keep some responsibilities in mind when communicating. Some of these specific strategies may include:

- Performance management (advertising or otherwise)
- Making the audience know the goal

What has the greatest impact can be when a good mood and strong character are present and related to.

So, here are some Sanathan practices to remember:

Dharma:

Refers to one's duty, honesty and morality in various roles and relationships. It is considered a way of behaving ethically and is considered essential for maintaining harmony and balance in personal and social life.

Ahimsa:

Ahimsa, or non-violence, is the moral foundation of Sanathan Dharma. It encourages people not to harm or harm any living being. It also includes refraining from causing harm through thought, word, and action.

Satya:

Satya or honesty refers to the importance of honesty, truthfulness and telling the truth. It is considered a virtue that promotes trust, harmony and truth in relationships and relationships.

Karma:

Karma is also known as the law of cause and effect. This means that every action has consequences, and people are responsible for their moral behaviour.

Compassion and charity:

Many of these involve compassion, kindness, and caring for others irrespective of their background, caste, or creed. It encourages people to see the divinity in all living things and to approach them with respect and compassion.

Personal Education and Self-Control:

Join the fight against desires, thoughts and emotions that may be harmful or unjust. Self-discipline is seen as a means of attaining inner peace, enlightenment, and morality. Respect for nature and the environment: explains the relationship between all forms of life and the need for environmental management, suggests ways to improve the environment, practices freezing while respecting sustainable living, and minimising damage to nature.

Decide for yourself how to use IKS media.

- IKS has much ancient wisdom, including meditation principles, leadership actions and behaviours as mentioned above

- People provide insight into their thoughts, behaviours, and reality. By integrating IKS principles with media literacy and critical thinking, individuals can develop knowledge and insight to analyse and respond to media strategies. This chapter focuses on the further development of personal abilities through Satya.

Yoga

Yoga is an ancient practice that combines physical posture, breathing control, meditation, and ethics to ensure harmony with one's body, mind and soul and provides the development of personal awareness, insight power and promotion challenge manipulation. People can use yoga practice to improve mental health, emotional balance, and meditation skills. Through regular practice, people can improve their concentration and focus, allowing them to look at things more objectively and impartially.

Seventh Sense: Hypnotism

In Ayurveda and Indian philosophy, the concept of "seventh sense" refers to a state of increased consciousness over the 5 senses. This concept can be understood in the context of social media management as a developmental theory aimed at revealing negative information about persuasion and control in media content. By developing these perspectives, people can become more sensitive to the manipulation of emotions, sensationalism, and misinformation that can appear in media narratives.

Colour Conveys Ayurveda and Psychology

Ayurveda is an ancient Indian medical system that recognises the colour of the human body whose health is good. We can find clues of this in Aharya Abhinaya, where clothing and appearance are taken into consideration. This is how many platforms use or misuse the colour or "apparent" thought and content of different Abhinayas to make information false. ***Ayurveda and Yoga***

Abhinayas are directly related to one's overall health, and their benefits are also seen in western science. The principles of colour communication and psychology and their application to understanding media aesthetics and colour perception in visual advertising explore how the choice of colour in content media evokes specific emotions, influences thoughts, and controls the subconscious.

Benefits of IKS

Indian Knowledge System (IKS) principles such as *Natyashastra* can be used in daily communication, education and Natyashastra's own social media. IKS can promote effective communication and ethics, promote leadership, and encourage individuals to resist control and maintain a sense of self. Additional benefits include strengthening public relations, promoting cultural diversity and integration, developing emotional intelligence, and preserving India's rich heritage and cultural wisdom.

Conclusion

This study shows the impact of verbal and non-verbal communication on the mind and the reason for the loss of originality in Indian culture due to external factors. However, this study shows that through the use of IKS, particularly through practices such as hypnosis, Ayurveda, yoga, and colour communication, people can regain their identity or reality.

The research paper also highlights the benefits of IKS in enabling people to get rid of social media and create a healthier, smarter nation. By incorporating IKS principles such as the development of the 7 senses and the psychological understanding of colour according to Ayurveda, yoga enables individuals to develop their emotions, thoughts and views while watching media content to do. We must make informed decisions and actively contribute to a fair and balanced media.

In Context or Rasa, this article is intended as a call to action to embrace IKS in character and nation. Finally, this article contributes to the ongoing debate around the preservation and promotion of Indian culture and explores once again the difference between living in Natyashastra and the power of ancient wisdom to create a future for our country.

References

Bharata, Muni. (2008). Nadia Chastra. (M. Ghosh, trans.). New Delhi: Munshiram Manoharlal Publishers.

Bandura, A. (2001). Social cognitive theory: An organisational perspective. Annual Review of Depression, 52 (1), 1-26.3.

Cialdini, R. B. (2007). Impact: The Psychology of Persuasion. Harper Business Journal.

Pavis, P. (2016). Routledge Guide to Arts and Culture. Routledge.

Nussbaum, M.C. (1997). Cultivating Humanity: A classic defence of educational change. Harvard University Press.

Iyengar, B.K.S. (2014). The Light of Yoga: The Gospel of Yoga Today. Harper Collins. Desikachar, T.K.V. (1995). Heart Yoga: Cultivating the Self.

Chapter 22

Relevance of the Gurukul System in the 21st Century

Rajeshwar Werulkar,
Senior Faculty, Podar International, Nanded, Maharashtra.

Actually, all educational systems are classified on 2 basic levels at all times and everywhere: informal education and formal education. Basically, an informal education begins at the family level, and it forms a stereotype of an individual's mental and psychological state of conduct. A person thinks, speaks, acts, and reacts according to his/her lineage and parental context. A person informally gets basic values and a code of conduct initially in his family, by which his inner self is developed automatically. On the other hand, Formal education has its fixed curriculum organised and implemented by an organisation or an institution. Here, a person has to learn according to the norms and conditions of the institution. Both formal and informal education systems are fundamental resources for the development of an individual.

If we look back at the Vedic period and its educational system in India, we find the references '*Gurukul System' and 'Guru Ashramas'* to provide contemporary basic education to only the interested pupils and people who belong to the particular dynasties or the Royal families. Here, one point is to be noted: both the informal and formal education was given to them in one place, Gurukul or the houses of their Gurus. Among them, the members of the Royal family used to go to the particular Gurukul or ashrams where they would get the necessary education in Vedas, Puranas, Upanishads, Dharma sutras and Dhanur vidya (archery).

As we know, Lord Shri Ram and Laxman went to Guru Vasistha, Lord Shri Krisha and his brother Lord Balaram went to Guru Sandipani, and Pandavas and Kauravas went to Guru Dron Acharya. It was so because the Royal family got the 'Royal education' to run their Royal states and kingdoms. This means that in the Vedic period, the Gurukul systems were available for the Royal family people according to their status and state, and they got multiple types of education under one roof at a specific age and time. It was the whole and sole responsibility of a *Guru* to make his *shishya,* a disciple, perfect one in every branch of knowledge. The disciples were admitted to the Gurukuls at the ages between 8 and 12 years only. Here, they used to get spiritual, intellectual, moral, physical, and value-based education, even though there was no prescribed subject like value education. Students were taught to maintain the balance between the self and nature because nature is considered a God or Goddess. It means the Environment Science.

Gurus and their shishyas used to work together in Gurukuls, which were situated in the forests and remote serine places. Even the parents were not allowed to visit the places or meet their children before the completion of the specific duration of time. Here, under the observation and guidance of the Guru, the pupils grow by learning basic values of life, which would help them to live a better life further. As referred to above, the informal education in the family in his early childhood. Sets up the basic thinking of a person; here, one of the Kauravas, Duryodhana, could not accept the moral value education in Gurukul, and his wicked self was not being controlled by Gurus and the Gurukul values even though Kauravas and Pandavas learned together in the same atmosphere at Gutu Drona's Ashram. It means that even if Gurus were trying their best to give their best, somewhere and somehow it is, the 'family background' or 'surrounding' also plays an important role in the development of a personality. This means that in the Vedic period, the triangle of education would also be completed from these 3 angles: first students, second family or parents, and third Gurukuls and Gurus.

So, Gurukuls, which were known as ashrams, later in the ancient period, were transformed into another form, such as Viharas or universities. During the period, the kings and the society tried their best to promote education and educational institutions. So, during this period, many famous educational centres and universities came into existence in Takshashila, Vikramshila, Odantpuri, Nalanda, Valbhai, and many others. In these institutions, higher level education was provided. Panini and Arya Chanakya were some of the outstanding students of Takshashila University.

Kings and contemporary rulers used to invite these scholars to deliver speeches on different occasions. Here, they discuss and debate different subjects like spiritualities, ethics, politics, mathematics, medicine, astronomy, arts, yoga, and even grammar. All the journey of those scholars was full of morality and spirituality. So, they were at the places of Gurus and good guides. They stood as an ideal person where the people used to take inspiration from their lives. Their words and actions had great prestige and weight and also had a great impact on the minds of the people. So, the kings and the emperors used to take their help in judgemental issues and even state affairs. Ethical and unethical, moral, and immoral concepts were deeply rooted among the Indian masses during this period. So, society was safe and secure under the flags of righteousness and rulers who were so-called representatives of God.

The Indian Education System during the medieval period turned towards the Madrasas or Mastabas. Here, pupils also used to go to madrasas and learn different languages like Arabi, Farsi, and Urdu. This medieval period in Indian history was covered by the Mughal emperors, and the scope was also given to art, languages, and warfare.

The colonial period of Indian history actually involved formal education. Previously, the informal education system concentrated on moral and spiritual values. It was holistic education, and exchanging and obtaining knowledge was the holy and sacred task. On the other hand, during British rule, education became formal, and it concentrated on the modernisation of education, which was attached to administrative roles and compelled to learn the English language, British literature, western sciences, and public administration. They opened missionary schools and colleges to teach the above-mentioned subjects. Here, Indian cultural and traditional values were less weighted. Under the name of modernisation and modification of the Indian educational system, Britishers tried to root out the Indian values and traditional and conventional foundation of the Indian Educational system.

Ultimately, they also became successful when they stopped the Gurukul systems of India and started missionary schools and colleges there. Indian people are also greatly attracted to these new forms of formal education where they can learn foreign languages, especially English, and can speak and write English in so-called dialects, such as Sahib or Saheb (Sir). No doubt, the Modern British Education System opened various new branches of learning and broadened the scope of thinking of Indian people, but today, the time has come again to teach the Value of Education Subjects in the school curriculum. In ancient times, education was only for learning, adopting, and implementing values in the Gurukuls and later in real life. It may not be an exaggeration to say that Gurukuls stood for the values only.

Today, in the 21st century, the question arises about the relevance of the Gurukul Education System all over the world. First of all, a simple question to be answered is whether there is a need for such an educational system, especially in India. Absolutely, the answer is positive. Yes, it's a need of the time and situation that the gurukul system to be adopted in India. As we roam the global world and call it the process of globalisation, the whole world appears so close that it becomes just like a small 'village.' Here in the modern time, the young generation has become hungrier about the new branches of knowledge. They are ready to move anywhere and everywhere to fulfil their ambition or dream. They want to prove themselves in every aspect of life, but they cannot because they lack a proper platform to prove themselves at the proper time and proper place. So, it can be available in the form of Gurukuls.

Today's Indian youth is going to be so baffled and confused that he can't get opportunities to prove himself/herself anywhere. If such students get the proper platform in the form of Gurukul, their future will be bright in India only. They need the proper guidance to tread the specific path that will lead them to the proper destination. It will be provided by the Gurukul educational system. It doesn't mean that today's schools, colleges, and universities are not providing the right education, but an interrogation is about its output, its outcome, and its ultimate results of making a person or an individual a successful or perfect one in all aspects of life.

In the Gurukul system, students have to follow the given peculiar format of life, where the first difficult word, discipline, is taught very seriously. Today, discipline is quite far from students, so they immediately go away from their aims. Forbearance, endurance, honesty, hard work, respect, optimism, and hopefulness, such essential principles of life, are going away from students who were taught by actions and evidence in Gurukuls. If the Gurukul systems provide such concrete morals, these systems are essential even today.

Today, in the modern education system, students are searching for institutions where they can live and study together. They are ready to leave their homes and ready to join such hostels or campuses of any university or institution where they can obtain an education under the one roof. They are not only interested to learn languages and social science but also to learn the modern natural sciences and technology. According to the need and demand of the time modern gurukuls are being established in our country.

So, in the modern education system, the modern gurukuls are uprising everywhere in our country in the form of well-reputed university campuses or hostels, where many students join with trust and confidence. In Kota (Rajasthan), Hyderabad, Chennai, and Vellore, such newly formed Gurukuls, i.e., residential schools, colleges, and universities, have been opened. Allen Career Institute Kota has more than 1.25 lakh strength, SRM Chanai has more than 52000 students taking education., VIT, Vellore has more than 8000 students in a year, Shri Chaitanya Hyderabad has 700 plus branches in the state and more than 6 lakh students, Narayana Institutions has more than 800 branches, 6.5 lakh students are taking education, Loyola Academy Chennai has 10381 students, Lovely University. Punjab has more than 32000 students. These are some of the nominal examples of modern gurukuls. These institutions provide hostel facilities and digital classrooms and take responsibility for the overall development of students. Along with accommodation, they have gyms, yoga, and fitness centres, which provide essential food and take care of their health. These educational hubs are the modern gurukuls of modern times.

Only the most important thing to be considered about these institutions is that these institutions are teaching the modern sciences like Physics, Chemistry, Biology, and information technology, and student's interest is completely shifted towards the Engineering and Medical Sciences, but while doing this, they should not avoid and forget the humanistic approach. By persuading formal education, they should not be so formal about the values and the life skills. They should not forget that they are human first and later, whatsoever they become or want to become. This means that by learning these technical sciences and technologies, they should not be like machines or only mechanical figures. They should know the difference between a man and a machine. As these modern gurukuls are providing holistic and multidisciplinary education, they should not overlook the basic aims of ethics and value education like stimulating ethical reflection, awareness, autonomy, responsibility, and compassion in children, to provide children with insight into important ethical principles and values, equip them with intellectual capacities and critical thinking.

In NEP 2020 Part II entitled 'Higher Education' section 9 Quality Universities and Colleges: A New and Forward-looking Vision for India's Higher Education System, it is stated that "Higher education plays an extremely important role in promoting human as well as societal well-being and in developing India as envisioned in its Constitution - a democratic, just, socially conscious, cultured, and humane nation upholding liberty, equality, fraternity, and justice for all. Higher education significantly contributes towards sustainable livelihoods and economic development of the nation. As India moves towards becoming a knowledge economy and society, more and younger Indians are likely to aspire for higher education."

It also highlights, "Given the 21st century requirements, quality higher education must aim to develop good, thoughtful, well-rounded, and creative individuals. It must enable an individual to study one or more specialised areas of interest at a deep level and also develop character, ethical and Constitutional values, intellectual curiosity, scientific temper, creativity, spirit of service, and 21st-century capabilities across a range of disciplines, including sciences, social sciences, arts, humanities, languages, as well as professional, technical, and vocational subjects. A quality higher education must enable personal accomplishment and enlightenment, constructive public engagement, and productive contribution to society. It must prepare students for more meaningful and satisfying lives and work roles and enable economic independence."

It refers the purpose or objective of the higher education, "For the purpose of developing holistic individuals, it is essential that an identified set of skills and values will be incorporated at each stage of learning, from pre-school to higher education."

If these modern gurukuls try to obtain these goals and objectives, then only our country, India, will be the Vishwa Guru in the coming time, and this modern system of Gurukuls will be successful. This means that they should carry on with traditional values and modern thoughts along with informal and formal education.

References

Altekar A.S. (1944) *Education in India*. Isha Books, Delhi.

Singh, Shahna (2017) *The Educational Heritagre of Ancient India*. Notion Press, Chennai.

National Education Policy 2020. Ministry of Human Resources, Government of India. https://www.education.gov.in/sites/upload_files/mhrd/files/NEP_Final_English_0.pdf

https://ncert.nic.in/textbook/pdf/heih111.pdf

https://www.google.com/search?q=basic+aim+of+education+in+ethics+and+values&sourceid=chrome&ie=UTF-8

Chapter 23

Indian Knowledge System in the Light of NEP 2020

Yewle Sunita Uttamrao,
Research Scholar, Department of English,
Dr. Babasaheb Ambedkar Marathwada University, Aurangabad,
Maharashtra.

India is a country with ancient civilisations and practices that are known to mankind. It is expected to accumulate some knowledge throughout its existence. This ancient knowledge is preserved on palm trees and transferred from generation to generation orally. However, over a period of time, there were abrupt changes in the knowledge transformation process, and this indigenous knowledge was lost. The newly introduced education system has tried to provide this knowledge to society. Indian Knowledge System comprises 3 words: Indian, Knowledge, and System.

Indian:

It refers to Akhanda Bharata, an undivided Indian sub-continent. It covers the area that spans from Burma on the east as well as modern-day Afghanistan on the west, the Himalayas on the north, as well as the Indian Ocean on the south. The Chanakya was instrumental in the establishment of the Mauryan Empire, as was Panini, who wrote Sanskrit Grammar; both of them got their education at Takshashila University of ancient India, which is now in Pakistan. Ancient Indian education included the teaching of 18 Vidya Sthanas, or schools of learning, which were imparted in renowned centres such as Nalanda and Takshashila. India's global reputation has been derived from its contributions in the fields of Art as well as Architecture, Science, Technology, Engineering, Philosophy, and Practices. Most of the foreigners who visited India for knowledge disseminated the same to the west and other parts of the world.

Knowledge:

Knowledge refers to tacit knowledge, and it lies in the wisdom of knowledge seekers. It is gained by insights into personal experiences, through observations, facing real-life problems, as well as solving them. Knowledge may exist in literary as well as non-literary forms. This tacit knowledge is transferred systematically by way of proposing new theories and frameworks, and in the form of literary work in the form of explicit knowledge.

System:

A system means a well-organised methodology and a classification scheme used to access a body of knowledge. The codification and classification are based on the need, interest, and capacity of the knowledge seeker so that he may access the inherent knowledge. This will help them gain insights from overall knowledge and know-how that different knowledge components logically complement each other.

The Indian Knowledge System is the systematic transfer of ancient and contemporary knowledge from one generation to another. It covers ancient knowledge from various domains to address current as well as future challenges.

These research centres are interdisciplinary, and they will preserve and disseminate knowledge for further research and societal applications. The Indian Knowledge System teacher training centres will provide necessary training to teachers to understand indigenous and traditional knowledge, and the Indian Knowledge System Bhasha

Kendras will act as centres to promote linguistics as well as literary knowledge. These centres will rejuvenate the languages that are on the verge of extinction and contain the knowledge needed to transform the nation.

Activities under the IKS Division:

To provide funding support of Rs. 30-40 lakh over 2 years by considering the need to establish Indian Knowledge System centres in traditional schools and STEM educational institutions that will promote Indian Knowledge System as well as related activities. To pair up students with Indian Knowledge System experts under the Indian Knowledge System Internship Programme to carry out short-term research projects/ activities with a stipend for 2 months.

To establish a more structured approach to Indian Knowledge System teaching, the regulatory body for technical education has authorised the creation of a textbook title 'Introduction to Indian Knowledge System, Concepts and Applications' authored by B Mahadevan. Some IITs have shown a keen interest in Indian Knowledge System. IIT Guwahati has been offering Ph.D. in spoken Sanskrit and Assamese since its inception in November 2021. IIT Gandhinagar introduced the Indian Knowledge System optional course in 2016, well in advance of the NEP's rise in prominence.

Challenges of the Indian Knowledge System:

With the advent of globalisation, there is a race to change the traditional education system and make it a global standard through modernisation. There is a dramatic change in pedagogy, curriculum, and medium of instruction. In cultural imperialism, countries with high social status dominate the societies and cultures of countries with low social status (Coleman, 2010). The Indian education system is of Macaulay origin, and we are still following it. In the age of vast information systems and following this education system, we have lost our culturally based knowledge and heritage. We have lost our agricultural biodiversity, and this has put pressure on food security, nutrition, and overall agricultural development. There is a massive loss of intellectual capital. Our IKS has more than 7000 medicinal plant species and over 15,000 herbal formulations. It has not only made it popular, but it is also drawing attention to biopiracy and patenting it within or outside of the country. This amplifies the wrong ownership.

NEP and IKS Inclusion:

The NEP 2020 has emphasised that IKS will be part of the curriculum and will be incorporated scientifically. These inputs will be delivered through modern technologies, fun games, and cultural exchange programmes in different states. NEP focuses on multilingualism, and the IKS repository has many languages. Under NEP, students will be delivered curriculum in their native languages as well as Sanskrit, the most ancient language, which will be taught to all. The Multilanguage formula will cover the aspects of Constitutional provisions, and it will create unity and integrity across the nation. It would be easy to include the history of Indian mathematics in normal math classes. The same could be done for architecture, philosophy, and Ayurveda. This is the goal of the NEP, but it will have to be done slowly.

Challenges of Implementation:

There are certain challenges when it comes to integrating IKS with NEP. There is a lack of awareness among the community and stakeholders about the importance of IKS. IKS is generally present in non-literary form, and it has been passed orally from one generation to another. It makes it difficult to develop and implement IKS-based courses and programmes in educational institutions. There is no clear-cut curriculum about IKS, and it is leaving educationists perplexed. Many stakeholders may see it as irrelevant or outdated. As IKS is available in different languages, it may create barriers for those who are not well-versed in these languages. Moreover, the colonial system of education has created a bias against the IKS in the Indian Education system. It can create difficulty in accommodating this system. There is also a shortage of well-qualified teachers to teach the IKS because it is not widely adopted yet.

Conclusion:

The inclusion of IKS in India may help the stakeholders understand their cultural heritage and develop a deep understanding of the environment. IKS is based on tacit knowledge. It can help students face and tackle the challenges they are going to face in their real lives, such as challenges of climate change and food security. This inclusion of IKS has certain challenges, and these challenges need to be addressed before inclusion. The data available about IKS needs to be streamlined with the help of information technology and made available as per the needs and capacity of the stakeholders. This cannot be done overnight, as the Indigenous Knowledge Systems have evolved in India over thousands of years. It will be replaced gradually over time.

References

Autonomous colleges in the state face challenges in implementing. January 5, 2024. https://www.hindustantimes.com/cities/mumbai-news/autonomous-colleges-in-state-face-challenges-in-implementing-indian-knowledge-system-101695582233165.

Coleman, M. A. (2010). The impact of negative acculturation on cultural dominance in multiple acquisitions (Doctoral dissertation, University of St. Thomas (Saint Paul, Minn.)

Ghosh, A. (2015). Traditional Knowledge: Problems and Prospects. *Lokodarpan - A Peer-Reviewed Bilingual Annual Research Journal Of Folklore*, V.

Indian Knowledge Systems (IKS). January 2, 2024. https://iksindia.org/

National Education Policy 2020. January 3, 2024. https://www.education.gov.in/sites/upload_files/mhrd/files/NEP_Final_English_0.pdf

About the Editor

Vitthal Gore holds an impressive academic profile with M.A., M.Phil., and Ph.D. degrees in English, boasting a distinguished career spanning 26 years in higher education. His expertise encompasses roles as an administrator, resource person, research supervisor, former BoS Member, YouTuber, and prolific academic writer.

Dr. Gore's contributions extend beyond academia; he has served as a Research Associate for UGC-IUC at the Indian Institute of Advanced Study, Shimla. He has delivered 109 professional presentations as a resource person for UGC E-Content Development, UGC HRDCs, UGC MMTTC, and various national and international academic events.

Presently, Dr. Gore serves as an Assistant Professor and Head of the Department of English, as well as the IQAC Coordinator and NSS Programme Officer at Shri Havagiswami College, Udgir, M.S. He has developed academic content for several universities across India and has authored numerous research articles and three books published by esteemed national and international publishers.

Other Titles of the Author:

1. Editor, *English Language Communication Skills Lab Manual* (2008).

2. Editor, *IPR and Research Ethics* (2023)

3. Author, *Professional Skills for 21st Century* (2023)